DETAILS

OF

AERIAL BOMBS

*Air Ministry,
September 1918*

The Naval & Military Press Ltd

Published by
The Naval & Military Press Ltd
5 Riverside, Brambleside, Bellbrook
Industrial Estate, Uckfield, East Sussex,
TN22 1QQ England
Tel: +44 (0) 1825 749494
Fax: +44 (0) 1825 765701
www.naval-military-press.com

In reprinting in facsimile from the original, any imperfections are inevitably reproduced and the quality may fall short of modern type and cartographic standards.

DETAILS OF AERIAL BOMBS.

The following notes and diagrams include full description and instructions for the loading and fuzing of High Explosive and Incendiary Bombs, also instructions for the use of parachute flares and other miscellaneous flares, smoke bombs, and ground flares.

Details of Bomb Racks are also included.

These instructions and diagrams will as far as possible be kept up to date by the issue of fresh leaflets and diagrams, as required from time to time by the introduction of modifications in the existing type of bombs or by the advent of entirely new designs

H.63.
DETAILS OF AERIAL BOMBS.
CONTENTS.
(Complete to 22nd July, 1918.)

Preface.
Contents Sheet.
Introductory Chapter. (1/1918.)
Supplement I. to Introductory Chapter. (3/1918.)
Leaflet No. 0A. Supplementary to Introductory Chapter. (7/1918.)
,, ,, 1.   Bomb H.E.R.L. 250 lbs. Mk. I. (1/1918.)
,, ,, 1A.   ,,   H.E.R.L. 250 lbs. Mk. I. (New fuzing.)
,, ,, 2.   ,,   H.E.R.L. 112 lbs. Mks. III. and V. (1/1918.)
,, ,, 3.*   ,,   H.E.R.L. 16 lbs. Mk. I/C.
,, ,, 4.   ,,   H.E.R.L. 100 lbs. (1/1918.)
,, ,, 4A.   ,,   H.E.R.L. 65 lbs. (1/1918.)
,, ,, 5.   ,,   Incendiary Carcass. (1/1918.)
,, ,, 6.*   ,,   H.E. Hales 20 lbs.
,, ,, 7.   ,,   H.E. R.F.C. 230 lbs. (1/1918.)
,, ,, 7A.   ,,   H.E. R.F.C. 230 lbs. (Light case.) Mk. III. (5/1918.)
,, ,, 8.   ,,   H.E. R.A.F. 336 lbs. (7/1918.)
,, ,, 9.   ,,   Aeroplane Demolition. (1/1918.)
,, ,, 10.   ,,   H.E. Cooper. 20 lbs. (1/1918.)
,, ,, 10A. ,,   Cooper Fuze. (1/1918.)
,, ,, 11.   ,,   40 lbs Phosphorus Mk. II/L, Type B. Special Fuze, Midgeley Fuze, 20 lbs. C.F.S. Carrier and Safety Device. (1918). (Corrected 7/1918.)
,, ,, 11A. ,,   40 lbs. Phosphorus Mk. I/L, Type A. (1/1918.)
,, ,, 12.   ,,   Baby Incendiary 6½ ozs. or Mk. IV. (3/1918.)
,, ,, 12A. ,,   B.I. Bomb Gear, and Operations Scheme
,, ,, 13.   ,,   H.E.R.L. 112 lbs. Mk. III. and V. (with new fuzing). (3/1918.)
,, ,, 14.   ,,   H.E.R.L. 112 lbs. Mk. VI and VII. (3/1918.)
,, ,, 15.   ,,   H.E. 50 lbs. Mk. IV. (3/1918.)
Leaflet No. 15A. Bomb Special Note. (Ref. Leaflets 13, 14, 15 and 17.)

DETAILS OF AERIAL BOMBS.—Continued.

,, ,, 15B. Supplementary Leaflet, additional to Nos. 14 and 15. (5/1918.)
,, ,, 15C. Bomb Supplementary Leaflet, additional to Leaflets Nos. 14 and 15. (6/1918.)
,, ,, 15D. Flanged Detonator, H.E. Bomb, 45 grains. (7/1918.)
,, ,, 16. Exploder, long. No. 1. Mk. I/C. (1/1918.)
,, ,, 17. New Type Suspension Nose and Tail Fuze. (3/1918.)
,, ,, 18. (5/1918.) Exploders. [Cancelling Leaflet No. 18 (1/1918.)]
,, ,, 19. (5/1918.) Tail Fuzes. [Cancelling Leaflet No. 19 (1/1918.)]
,, ,, 19A. Supplementary Note to Leaflet No. 19 on Relays and Detonators.
,, ,, 19B. Nomenclature. (6/1918.)
,, ,, 19C. Erratum Slip. (7/1918.)
,, ,, 20. Fuze Bomb D.A. No. 1. (1/1918.)
,, ,, 21. Holt's Wing Tip Flares. (1/1918.)
,, ,, 22. Michelin Flare and Carrier. (1/1918.)
,, ,, 23. T.W.R. Flares. (1/1918.)
,, ,, 24. Very Cartridges. (1/1918.)
,, ,, 25. H.E. Bomb Components. (3/1918.)
,, ,, 26. 20 lbs., 112 lbs., and 230 lbs. Bomb Carriers. (5/1918.)
,, ,, 26A. Bomb Carriers. Supplementary to Leaflet No. 26. (6/1918.)
,, ,, 26B. Bomb Carriers. (7/1918.)
,, ,, 27. Gledhill Bomb Gear. (3/1918.)
,, ,, 28. Handley Page Bomb Gear. (5/1918.)
,, ,, 29. Negative Lens Bomb Sight. (3/1918.)
,, ,, 30. Bomb. H.E., 520 lbs. (Light Case.) (5/1918.)
,, ,, 31. ,, H.E., 550 lbs. (Heavy Case.) (5/1918.)
,, ,, 32.† ,, Thermalloy Incendiary, 34 lbs.
,, ,, 33. ,, H.E., 9.45 in. Trench Howitzer (Converted).
,, ,, 34.† ,, Incendiary Mark III.
,, ,, 35.† ,, H.E.R.L. 180 lbs. Mk. I.
,, ,, 36.† ,, H.E.R.L. 50 lbs. Mk. II.

* These Leaflets refer to obsolete Bombs, and will no longer be issued.
† In course of preparation.

DETAILS OF AERIAL BOMBS.

INTRODUCTORY CHAPTER.

Classification of Bombs.

Bombs are briefly divided into three classes.

(1) High Explosive Bombs (Bombs H.E.).

(2) Incendiary Bombs (Bombs I.).

(3) Parachute Flares (Bombs Parachute).

The present bombing policy is based on the assumption that only four types of high explosive bombs are required for use overseas. These four types may be illustrated as follows:—

(A) A small heavy case bomb of about 20 lbs. weight for use in the attack of personnel, aerodromes, and road transport, also to be suitable for carrying on light machines.

These requirements are fulfilled by the 20 lb. Cooper bomb.

(B) A medium weight heavy case bomb of about 50 lb. weight. This bomb to be used more particularly against *materiel*, but also for general use.

These bombs will be used in conjunction with new fuses, and be made in cast iron (no steel being available). Since bombs manufactured in this substance are on impact with hard surfaces liable to break up, it is essential that they should be fitted with both nose and tail fuses. (*See* end of Chapter for fuses.)

These bombs may be used by the smaller bombing machines on long-distance raids when full fuel is needed, so precluding the carrying of a heavier class of bomb. They are fitted for stowing internally in D.H.9.

The 50 lb. R.L. Bomb, Mk. IV., will fulfil these requirements.

(C) A large heavy case bomb, about 112 lb. in weight, to be used against *materiel* and for general purposes.

The 112 lb. bombs, Mks. VI. and VII., will fulfil these requirements.

For fusing, the same remarks apply as for "B."

(D) A large light case bomb, about 230 lb. in weight, for crater production in the attack of railways or buildings. The bomb to be fitted with tail fuse only.

The 230 lb. R.F.C. light case bomb fulfils this requirement.

Note.—For internal stowage in the H.P. machine, a converted 9·45-inch shell bomb is being experimented with, and if trials are satisfactory, it will be provided. It is fitted with nose fuse, and will be useful against personnel or *materiel*.

At the date of writing (January, 1918), a transition stage has been arrived at where the multiplicity of types of H.E. bombs is to be reduced to four, or thereabouts, on the lines already illustrated. There are, however, considerable supplies of the older types of bombs still to be issued before the later bombs, as instanced by the 112 lb. Mk. VI. and VII. 230 lb. R.F.C. Light Case, 50 lb., Mk. IV., and Cooper 20 lb. bombs become an approximately standardised issue.

Until this takes effect, the reading of the leaflets on those bombs marked at their foot "obsolescent—no more being made "—will be necessary to obtain a comprehensive knowledge of all types of bombs as at present issued.

Explosive System of Bombs.

It is now intended roughly to illustrate the nature of bombs, and the components necessary to their construction and effective action.

All H.E. bombs in use contain three different types of explosive, namely, a bursting charge, a primer or exploder, and a detonator or cap.

The Bursting Charge is always some safe and insensitive explosive such as TNT or amatol. This can only be detonated by a violent explosion, and consequently all bombs are fitted with a primer or exploder.

Exploders or Primers contain tetryl. This explosive resembles TNT, but is more sensitive and is easily detonated by a detonator.

Detonators all contain fulminate of mercury. This explosive is very sensitive, and all detonators must be handled carefully and not dropped or knocked in any way.

All bombs contain a detonator which is fired on being struck or pierced by the striker of the fuse. In nose fuses this detonator is in contact with a primer and no further detonators are essential; though to ensure detonation detonators are generally used in the exploder. But in tail fuses there is usually a considerable distance between the fuse and the exploder. Consequently the cap in the fuse is caused to fire one end of a piece of safety or instantaneous fuse. The other end of this piece of fuse is crimped into a detonator, which sets off the detonator in the exploder.

BOMB FUSES.

Classification and Use.

There are two classes of bomb fuses:—

(1) *Nose Fuses.*—All nose fuses work by direct percussion and are instantaneous.

(2) *Tail Fuses.*—No tail fuse can be instantaneous. The delays in use are ·05 secs., 2·5 secs., and 15 secs.

1. *Nose Fuses.*—In these fuses the striker spindle is the first portion of the bomb to hit the ground, and in consequence the striker is driven directly on to a detonator or cap, which ignites the exploder. These fuses are practically instantaneous (delay, less than 1/400 second), and bombs fired by them explode on impact and so do not enter the ground. This results in the formation of a shallow crater, but the fragments of the bomb are scattered over a wide area. In consequence, these fuses should be used only in thick case bombs and for attacking personnel and light structures, such as aeroplanes or transport, where crater production is not desired.

2. *Tail Fuses.*—All tail fuses have a delay action, because they only act after the whole bomb has had its speed reduced considerably by meeting with some serious resistance. When the bomb has been slowed up appreciably, the striker, which still travels with its own momentum, hits the cap of the igniter and so fires the bomb. Owing to their method of action, the smallest delay occurring with tail fuses is about 1/20 second. This occurs even with the so called "instantaneous fuses," and consequently all bombs fired by tail fuses bury themselves in the ground before exploding and produce a considerable crater, but do not scatter their fragments at all. For this reason, tail fuses should only be used in the attack of railways, dumps, and buildings or factories, where a violent local destruction is needed rather than a scattering of small pieces of steel over a large area. As a result, tail fuses should be used only in light cased bombs, or in special cases as a safeguard against the failure of a nose fuse.

3. *New Types of Nose and Tail Fuse.*—It should be noted that the new types of fuses (to be illustrated later) are designed with the intention that the shearing pins in the nose fuse should not be sheared on impact with a roof in the attack

of buildings, but the tail fuse is so arranged that under these conditions it will function with a delay action as influenced by the igniter used, so producing an explosion within the structure attacked.

In the attack of towns it should be borne in mind that only 40 per cent. of a town area is covered by buildings, the balance of 60 per cent. being covered by streets and open spaces. It may, therefore, be anticipated that in the attack of towns, 60 per cent. of the bombs released will fall in streets or in open ground. In this event the nose fuse will function before the complete detonation of the bomb can be influenced by the possibility of its breaking up.

If a tail fuse alone were used, and the bomb case broke down on impact, the delay action caused by the use of the tail fuse would involve either incomplete detonation, or, in the case of a complete breaking up of the walls of the bomb, no detonation at all.

Incendiary Bombs.—These will be dealt with in a subsequent issue.

AIR MINISTRY,
January, 1918.

Supplement I.

TO

Introductory Chapter.

DETAILS OF AERIAL BOMBS.

HIGH EXPLOSIVES AND INCENDIARY MIXTURES USED IN THE FILLING OF BOMBS.

Trinitrotoluene.

1. Trinitrotoluene, variously called trotyl, trinol, trilite, &c., has been used on a large scale in this country only comparatively recently.

Disadvantages and Advantages as Compared with Picric Acid.—For some years previously picric acid, known as lyddite, was almost universally employed for the filling of shell, and although trotyl is less sensitive it has nevertheless been able to displace picric acid for the following reasons:—

(1) It has a lower melting point.

(2) It does not form sensitive metallic salts as does picric acid.

2. *Manufacture.*—Trotyl — $C_6H_2CH_3(NO_2)_3$ — is obtained by nitrating toluene, which is a liquid hydrocarbon, obtained along with benzene from coal tar.

Filling.—It can be melted at a temperature below steam heat, and is then poured into the bomb, where it rapidly solidifies.

In its cast form it is a crystalline solid mass, of a buff colour.

3. *Properties.*—The melting point of trotyl is 81° C.; it is nearly insoluble in water, and only slightly so in cold alcohol.

Frost or damp do not affect it, and it does not deteriorate with age.

It can be safely lighted in the open with a match, when it burns with a dull red flame accompanied by a thick, sooty smoke, but detonates with extreme violence when the ordinary fulminate detonator used in conjunction with a tetryl or other suitable exploder is employed.

It must be remembered that trotyl is an explosive, and that as such it must be treated with the utmost care; handling it, or the bomb filled with it, carelessly, will inevitably lead to disaster.

Trotyl is one of the most stable explosives; when heated it does not ignite until a temperature of 240° C. is reached. It is also one of the least sensitive of powerful explosives in common use. By mechanical treatment it is with difficulty affected. Even with a light compression, and markedly when in the cast state, it requires a detonant at the same time powerful and possessing a high rate of detonation to bring out its full effect, and unless the initiating detonant be in close contact there will be failure of the trotyl to respond with the full violence of which it is capable. The following experiment carried out lately illustrates the necessity of having close contact for purposes of obtaining detonation; a 65 lb. bomb filled with 40 lbs. T.N.T., fitted with a 22-seconds delay fuze, was dropped from a height of 50 feet, but failed to explode owing to a damp relay; a second bomb of the same kind was then dropped from a similar height and detonated within 10 feet of the first, which was unaffected by the explosion.

4. *Velocity of Detonation: Density.*—The velocity of detonation of an explosive is not constant, but is affected by various conditions, the most important of which is its density. The lower the density the lower the velocity of detonation, but the easier it is to detonate, and *vice versâ*, e.g., with pressed trotyl, density 1, the velocity of detonation is 6,483 metres per second; with density 1.57, velocity is 6,950 metres per second.

The density of trotyl when cast is from 1.54 to 1.59 of that of water, or roughly 100 lbs. per cubic foot, and its velocity of detonation is from 6,800 to 6,900 metres per second.

For the detonation of cast trotyl a primer of tetryl or other more sensitive explosive is required; a fulminate detonator by itself is not sufficient. Compressed trotyl crystals may be detonated by the detonation of mixed fulminate and tetryl and, when so detonated, will serve as a primer for the detonation of cast trotyl. The exploders used in bombs generally consist of a tube containing compressed trotyl with a pellet of tetryl at the end into which the fulminate detonator is inserted.

Tetryl.

5. **Tetranitro-methylaniline**, known as tetryl, tetralite, C.E., &c., is, with the ordinary fulminate detonator, used extensively for the detonation of trotyl.

Manufacture.—Tetryl is obtained by nitrating dimethylaniline.

Properties.—The melting point of the pure substance is from 128.5° to 129.5°C. It is more violent in its action and more sensitive than trotyl. When lighted in the open it burns quietly with a bright flame.

It is a pale yellow colour.

Density.—When compressed to a density of 1.63 the velocity of detonation of tetryl is 7,520 metres per second.

Ammonium Nitrate.

Ammonium nitrate is in itself an explosive, but can only be detonated with extreme difficulty, unless it is mixed with oxidisable matter. The mixtures made with it are not very sensitive, and are accordingly well adapted to military uses.

Ammonium nitrate has the disadvantage of being hygroscopic, and on this account explosive mixtures of which it forms an ingredient must not be exposed to the air as they will when so situated absorb moisture and become damp, and thus be rendered useless.

Supplement I. (continued).

Ammonium nitrate when mixed with T.N.T. is known as amatol, in which form it is used in filling the later types of bombs.

Manufacture.—Ammonium nitrate is a compound formed by the combination of ammonia with nitric acid. It is a crystalline solid resembling ordinary nitre.

Amatol

Amatol is a mixture of T.N.T. and ammonium nitrate. It is used in filling bombs in two forms; these are known as 40/60 and 80/20 amatol. The figures 40/60 and 80/20 denote the proportions of T.N.T. and ammonium nitrate contained in the amatol. The first figure represents the percentage of ammonium nitrate, the second the percentage of T.N.T.; thus 40/60 amatol represents a mixture made up of 40% ammonium nitrate and 60% T.N.T.

The reason for employing amatol in place of simple T.N.T. is due to the growing scarcity of the latter.

The density of amatol is somewhat less than that of T.N.T., and on this account bombs filled with amatol will contain a relatively smaller bursting charge than T.N.T. filled bombs.

In illustration, the case of the 112 lb. bomb is taken. This bomb, when filled with pure T.N.T., contains approximately 35 lbs. of explosive, but when filled with 80/20 amatol it contains approximately 28 lbs. of explosive. From this example it is seen that bombs filled with 80/20 amatol will contain 25% by weight less explosive than bombs filled with T.N.T.

These figures are not exact; they are obtained by striking an average, but are sufficient to afford an approximate illustration. It should be noted that the bombs filled with T.N.T., or 40/60 amatol are cast filled, *i.e.*, the mixture is melted and poured in liquid, while bombs filled with 80/20 are stem filled, *i.e.*, the dry powdered mixture is pressed in.

Properties of Amatol.—Generally speaking, the properties of amatol are similar to those of trotyl except that, ammonium nitrate being hygroscopic, the mixture is affected by damp. Amatol is slightly less sensitive than trotyl. It can be detonated by means of a primer of tetryl or compressed trotyl. When enclosed in a strong steel casing it is slightly more powerful, but when not so enclosed is less powerful than trotyl.

Ammonal.

7. Ammonal is a mixture of trotyl, ammonium nitrate, carbon, and aluminium.

It is possible that it may be used in future for filling bombs.

INCENDIARY MIXTURES.

Carcass Composition.

This composition is used in the filling of the 15 lb. carcass incendiary bombs.

It is made up of the following substances:—

	Per cent.
Saltpetre	37.88
Sulphur	15.45
Resin	11.36
Antimony sulphide	3.79
Tallow	3.79
Venice turpentine	3.49
Black powder mealed	6.06
Aluminium powder	18.18

It is primed with magnesium powder.

Thermit.

This mixture is at present used in the aeronautical service, in the Baby Incendiary Bomb, and may soon be more extensively used.

Thermit is composed of practically any metallic oxide (iron oxide is generally used) mixed to a fine powder with aluminium.

For ignition a primer of magnesium and barium peroxide is generally employed.

COMPONENTS OF H.E. BOMBS.

The main mass of the explosive in the earlier marks of H.E. bombs, as issued in 1915 or early in 1916, is either trotyl (T.N.T.) or 40/60 amatol. In all modern H.E. bombs the main mass of the explosive or bursting charge is formed of 80/20 amatol. Both T.N.T. and amatol are insensitive to any but the most violent mechanical shock. To secure detonation by impact on the ground the following "components" are necessary. The details and arrangement vary in different types, but the essential features are the same.

(1) *The Detonator.*—This consists of a few grains of violent and sensitive explosive, in which fulminate of mercury is an ingredient, contained in a copper capsule It can be detonated by slight shock, such as the impact of a striker when the bomb hits the ground. The detonator may be incorporated in the fuze and struck direct, or it may be fired by a flash started by the fuze. Since the whole process of detonation when once started is practically instantaneous, the latter method must be used if any delay is desired between the moment of impact and that of detonation.

(2) *The Exploder.*—The shock caused by the firing of the detonator alone is not usually sufficient to detonate the main mass properly. An intermediate "exploder" is therefore employed, consisting of a pound or more of some more sensitive explosive, such as tetryl, surrounding the detonator, and itself surrounded by the main charge. The exploder is detonated by the firing of the detonator when the bomb strikes, and in its turn detonates the main mass.

Effects of H.E. Bombs.

The destructive action of a bomb depends partly on the direct "blast" action of the gases generated and partly on the fragments of the case which are projected with very high velocity. Blast action is very local except on fragile structures such as glass windows, tiled roofs and the like; the effect of fragments depends on their size.

Many experiments have been made on the effect of bombs, largely by the use of models on reduced scale. Actual comparison of large and small bombs has shown that the effects are closely similar if the linear dimensions of the bomb, of its distance from the target and of the target itself, are all reduced in the same proportion. This means that to cause similar damage the weight of the bomb must be in proportion to the cube of the linear dimensions. For instance, if a 100 lb. bomb will just blow a hole in a 9 inch wall when detonated at a distance of 5 feet, a bomb of similar construction weighing 800 lbs. will blow a hole in an 18 inch wall from a distance of 10 feet.

The following are a few results of observation and experiment from which the effects of bombs may be roughly estimated:—

(1) A bomb containing 200 lbs. of trotyl in a thin case and detonated well within a building like a factory workshop 36 feet high, 150 feet long and say, 110 feet wide (two bays each 55 feet wide), would blow off a good deal of the roof. The walls if of ordinary strength, say 14 inches thick, strengthened by brick buttresses would not be much damaged; neither would any heavy machinery which happened to be in the shop.

Experience has shown that one of the smaller H.E. bombs detonated instantaneously on the roof of a substantial building has only a very local effect on the roof itself and objects within will probably not be much damaged. To get the best effect on such a target some form of fuze giving delay action is necessary. In addition to the added "blast" effect thereby obtained the fragments of the case, of which a large proportion are projected roughly horizontally, do more useful work.

(2) The penetration and size of fragments from 112 lb. R.L. bombs are shown by an experiment in which a bomb was fired 6 feet from a ½ inch steel plate about 8 feet by 4 feet. Of the 56 pieces which passed through, 28 made holes of less than 1½ square inches area, and the 10 largest made holes between 2 and 4 square inches. Two of the fragments penetrated a second ½ inch steel plate placed just behind the first.

(3) The initial velocity of the bars of the 336 lb. bomb is about 2,300 feet-sec., and they will penetrate two 1 inch steel plates in succession at close range, making holes about 12 inches by 6 inches.

(4) One of the 230 lb. bombs detonated well below the surface of the water on the up-stream side of a double lock gate, the lock being 12 feet deep and 17 feet wide, would very seriously damage the gate if it fell within 20 feet of it.

(5) In the attack of railways the resultant delay is chiefly due to the loss of time in bringing up materials and men to effect the necessary repairs, rather than to the actual time taken in completing the repairing of the damage itself. It is not unreasonable to suppose that at least six hours would be lost in bringing up the men and materials necessary to carry out repairs to the permanent way, in the event of a direct hit having been registered with a 230 lb. bomb. The time taken to repair the damage to the track *alone* is estimated below. To these figures should be added the time which it is anticipated will elapse between the time of the dropping of the bomb and the arrival of the repair section.

In the event of a direct hit being registered on the permanent way with a 112 lb. bomb, the damage so caused can usually be made good by a party of ten men in one to one and a half hours. The damage caused by a 112 lb. bomb will seldom consist of more than one rail being broken, and some fifteen feet of permanent way being disturbed. The crater will require 10 to 12 tons of filling, or possibly more on very soft ground.

It should be noted that a 112 lb. bomb will cause no damage whatever to the permanent way if dropped a greater distance than 7 feet from the centre of the track.

A 230 lb. bomb has a larger radius of action, and may, if it falls within 12 feet of the centre of the track, cause some damage, and should probably break at least one rail.

Further than 12 feet from the centre of the track a 230 lb. bomb will do no more serious damage than cover the rails with earth and stones.

The maximum damage caused by a direct hit with a 230 lb. bomb would take two to three hours to repair with ten men available. Forty to fifty tons of filling would be required. A direct hit will invariably cut both rails and displace a considerable length of permanent way.

These figures are the result of actual operations and are based on the assumption that materials are at hand for repair. The time given for executing the repairs is the actual time taken to render the line fit for the passage of a train. The filling in of craters temporarily bridged would be done at leisure after the initial repairs had been completed.

The most effective method of causing delay on a railway is to derail a moving train, this being done if possible on an embankment.

AIR MINISTRY,
  MARCH, 1918.

LEAFLET No. 0. (A).

Supplementary to Introductory Chapter.

A. All H.E. Bombs where provided for, should normally be fuzed nose and tail—cast iron bombs invariably so.

B. In certain special cases steel bombs which can be fuzed nose and tail, may be employed with tail fuze only, where either a certain definite time delay is required or crater effect only is the object in view.

The following points are in elucidation of the above:—

1. Penetrative effect, as distinct from crater effect is given by Fuzes, Bomb, D.A. Nos. 8 and 9 Mark I. and thus their use is not precluded under Section B above, in attacks on towns, aerodromes, factory buildings and such like.

2. A nose fuze is always fitted with an instantaneous " detonator aerial bomb."

3. A tail fuze can be fitted with a definite time delay " detonator aerial bomb " for reasons under B above; but even if fitted with an instantaneous " detonator aerial bomb " has still an appreciable delay action.

(*See* Introductory Chapter.)

ERRATUM.

Line 9. For " Fuzes " read " Pistols."

AIR MINISTRY,
JULY, 1918.

Leaflet No. 1.

BOMB :—H.E.R.L., 250 lb.

HEAVY CASE.
Mk. I.

General Description.
    Actual Weight of Bomb.—250 lbs.
    Weight of Case.—139 lbs.
    Weight of Explosive.—111 lbs.
    Explosive Substance.—Amatol 40/60.
    Case Material.—Cast Steel.
    Thickness of Case.—All over, ·5 inches.
    Overall Dimension.—Bomb. 36·3 inches long × 12·5 inches maximum diameter.
        ,,   ,,   .—Fins. Side of square containing fins, 12·6 inches.
    How Stowed.—Horizontally, with nose or tail fuse; Vertically, nose up with tail fuse only.
    Type of Fuse.—Nose fuse or tail fuse (Fig. 1).
    Construction.—See diagram.

To Prepare for Action.
    The following will be required:—
    (A) For nose fuse.
    (B) For tail fuse.
    (C) For use with A and B.

(A). *Nose Fuse.*	(B). *Tail Fuse.*
Nose Fuse D.A., No. 1, Mk. 1.	(1) 1 Tail Fuze, No. 3 or No. 4.
	(2) 1 Nose Plug.
	(3) 1 Relay, 12 inches.

(For use with either A or B.)

Exploders.—1 long No. 2, Mk. I or II.

Detonators.—2 56 gr. Mk. I or II, according to exploder used.

Fusing Bomb.

Nose Fuse.—1. Remove nose plug from bomb.

2. Remove exploder (and if Mk. II, detonators also) from its tin. (If Mk. II, screw detonators into exploder.) Gently push exploder into central tube from nose end.

3. Remove safety pin, safety collar, and striker spindle from nose fuse, and test striker spindle for ease of spinning. Screw nose fuse into bomb, and replace striker spindle, safety collar, and safety pin, seeing that red line on striker spindle is flush with face of pressure plate, and that short end of vane stop engages in castellation on nose of bomb.

4. Wire safety collar to bomb carrier.

5. Just before leaving ground, remove safety pin from nose fuse.

Tail Fuse.—1. Remove nose plug from bomb.

2. Remove exploder (and if Mk. II, detonators also) from its tin. (If Mk. II, screw detonators into exploder.) Gently push exploder into central tube, nose end, and replace nose plug.

Note.—If any nose plug is not long enough to press exploder against diaphragm in the central tube, a wood plug or some felt washers must be inserted between exploder and nose plug.

3. Remove plug from tail of bomb. (If bomb is to be stowed vertically replace standard nose plug by a special nose plug and eye bolt.)

4. Through tail end of bomb insert relay.

5. Untie cord becket on tail fuse, and test vane for ease of spinning.

6. Screw tail fuse into tail of bomb and tighten grub screw.

7. Just before leaving ground, remove safety pin from tail fuse.

Action of Fuse and Safety Device.

On the horizontal carrier, vane of nose fuse is held from rotating by vane-stop on safety collar; that of tail fuse by vane-stop on carrier.

Nose Fuse (see Leaflet 20).

1. On dropping, safety collar is pulled off nose fuse by wire attached to carrier, and vane is spun round by air pressure.

2. On striking the ground, blow comes on vane and pressure plate, shearing pins are sheared and striker hits cap. This detonates the Tetryl in nose fuse and this in its turn detonates 56 grain detonator and exploder, which sets off the bomb.

Tail Fuse.—1. On dropping, the vane is free to rotate and spins off, the striker being held from hitting cap by striker spring.

2. On striking ground, bomb is checked, but striker being free to move forward, compresses striker spring and pierces cap. This fires the powder pellets in fuse. The flash from the fuse lights fuse in relay, which in its turn fires 56 grain detonator and exploder, which sets off the bomb.

Loading Bomb on Carrier.

The bomb must be securely housed on the carrier, and on no account be free to move in either the horizontal or vertical planes.

This object is attained by the adjustment of the nose and tail pieces. This adjustment must be repeated in the case of every bomb loaded.

Before the bomb is fused, it must be loaded on the carrier and dropped at least once, to ascertain that the carrier is functioning correctly. When this has been done, and provided the carrier is found to be working satisfactorily, the bomb is to be reloaded on the carrier, and made live by the insertion of the exploders and detonators and the subsequent screwing of the fuses into position.

Unloading.

1. Replace safety pins in fuses.
2. Drop bomb off carrier.
3. Carefully unscrew fuses from bomb, and replace them in their tins. (In unscrewing nose fuse, first remove safety collar and striker.)
4. Gently shake out exploder and relay, and replace them in their tins. (If Mk. II exploder, remove detonators.)
5. Replace nose and tail plugs in bomb.

Targets Engaged.

Nose Fuse.—Personnel, Transport, Aerodromes.

Tail Fuse.—*Materiel*, Buildings.

Note.—This bomb is obsolescent—no more being made

AIR MINISTRY,
January, 1918.

[OVER

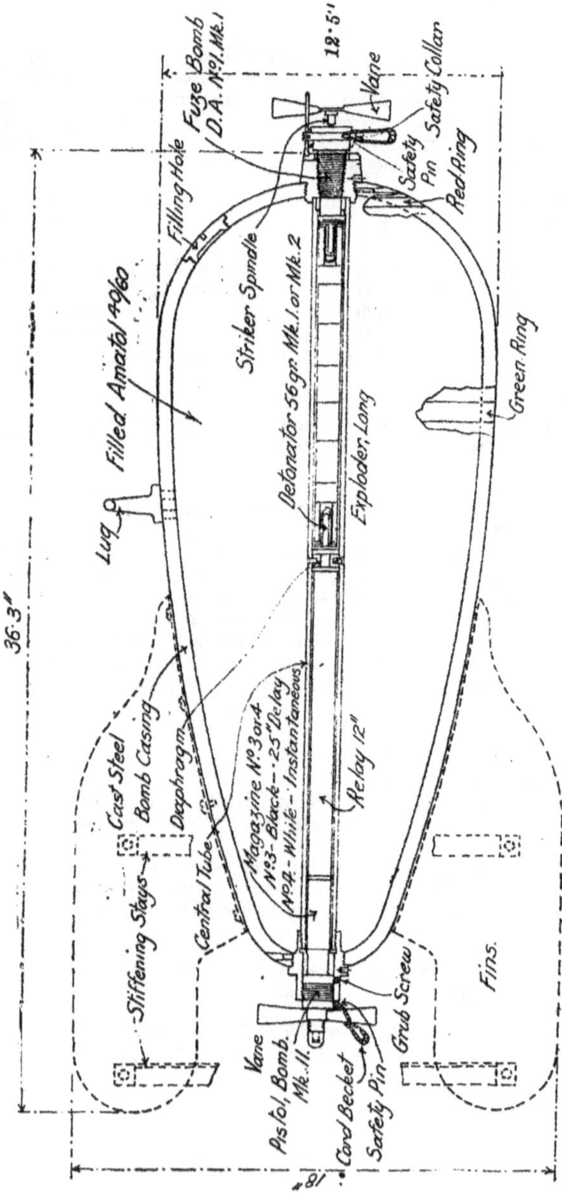

4

Diagram labels:
- 18·5"
- Vane
- Safety Pin
- Safety Collar
- Red Ring
- Filling Hole
- Fuze Bomb (D.A. No.1.Mk.1)
- Filled Amatol 40/60
- Lug
- Striker Spindle
- Detonator 56 gr. Mk.I or Mk.2
- Exploder, Long
- Green Ring
- 36·3"
- Cast Steel Bomb Casing
- Diaphragm
- Magazine No.3 or 4, No.3 – Black – 2·5 Delay, No.4 – White – Instantaneous
- Relay 12"
- Stiffening Stays
- Central Tube
- Fins
- Vane
- Pistol, Bomb. Mk.II.
- Cord Becket
- Safety Pin
- Grub Screw
- 18"

Leaflet No. 1.

BOMB :—H.E.R.L., 250 lbs.

MARK I.

Heavy Case.

GENERAL DESCRIPTION.

Actual weight of bomb ...	250 lbs.
Weight of case	139 lbs.
Weight of explosive ...	111 lbs.
Explosive substance ...	Amatol 40/60.
Case material	Cast steel.
Thickness of case ...	All over, .5 inches.
Overall dimensions	
Bomb	36.3″ long × 12.5″ maximum diameter.
Fins	Side of square containing fins, 12.6″.
How stowed	Horizontally, with nose or tail fuse; vertically, nose up with tail fuse only.
Type of fuse	Nose fuse or tail fuse.
Construction	See diagram.

TO PREPARE FOR ACTION.

    The following will be required :—
        (A) For nose fuse.
        (B) For tail fuse.
        (C) For use with A and B.

T.5.

(A).	(B).
Nose Fuse.	*Tail Fuse.*
Nose Fuse D.A., No. 1, Mk. 1.	(1) 1 Tail Fuse, No. 3 or No. 4.
	(2) 1 Nose Plug.
	(3) 1 Relay, 12 inches.

(For use with either A or B.)

Exploders.—I long No. 2, Mk. I. or II.

Detonators.—2,56 gr. Mk. I. or II., according to exploder used.

FUSING BOMB.

Nose Fuse.—1. Remove nose plug from bomb.

2. Remove exploder (and if Mk. II., detonators also) from its tin. (If Mk. II., screw detonators into exploder.) Gently push exploder into central tube from nose end.

3. Remove safety pin, safety collar, and striker spindle from nose fuse, and test striker spindle for ease of spinning. Screw nose fuse into bomb, and replace striker spindle, safety collar, and safety pin, seeing that red line on striker spindle is flush with face of pressure plate, and that short end of vane stop engages in castellation on nose of bomb.

4. Wire safety collar to bomb carrier.

5. Just before leaving ground, remove safety pin from nose fuse.

Tail Fuse.—1. Remove nose plug from bomb.

2. Remove exploder (and if Mk. II., detonators also) from its tin. (If Mk. II., screw detonators into exploder.) Gently push exploder into central tube, nose end, and replace nose plug.

> NOTE.—If any nose plug is not long enough to press exploder against diaphragm in the central tube, a wood plug or some felt washers must be inserted between exploder and nose plug.

3. Remove plug from tail of bomb. (If bomb is to be stowed vertically, replace standard nose plug by a special nose plug and eye bolt.)

4. Through tail end of bomb insert relay.

Leaflet No. 1 (continued).

5. Untie cord becket on tail fuse, and test vane for ease of spinning.

6. Screw tail fuse into tail of bomb and tighten grub screw.

7. Just before leaving ground, remove safety pin from tail fuse.

ACTION OF FUSE AND SAFETY DEVICE.

On the horizontal carrier, vane of nose fuse is held from rotating by vane-stop on safety collar; that of tail fuse by vane-stop on carrier.

NOSE FUSE (See Leaflet 20).

1. On dropping, safety collar is pulled off nose fuse by wire attached to carrier, and vane is spun round by air pressure.

2. On striking the ground, blow comes on vane and pressure plate, shearing pins are sheared and striker hits cap. This detonates the Tetryl in nose fuse and this in its turn detonates 56 grain detonator and exploder, which sets off the bomb.

Tail Fuse.—1. On dropping, the vane is free to rotate and spins off, the striker being held from hitting cap by striker spring.

2. On striking ground, bomb is checked, but striker being free to move forward, compresses striker spring and pierces cap. This fires the powder pellets in fuse. The flash from the fuse lights fuse in relay, which in its turn fires 56 grain detonator and exploder, which sets off the bomb.

LOADING BOMB ON CARRIER.

The bomb must be securely housed on the carrier, and on no account be free to move in either the horizontal or vertical planes.

This object is attained by the adjustment of the nose and tail pieces. This adjustment must be repeated in the case of every bomb loaded.

Before the bomb is fused, it must be loaded on the carrier and dropped at least once, to ascertain that the carrier is functioning correctly. When this has been done, and provided the carrier is found to be working satisfactorily, the bomb is to be reloaded on the carrier, and made live by the insertion of the exploders and detonators and the subsequent screwing of the fuses into position.

UNLOADING.

1. Replace safety pins in fuses.
2. Drop bomb off carrier.
3. Carefully unscrew fuses from bomb, and replace them in their tins. (In unscrewing nose fuse, first remove safety collar and striker.)
4. Gently shake out exploder and relay, and replace them in their tins. (If Mk. II. exploder, remove detonators.)
5. Replace nose and tail plugs in bomb.

TARGETS ENGAGED.

Nose Fuse.—Personnel, Transport, Aerodromes.

Tail Fuse.—Materiel, Buildings.

NOTE.—This bomb is obsolescent—no more being made.

AIR MINISTRY,
January, 1918.

NOTE.—Mark I. is obsolescent. A modified bomb of this type will shortly be in production, and a leaflet describing it will be issued to cancel the above.

Bomb, H.E.R.L., 250 lbs., Mk. I.

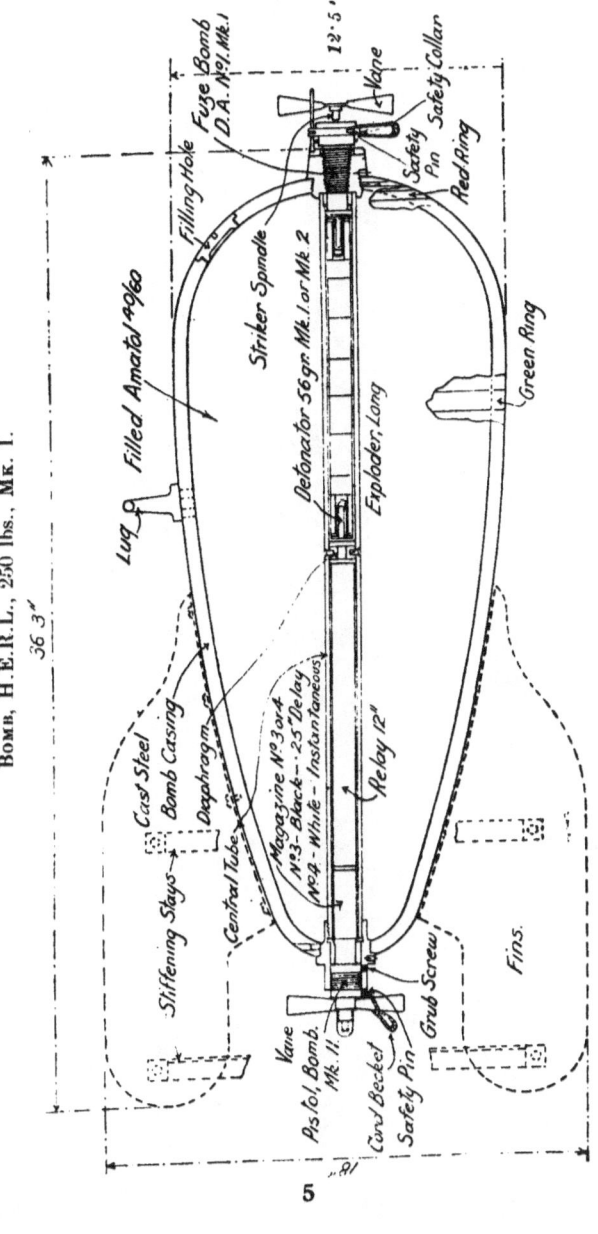

5

Leaflet No. 2.

BOMB :—H.E.R.L., 112 lb.

Heavy Case.
Mk. III and V.

General Description.

    Actual Weight of Bomb.—106 lb.
    Weight of Case.—79 lb.
    Weight of Explosive.—27 lbs.
    Explosive Substance.—Amatol 80/20 (if filled Amatol 40/60 38 lbs).
    Case Material.—Cast steel.
    Thickness of Case.—All over ·5 inch.
    Overall Dimensions.—Bomb.—29·1 inches long × 9 inches, maximum diameter.
    ,,   ,,   *Fins.*—Side of square containing fins, 12·9 inches.
    How Stowed.—Horizontally, with nose or tail fuse; vertically, nose up with tail fuse only.
    Type of Fuse.—Nose fuse or tail fuse.
    Construction.—See diagram.

To Prepare for Action.

    The following will be required:—
    (A) For nose fuse.
    (B) For tail fuse.
    (C) For use with both A and B.

(A). *Nose Fuse.*	(B). *Tail Fuse.*
(1) Nose Fuse, D.A., No. 1, Mk. I.	(1) 1 Pistol, No. 5, Mk. I.
	(2) 1 Pistol Adapter (for Mk. III. only).
	(3) 1 Relay Detonating, 7·39-in.
	(4) 1 Igniter.
	(5) 1 Long Nose Plug.

(15577.) Wt. W. 3982—P.P. 598. 5000. 2/18. D & S. G. 2. P. 18/73 (2).

(C).

(1) Exploders ... ... 1 Long No. 2 Mk. I or II.
(2) Detonators ... ... 2 56 gr., Mk. I or II.

Fusing Bomb.

Nose Fuse.—1. Remove nose plug from bomb.

2. Remove exploder (and if Mk. II, detonators also) from its tin. (If Mk. II, screw detonators into exploder.) Gently push exploder into central tube from nose end.

3. Remove safety pin, safety collar, and striker spindle from nose fuse, and test striker spindle for ease of spinning. Screw nose fuse into bomb, and replace striker spindle, safety collar and safety pin, seeing that red line on striker spindle is flush with face of pressure plate, and that short end of vane stop engages in castellation on nose of bomb.

4. Wire safety collar to bomb carrier.

5. Just before leaving ground, remove safety pin from nose fuse.

Tail Fuse.

1. Remove exploder and detonators from their tins, and screw detonators into exploder (if Mk. II).

2. Remove nose plug and gently push exploder into vertical tube from nose end. Replace nose plug. (If stowed vertically replace standard nose plug with special nose plug and eye bolt.

3. Untie cord becket from pistol vane and test vane for ease of spinning.

4. Push igniter into detonating relay, and screw pistol on to relay.

5. Screw adapter on to pistol and screw fuse into tail of bomb. Tighten grub screw. (If Mk. V, no adapter is required and the fuse may be screwed direct into tail of bomb and grub screw be tightened.)

6. Just before leaving ground, remove safety pin from fuse.

Action of Fuse and Safety Device.

On the horizontal carrier, vane of nose fuse is held from rotating by vane-stop on safety collar; that of tail fuse by vane-stop on carrier.

Nose Fuse (*See* LEAFLET 20).—1. On dropping, safety collar is pulled off nose fuse by wire attached to carrier, and vane is spun round by air pressure.

2. On striking the ground, blow comes on vane and pressure plate, shearing pins are sheared and striker hits cap. This detonates the Tetryl in nose fuse and this in its turn detonates 56-grain detonator and exploder, which sets off the bomb.

Tail Fuse.

When the bomb is dropped the vane is free to rotate and spins off.

On impact the bomb is checked, but the striker being free to move forward, compresses the striker spring and fires the cap of the igniter. This burns for 15 seconds, 2·5 seconds, or ·05 second, according to type, and then fires its detonator which in its turn fires the detonator in exploder, and so sets off the bomb.

Loading Bomb on Carrier.

The bomb must be securely housed on the carrier, and on no account be free to move either in the horizontal or vertical planes.

This object is attained by the adjustment of the nose and tail pieces. This adjustment must be repeated in the case of every bomb loaded.

Before the bomb is fused, it must be loaded on the carrier and dropped at least once, to ascertain that the carrier is functioning correctly. When this has been done, and provided the carrier is found to be working satisfactorily, the bomb is to be re-loaded on the carrier, and made live by the insertion of the exploders and detonators and the subsequent screwing of the fuses into position.

Unloading.

1. Replace safety pins in fuses.

2. Drop bomb off carrier.

3. Unscrew and remove fuses or nose plug. (In removing nose fuse, first take off safety collar, and unscrew striker spindle.) Replace fuses in their tins.

4. Gently shake exploders out of central tube, and if Mk. II remove detonators. Replace exploder and detonators in their tins.

5. Replace nose plug in bomb.

Targets Engaged.

Nose Fuse.—Personnel, aerodromes, and road transport.

Tail Fuse.—Materiel, buildings, &c.

Note.—These bombs are obsolescent—to be replaced by **Mk. VI**, cast-iron, and **Mk. VII**, cast-steel, which are of a somewhat different pattern.

AIR MINISTRY,
January, 1918.

BOMB:—H.E.R.L., 112 lbs., Mk. III.

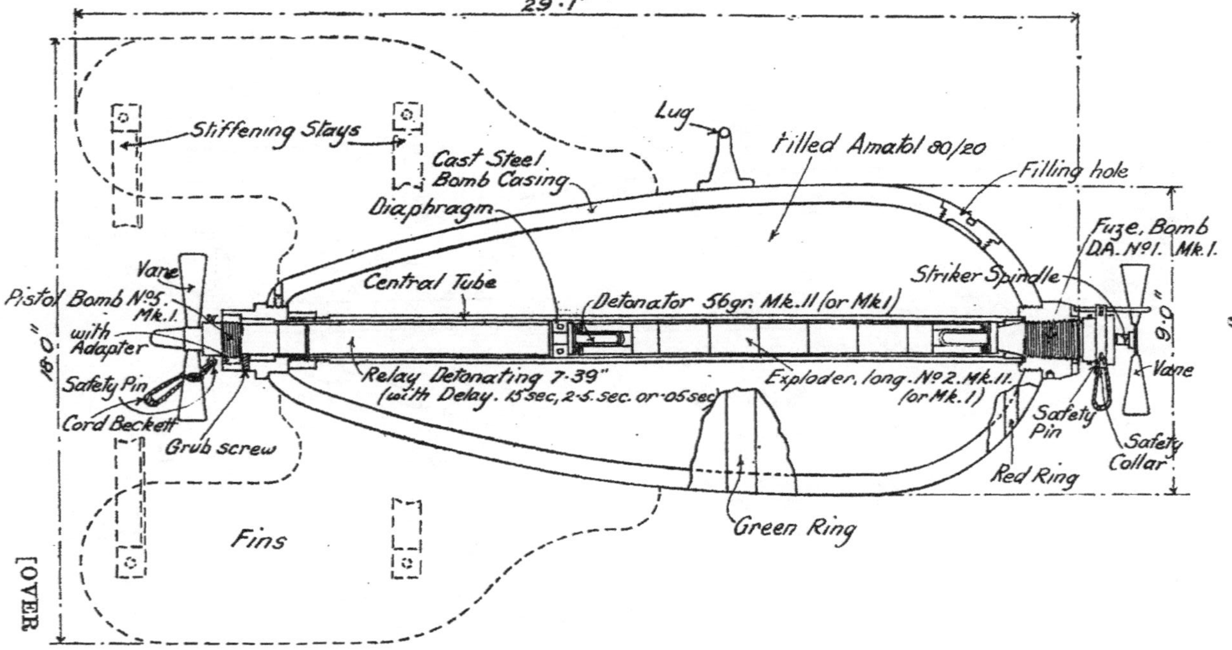

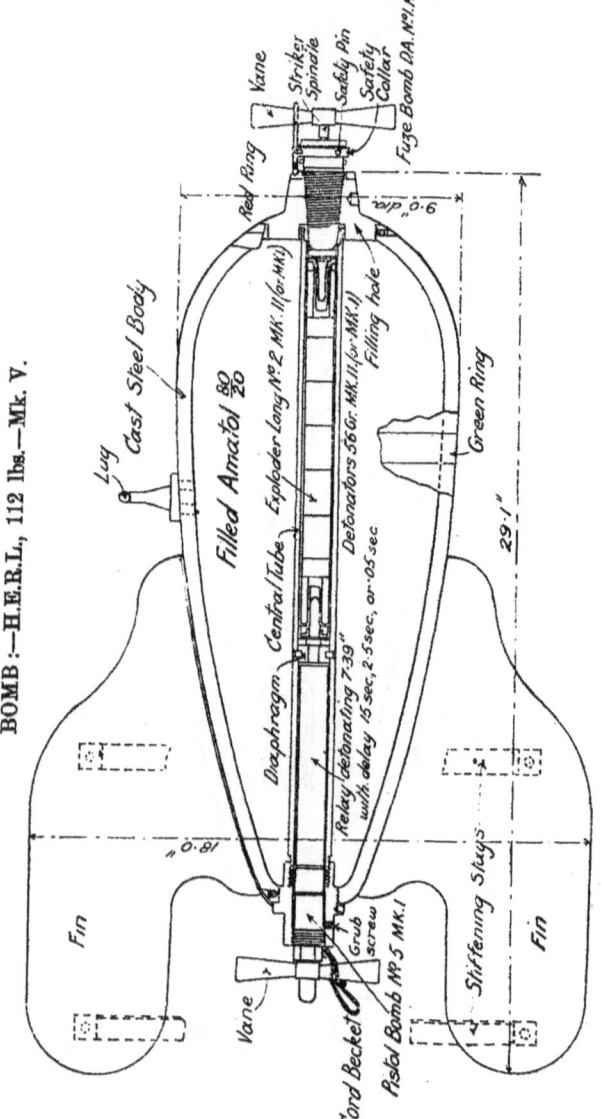

BOMB :—H.E.R.L., 112 lbs.—Mk. V.

Leaflet No. 3.

BOMB :—H.E.R.L., 16 lb.

Light Case.
Mk. I/C.

General Description.

    Actual Weight of Bomb.—16 lbs.
    Weight of Case.—9 lbs.
    Weight of Explosive.—7 lbs.
    Explosive Substance.—Amatol 40/60.
    Case Material.—Mild steel, sheet.
    Thickness of Case.—Nose: 10 S.W.G. ($\cdot$128 in. thick); Body: 16 S.W.G. ($\cdot$064 in. thick).
    Overall Dimensions.—Bomb. 25$\cdot$15 in. long by 5 in. diam.
            ,,   Fins: Side of square containing fins. 5 ins.
    How Stowed.—Horizontally.
    Type of Fuse.—Tail Fuse.
    Construction.—See diagram.

To Prepare for Action.

  The following will be required:—
    Pistols.—1 Mk. II.
    Exploders.—1 long No. 1, Mk. I.
    Detonators.—1 77 gr., Mk. I.

Fusing Bomb.

  1. Remove plug from tail of bomb.

  2. Take exploder and detonator from their tins and place detonator in the hole in end of exploder.

  3. Gently push exploder into bomb, taking care to see that detonator end goes in last.

  4. Untie cord becket from vane of pistol and test vane for ease of spinning.

5. Screw pistol into bomb and tighten grub screw.

6. Just before leaving ground remove safety pin from pistol.

Action of Fuse and Safety Device. (*See* Leaflet 19.)

On the carrier the vane of the pistol is held from rotating by a stop on the carrier.

When the bomb is released the vane is free to rotate and spins off. The striker is then supported on the striker spring.

On impact the bomb is slowed up, but the striker being free to move forward compresses the striker spring and pierces the detonator which fires the bomb.

Loading Bomb on Carrier.

The bomb must be securely housed on the carrier, and on no account be free to move in either the horizontal or vertical planes.

This object is attained by the adjustment of the nose and tail pieces. This adjustment must be repeated in the case of every bomb loaded.

Before the bomb is fused, it must be loaded on the carrier and dropped at least once, to ascertain that the carrier is functioning correctly. When this has been done the bomb is to be fused and replaced on the carrier.

Unloading.

(1) Replace safety pin in pistol.

(2) Drop bomb off carrier.

(3) Unscrew pistol and replace it in its tin.

(4) Gently shake exploder out of bomb, take out detonator and replace both in their tins.

(5) Replace plug in tail of bomb.

Targets Engaged.

Personnel—Aerodromes.

Note.—This bomb is obsolescent—no more being made.

AIR MINISTRY,
January, 1918.

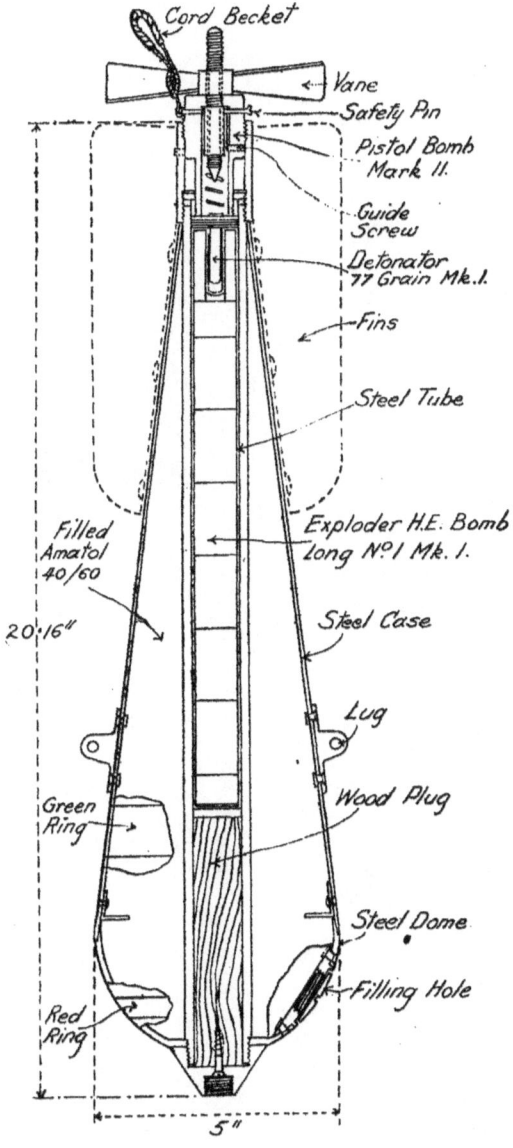

Leaflet No. 5.

BOMB:—INCENDIARY CARCASS.

Mark II.

General Description.

   Actual weight of bomb.—14·5 lb.
   Weight of Case.—6 lb.
   Weight of Incendiary Substance.—8·5 lb.
   Incendiary Substance.—Carcass.
   Case Material.—Tin plate.
   Overall Dimensions.—Bomb: 19·25 in. × 5 in. max. diam.
      ,,   ,,   Fins: Side of square containing fins, 5·2 in.
   How Stowed.—Horizontally.
   Type of Fuse.—Tail Fuse.
   Construction.—See diagram.

To Prepare for Action.
   The following will be required:—
      (1) Pistol Bomb No. 1 Mk. II.
      (2) 1 Special Very Cartridge.

Fusing Bomb.
   1. Place Very Cartridge cap uppermost in tail of bomb.
   2. Untie cord becket from bomb pistol and test vane for ease of spinning.
   3. Screw pistol into bomb.
   4. Just before leaving ground remove safety pin from pistol

Action of Fuse and Safety Device.
   When the bomb is loaded on carrier, the vane of fuse is held from rotating by a stop on the carrier.

When the bomb is dropped, the vane is free to rotate, and spins off.

On impact the bomb is checked, but the striker being free to move forward compresses the striker spring, and fires the cap of Very's Cartridge.

The star of cartridge is projected through the thin copper diaphragm and ignites magnesium composition pellet, which lights the bomb.

Loading Bomb on Carrier.

The bomb must be securely housed on the carrier, and on no account be free to move in either the horizontal or vertical planes.

This object is attained by the adjustment of the nose and tail pieces. This adjustment must be repeated in the case of every bomb loaded.

Before the bomb is fused it must be loaded on the carrier and dropped at least once, to ascertain that the carrier is functioning correctly. When this has been done, and provided the carrier is found to be working satisfactorily, the bomb is to be reloaded on the carrier, having first been made live by the insertion of Very's Cartridge and subsequent screwing of tail fuse into position.

Unloading.

1. Replace safety pin in fuse.
2. Drop bomb off carrier.
3. Unscrew fuse from bomb and remove Very's Cartridge, replacing Very's Cartridge in its box and Pistol Bomb in its tin.

Targets Engaged.

Buildings, Aerodromes, Forage Stores.

Note:—

Obsolescent in present form; may be re-introduced later with thermite filling.

AIR MINISTRY,
January, 1918.

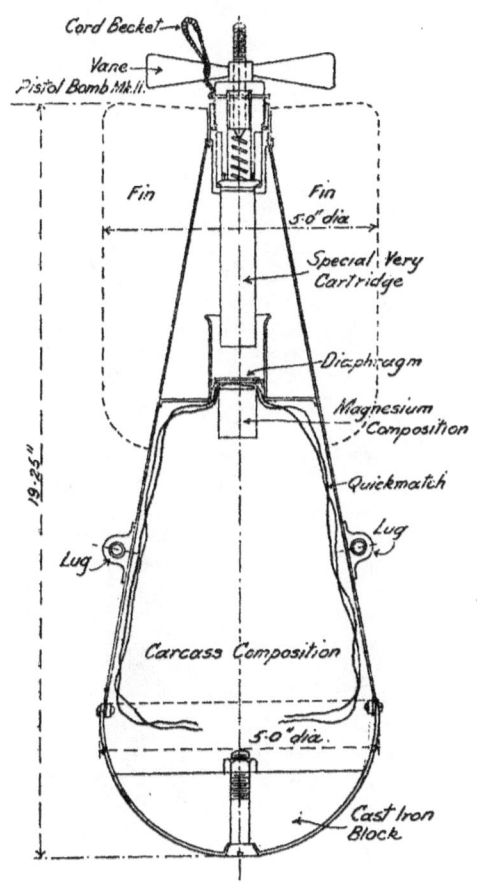

Leaflet No. 6.

BOMB :—H.E. "HALE," 20 lb.

HEAVY CASE.
Mk. II/C.

General Description.

   Actual Weight of Bomb.—18·5 lbs.
   Weight of Case.—14 lbs.
   Weight of Explosive.—4·5 lbs.
   Explosive Substance.—Amatol 80/60, some amatol 40/60.
   Case Material.—Cast steel or forged steel.
   Thickness of Case.—Nose, 1·3 inches; Body, $\frac{1}{4}$ inch.
   Overall Dimensions.—Bomb. $23\frac{1}{4}$ inches long × 5 inches diameter, maximum.
      ,,   ,,   .—Fins. Side of square containing fins, 5·1 inches.
   How Stowed.—Horizontally.
   Type of Fuse.—"Hales."
   Construction.—See diagram.

To Prepare for Action.
  The following will be required:—
    Detonators.   "Hales" Detonator (Mk. II).
Note.—The exploders are fixed so forming an integral portion of the bomb.

Fusing Bomb.
  This bomb must be fused before putting it on the carrier.
    (1) Unscrew knurled cap and remove tail.
    (2) Pull out safety pin and test vanes for ease of spinning, replace safety pin.
    (3) Screw detonator on to spindle seeing that slot on detonator is well engaged on spring pin on tail.

(4) Replace tail on bomb, seeing that fixed pin on tail enters hole provided in body of bomb.

(5) Just before leaving the ground remove safety pin and see that vane is free.

Action of Fuse and Safety Device.

On the carrier the vanes are held from rotating by a stop on the carrier. When the bomb is released the vanes are free to rotate and spin round. This draws the spindle up into the tail, and, as the detonator is held from rotating by spring pin, it unscrews and drops off on to detonator spring.

On impact the bomb is slowed up, but the detonator being free to move forward compresses the spring and strikes the point of the striker, thus firing the bomb.

Loading Bomb on Carrier.

The bomb must be securely housed on the carrier, and on no account be free to move in either the horizontal or vertical planes.

This object is attained by the adjustment of the nose and tail pieces. This adjustment must be repeated in the case of every bomb loaded.

Before the bomb is fused, it must be loaded on the carrier and dropped at least once, to ascertain that the carrier is functioning correctly. When this has been done, and provided the carrier is found to be working satisfactorily, the bomb is to be made live by the insertion of a " Hales " detonator, and be reloaded on the carrier.

Unloading.

1. Replace safety pin in bomb.
2. Release bomb from carrier.
3. Unscrew knurled cap, remove tail and unscrew detonator. Replace detonator in its tin.
4. Replace tail of bomb and screw up knurled cap.

Targets Engaged.

Personnel, aerodromes, road transport.

(*Note.*—This bomb is obsolescent—no more being made.)

AIR MINISTRY,
January, 1918.

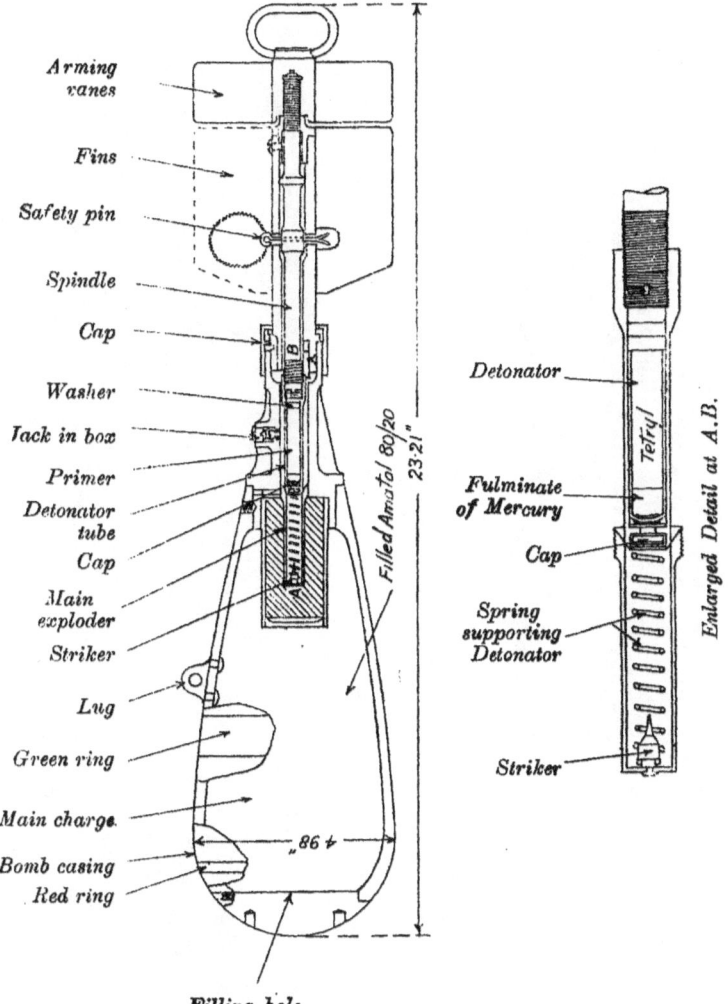

Leaflet No. 7.

BOMB:—H.E., R.F.C., 230 lb.

Light Case.
Mk. I.

General Description.

    Actual Weight of Bomb.—230 lbs.
    Weight of Case.—90 lbs.
    Weight of Explosive.—140 lbs.
    Explosive Substance.—Amatol 40/60.
    Case Material.—Mild Steel Sheet.
    Thickness of Case.—Nose: 1 inch.
         ,,   ,,   Body: 10 gauge (·128 inches thick).
    Overall Dimensions.—Bomb: 50·5 inches long × 10 inches diameter.
         ,,   ,,   Fins: Side of square containing fins: 13·6 inches.
    How Stowed.—Horizontally.
    Type of Fuse.—Tail fuse.
    Construction.—*See* Diagram.

To Prepare for Action.

  The following will be required:—
    (1) 1 Bomb Pistol, No. 5, Mk. I.
    (2) 1 Relay detonating.
    (3) 1 Igniter. 15 secs. 2·5 or ·05 secs., as required.
    Exploders: Two long No. 2 Mk. II.
    Detonators: Four 56 gr. Mk. II.

Fusing Bomb.

1. Remove plug from tail.

2. Remove exploders and detonators from their tins, and screw detonators into exploders.

3. Gently push exploders into central tube.

4. Untie cord becket from pistol vane, and test vane for ease of spinning.

5. Push igniter into detonating relay, and screw pistol on to relay.

6. Screw fuse into bomb, and tighten grub screw.

7. Just before leaving ground, remove safety pin from fuse.

Action of Fuse and Safety Devices.

When the bomb is loaded on carrier, the vane of fuse is held from rotating by a stop on the carrier.

When the bomb is dropped the vane is free to rotate, and spins off.

On impact the bomb is checked, but the striker being free to move forward compresses the striker spring and fires the cap of the igniter. This burns for 15 sec., 2·5 sec., or ·05 sec., according to type, and then fires its detonator, which in its turn fires the detonator in exploder, and so sets off the bomb.

Loading Bomb on Carrier.

The bomb must be securely housed on the carrier, and on no account be free to move in either the horizontal or vertical planes.

This object is attained by the adjustment of the nose and tail pieces. This adjustment must be repeated in the case of every bomb loaded.

Before the bomb is fused it must be loaded on the carrier and dropped at least once, to ascertain that the carrier is functioning correctly. When this has been done, and provided the carrier is found to be working satisfactorily, the bomb is to be reloaded on the carrier and made live by the insertion of the exploders and detonators, and the subsequent screwing of the fuse into position.

Unloading.

1. Replace safety pin in fuse.

2. Drop bomb off carrier.

3. Unscrew fuse from bomb and take it to pieces, replacing detonating relay, pistol, and igniter in their boxes.

4. Gently shake out exploders, unscrew detonators, and replace the whole in their tins.

5. Screw plug into tail.

Targets Engaged.

Buildings, railways and roads. Also used against submarines, for which purpose it is fitted with a nose cap.

AIR MINISTRY,
January, 1918.

[OVER

Diagram of a bomb/munition, labeled as follows:

- Steel Nose
- Red Ring
- Steel Rod
- Diaphragm
- Detonator 56 Gr. Mk II
- Body
- Filled Amatol 40/60
- Lug
- Central Tube
- Exploder Long No 2 Mk II
- Green Ring
- Detonator 56 Gr. Mk II
- Detonators 56 Gr. Mk II
- (Delay 1·5 sec Blue or 2·5 sec Green or ·05 sec White)
- Fin
- Filling Plug
- Relay Detonating (See Fig 2)
- Fin
- Stiffening Stays
- S·61
- Safety Pin
- Vane
- Cord
- Becket
- Pistol Bomb No 3 Mk I
- 50·5" Over all

Leaflet No. 7a. *Supplementary to No. 7.*

BOMB :—H.E., R.F.C., 230 lbs.

LIGHT CASE.
Mk. III.

GENERAL DESCRIPTION.

Approx. Weight of Bomb ...	200 lbs.
,, Weight of Case ...	100 lbs.
,, Weight of Explosive	100 lbs.
Explosive Substance	Amatol 80/20.
Case Material	Mild Steel Sheet.
Thickness of Case	Nose : .375 inch.
Thickness of Case	Body : 10 gauge (.128 inch thick).
Overall Dimensions	Bomb : 50.5 inches long × 10 inches diameter.
Overall Dimensions	Fins : Side of square containing fins : 13.6 inches.
How Stowed	Horizontally or vertically.
Type of Fuse...	Tail Fuse.
Construction	*See* Diagram.

The Mark II. Bomb is identical with the Mark I. except for very slight alterations to simplify manufacture.

The Mark III. is designed for stem filling from the nose, and thus has no filling hole and plug. It is fitted also with detachable vanes. The steel point X (*see* Fig.) is also drilled with a hole to take a pin for a shackle when the bomb is slung vertically by the nose.

TO PREPARE FOR ACTION.
The following will be required :—

Assemblage "A"
(1) 1, *Pistol, Bomb*, No. 3 or No. 5 Mark I. (When No. 3. Mark I is issued, the screwed gland must be removed for sea use.)
(2) 1, *Relay Detonating*, H.E. Bomb, 7.89" Mark I. or II.
(3) 1, *Detonator, Aerial Bomb*, Mark II, with .05 sec. or 15 secs. delay. (Sometimes called " Igniter.")

T.5. D.728.

Assemblage "B"

and

or
- (1) 1, *Pistol, Bomb*, No. 3 or No. 5, Mark I. (Where No. 3 Mark I is issued, the screwed gland must be removed for sea use.
- (2) 1, *Relay Detonating, H.E. Bomb*, 7.89" Mark III. (Mark, III only. Sometimes called " 7.39" Exploder.")
- (3) 1, *Detonator, Aerial Bomb*, Mark II with .05 sec. or 15 secs. delay.
  or
- (3) 1, *Detonator, Aerial Bomb*, No. 4 Mark I (instantaneous).
  or
- (3) 1, *Detonator, Aerial Bomb*, No. 5 Mark I. (2.5 secs. delay.)

together with :—
- 2, Exploders, H.E. Bomb, 12.75" No. 2. Mark II.
- 4, Detonators, H.E. Bomb, 56 grs. Mark II.

NOTE:—
  I. Interchange may not be made in fusing components between the two assemblages " A " and " B." Only alternatives stated within the individual assemblages are permitted.

  II. Detonators, Aerial Bomb, No. 4 Mark I and No. 5 Mark I may not be employed in Assemblage " A."

  III. Note should be made of the distinction between " Detonators Aerial Bomb " and " Detonators H.E. Bomb."

  IV. The important difference between Relays Detonating 7.39" Mark I or II and Mark III should be noted. The Marks I and II are identical as regards action, and contain 2 C.E. pellets and wood block, whereas the Mark III has 4 C.E. pellets.

  V. The above methods of fusing apply equally to the Mark I bomb where still in use, and supersede instructions in Leaflet No. 7.

Leaflet No. 7a (continued).

  VI. *Detonator*, Aerial Bomb, Mark II. (with 2.5 secs. delay) will no longer be used. For this length of delay, Detonator, Aerial Bomb, No. 5 Mk. I. will be employed, and then *only* with the Mark III. Relay Detonating 7.39″.

FUSING BOMB.

1. Remove plug from tail.

2. Remove exploders and "detonators, H.E. bomb," from their tins, and screw detonators into exploders.

3. Gently push exploders into central tube.

4. Untie cord becket from pistol vane, and test vane for ease of spinning.

5. Push the "detonator, aerial bomb," into detonating relay, and screw pistol on to relay.

6. Screw fuse into bomb, and tighten grub screw.

7. Just before leaving ground, remove safety pin from fuse.

ACTION OF FUSE AND SAFETY DEVICE.

When the bomb is loaded on carrier, the vane of fuse is held from rotating by a stop on the carrier.

When the bomb is dropped, the vane is free to rotate, and spins off.

On impact the bomb is checked, but the striker being free to move forward compresses the striker spring and fires the cap of the "detonator, aerial bomb." This burns for 15 secs., 2.5 secs., or ·.05 sec., according to type and then fires its detonator, which in its turn fires the "detonator, H.E. bomb," in exploder, and so sets off the bomb.

LOADING BOMB ON CARRIER.

The bomb must be securely housed on the carrier, and on no account be free to move in either the horizontal or vertical planes.

This object is attained by the adjustment of the nose and tail pieces. This adjustment must be repeated in the case of every bomb loaded.

Before the bomb is fused it must be loaded on the carrier and dropped at least once, to ascertain that the carrier is functioning correctly. When this has been done, and provided the carrier is found to be working satisfactorily, the bomb is to be reloaded on the carrier and made live by the insertion of the exploders and detonators, and the subsequent screwing of the fuse into position.

UNLOADING.

1. Replace safety pin in fuse.
2. Drop bomb off carrier.
3. Unscrew fuse from bomb and take it to pieces, replacing detonating relay, pistol, and detonator, aerial bomb, in their boxes.
4. Gently shake out exploders, unscrew detonators, H.E. bomb, and replace the whole in their tins.
5. Screw plug into tail.

TARGETS ENGAGED.

Buildings, railways and roads. Also used against submarines, for which purpose it is fitted with a nose cap.

MARK IV. BOMB.

For use in H.M. ships and storage in R.N.O. depots the two Exploders 12.75″ No. 2 Mk. II. are replaced by two special exploders, Nos. 5 and 7; each having only one 56 grain Detonator, H.E. Bomb, Mark II. When inserting these exploders care should be taken that the detonators are towards the tail of the bomb.

The above assemblage will not fit land service bombs, on account of a slight difference in the length of central tube.

Naval bombs fused this way are designated Mark IV. and stencilled " N " to denote naval service, and will only be issued to A.F. units serving in H.M. Ships.

Air Ministry,

May, 1918.

BOMB, H.E., R.F.C. 230 LBS, MARK III

A. CORD SOCKET
B. ARMING VANE
C. SAFETY PIN
D. STRIKER SPINDLE
E. STRIKER SPRING
F. .410 CAP OF IGNITER
G. ADAPTER
H. WOOD BLOCK
J. FUZE
K. CORK WASHER
L. C.E. PELLETS
M. DETONATOR
N. AMATOL
O. P. DETACHABLE METAL STRAP SECURING FINS
Q. FELT WASHER
R. DETONATOR 58 GRAIN
S. DETONATOR ENVELOPE
T. C.E. PELLETS
U. SUSPENSION LUG
V. STEEL ROD
W. FORGED SHELL STEEL NOSE
X. STEEL POINT THREADED
Y. CENTRAL TUBE
Z. FILLING 1/2 AMATOL
AA. SHEET STEEL BODY
BB. PIN
CC. FIN STIFFENING STAY

VIEW SHOWING POSITION OF SUSPENSION LUG, FINS, AND FIN STIFFENING STAYS.

Leaflet No. 7b.

REVISED VANES FOR 230 lb. BOMB.

These new vanes have been designed for the 230 lb. bomb, owing to insufficient vane area in existing ones, causing the bombs to oscillate in flight with consequent impact at an angle wide of the line of flight and the probability of lack of retardation.

For the Mark III. bomb with detachable vanes, the diagram shows the new pattern vane which is attached to circular bands by the lugs A and B as at present. In addition a lug C, is provided for an extra steadying band (shown on the right of diagram), owing to the additional length of vane. Stays from vane to vane will be fitted as at present, with an additional set towards the front.

In cases where the detachable vanes are not fitted, an extension should be rivetted on to the existing vanes to make them equivalent in size to new vanes, the steadying band being attached to the lugs C and bolted to body of the bomb by the bolt D. These alterations will be made by manufacturers as soon as possible, but can be carried out locally as a temporary measure.

In the case of the D.H.9 machines, in this connection, the small sighting view will not allow this alteration in width; an extension of 9" to the rear can, however, be fitted, which will also entail new stays.

Side of square containing vanes at present=18.6"
,,   ,,   ,,   ,,   ,,   new pattern=19.6"

Air Ministry,
August, 1918.

REVISED VANES & STEADYING BAND FOR 230 LB BOMB.

DIMENSIONS IN INCHES.

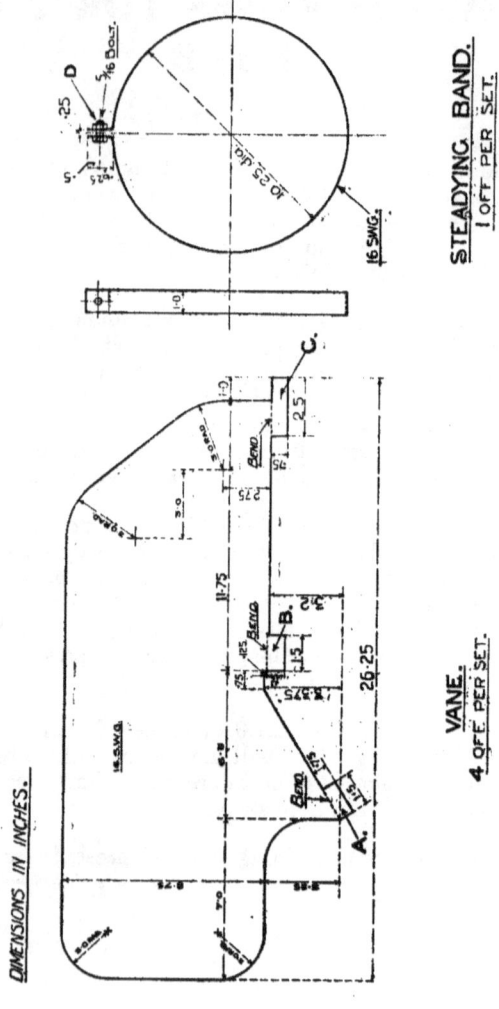

STEADYING BAND.
1 OFF PER SET.

VANE.
4 OFF PER SET.

Leaflet No. 8.

BOMB:—H.E, R.A.F, 336 lb.

HEAVY CASE.
Mk. I.

General Description.

Actual Weight of Bomb.—336 lbs.

Weight of Nose.—230 lbs.

Weight of Fairing and Central Tube.—36 lbs.

Weight of Explosive.—70 lbs.

Explosive Substance.—Cast or Compressed TNT.

Case Material.—Cast Steel.

Thickness of Case.—Nose: The nose of this bomb is made up of bulged segments (thickest part $1\frac{13}{16}$ in.).

Overall Dimensions.—Bomb   Long bomb: 6 ft. $9\frac{1}{2}$ ins. by 14 ins. max. diameter.

,,   Short bomb: 5 ft. $2\frac{5}{8}$ ins. by 14 ins. max. diameter.

,,   Fins: Side of square containing fins 15·6 ins.

How Stowed.—Horizontally.

Type of Fuse.—Nose fuse, D.A. No. 1, Mk. 1.

Construction.—See diagram.

To Prepare for Action, with Nose Fuse.

The following will be required:—

Fuses.—1 D.A. No. 1, Mk. 1.

Exploders.—1 No. 4, Mk. I/L.

Detonators.—Two 60 gr. No. 2, Mk. I/C for R.A.F. bombs.

Fusing Bomb, Nose Fuse.

1. Remove nose plug and nose adapter from bomb.
2. Remove exploder and detonators from their tins, and screw detonators into exploder.
3. Gently push exploder into central tube from nose end and replace nose adapter.
4. Remove safety pin, safety collar, and striker spindle from nose fuse, and test striker spindle for ease of spinning. Screw nose fuse into bomb, and replace striker spindle, safety collar, and safety pin, seeing that red line on striker spindle is flush with face of pressure plate, and that short end of vane stop engages in castellation on nose of bomb.
5. Wire safety collar to bomb carrier.
6. Just before leaving ground, remove safety pin from nose fuse.

Action of Fuse and Safety Device.

On the carrier the vane of the fuse is held from rotating by the vane-stop on safety collar.

Nose Fuse. (*See* LEAFLET 20.)

1. On dropping, safety collar is pulled off nose fuse by wire attached to carrier, and vane is spun round by air pressure.
2. On striking the ground, blow comes on vane and pressure plate, shearing pins are sheared and striker hits cap. This detonates the Tetryl in nose fuse and this in its turn detonates 60 grain detonator and exploder, which sets off the bomb.

Unloading.

1. Carefully remove nose fuse from bomb and replace it in its tin.
2. Drop bomb off carrier.
3. Unscrew nose adapter and shake out exploder. Remove detonators and replace exploder and detonators in their tins.
4. Replace nose adapter and nose plug in bomb.

Targets Engaged.

Railway stations, workshops, Aerodromes, personnel.

Note.—This bomb is obsolescent. No more will be made.

AIR MINISTRY,
January, 1918.

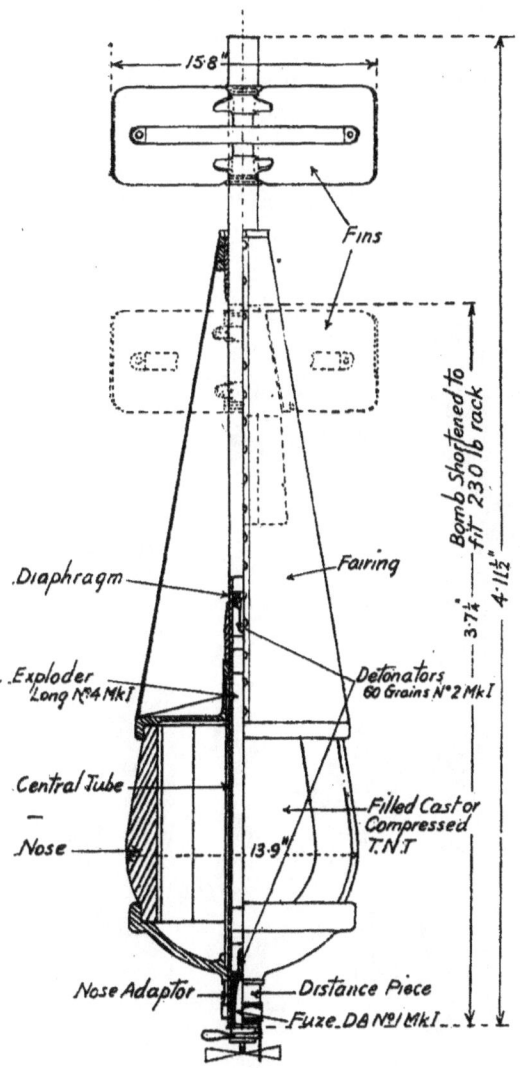

Leaflet No. 9.

BOMB AEROPLANE DEMOLITION.

Thin Case.

General Description.
  Actual Weight of Bomb.—4 lb. 14 oz.
  Weight of Case.—14 ozs.
  Weight of Explosive.—4 lbs.
  Explosive Substance.—80/20 Amatol.
  Case Material.—Tinplate.
  Overall Dimensions.—1 ft. 2½ ins. long by 3 ins. in diameter.
  How stowed.—As convenient. Special fitting.
  Type of Fuse.—Special Fuse.
  Construction.—See diagram.

To prepare for Action.
  The following will be required:—1 Special Fuse.

Fusing Bomb.
  (The fuse is kept in a tin wired to one of the outer interplane struts.)

  After a forced landing in enemy territory.
   (1) Remove fuse from its tin.
   (2) Push fuse into bomb, detonator first, and fix it in position by wire attached to bomb.
   (3) Place the bomb on the engine, between the cylinders if possible, pull out the safety pin and run away.
   (4) After one minute the bomb will explode.

(This is a specially designed bomb intended for the destruction of aeroplanes after forced landings in enemy territory, and is not otherwise used.)

Air Ministry,
January, 1918.

2

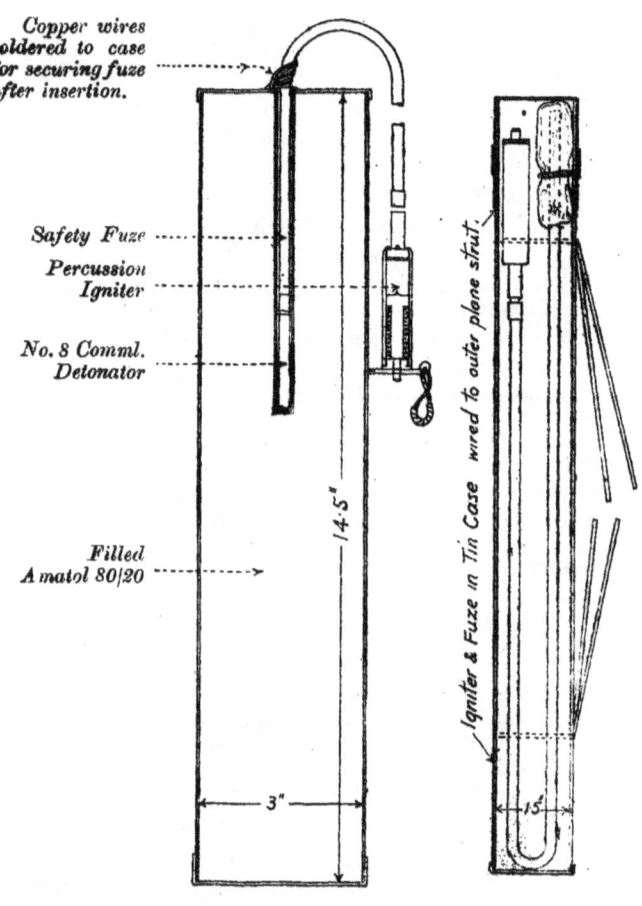

Leaflet No. 10.

BOMB :—H.E. COOPER, 20 lb.

Heavy Case.
Mk. I.

General Description.

Actual Weight of Bomb.—24 lbs.
Weight of Case.—20 lbs.
Weight of Explosive.—4 lbs.
Explosive Substance.—Amatol 80/20 (if filled Amatol 40/60 weight of charge 4 lbs. 9 ozs.).
Case Material.—Cast or forged steel—semi-steel.
Thickness of Case.—All over, $\frac{5}{16}$ inches.
Overall Dimensions.—Bomb. 24·4 inches long × 5·12 inches maximum diameter.
,, ,, —Fins. Side of square containing fins, 5·2 inches.
How Stowed.—Horizontally. Vertically, tail up.
Type of Fuse.—Cooper, nose fuse.
Construction.—See diagram.

The following will be required:—

1 Cooper Bomb Detonator.

(*Note.*—The exploders are fixed and form an integral portion of the bomb.)

Fusing Bomb.

1. Unscrew nose cap and fuse.
2. Insert detonator in hole in nose of bomb.
3. Screw home fuse.
4. Just before leaving the ground, cut the safety wire of fuse.

Action of Fuse and Safety Device.

(For action of fuse, *see* Leaflet 10A.)

On the carrier, the vane of the fuse is held from rotating by a stop on the carrier.

When the bomb is released, the vane (A) is free to rotate. By means of a series of cog wheels the vane spindle (B) rotates the striker carrier (C). After 25 turns of the vane spindle, the striker carrier has been rotated, so far that the striker (D) is opposite the striker way (E). At this point the striker carrier becomes unmeshed, and ceases to rotate.

On impact, the blow comes on the vane, the shearing wire (F) is sheared and the striker is forced out of its carrier, down the striker way and on to the cap (G) of the detonator (H) thus firing the bomb.

Loading Bomb on Carrier.

The bomb must be securely housed on carrier, and on no account be free to move in either the horizontal or vertical planes.

This object is attained by the adjustment of the nose piece. This adjustment must be repeated in the case of every bomb loaded.

Before the bomb is fused, it must be loaded on the carrier and dropped at least once, to ascertain that the carrier is functioning correctly. When this has been done, and provided the carrier is found to be working satisfactorily, the bomb is to be reloaded on the carrier, and made live by the insertion of the detonator, and screwing of fuse into position.

Unloading.

(1) Unscrew fuse, remove detonator and replace it in its tin.

(2) Drop bomb off carrier.

(3) Replace nose fuse and cover.

Targets Engaged.

Personnel and aerodromes.

AIR MINISTRY,
January, 1918.

3

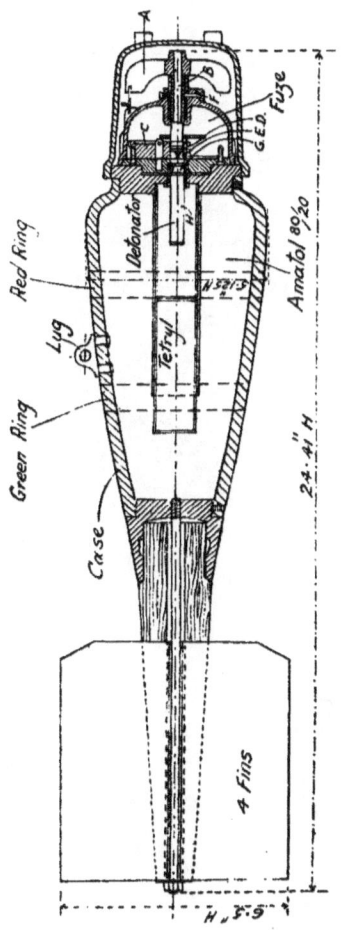

Leaflet No. 10a.

COOPER FUSE.

Weight Complete.—2 lb.

Construction.—*See* diagram.

This fuse is used in the 20-lb. Cooper bomb and may possibly also be used in converted shell bombs.

Method of Loading into Bomb.
  (1) Remove nose cap and fuse from bomb.
  (2) Place bomb on rack.
  (3) Insert detonator.
  (4) Replace fuse.
  (5) Just before leaving the ground, cut the safety wire which holds the vane A to the body of the fuse.

Safety Device and Method of Action.
  On the carrier the vane (A) is held from rotating by the stop on the carrier. On release the vane is free to rotate and spins round with its spindle (B).

  By means of a system of cog wheels, the vane spindle (B) rotates the striker carrier (C). When the spindle has made 25 revolutions, the striker carrier has reached the end of its travel and becomes unmeshed. In this position the striker (D) is opposite the striker way (E).

  On striking the ground, the blow comes on the vane, the shearing wire (F) is sheared and the vane spindle with its bush moves forward and drives the striker down the striker way (E) on to the cap (G) of the detonator (H) thus firing the bomb.

Unloading.
  In unloading first replace the safety wire and then remove the fuse from the bomb, remove the detonator replacing it in its tin, drop bomb off rack, and replace fuse and nose cap on bomb.

AIR MINISTRY,
January, 1918.

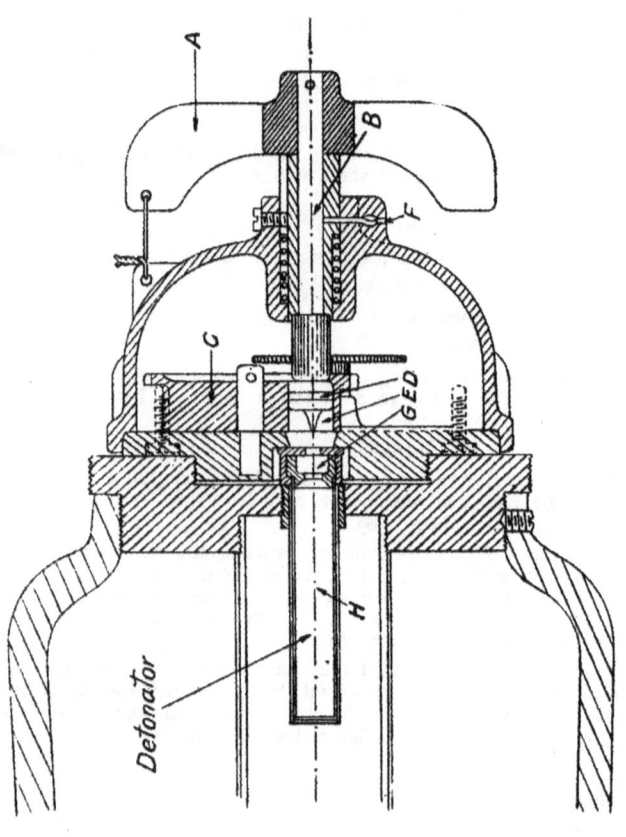

Leaflet 11.

BOMB
INCENDIARY AND SMOKE.
T.W. 40lbs.
Mk. II/L/TYPE B.

Ap.D. [P.]   D.397.   2/18.

2

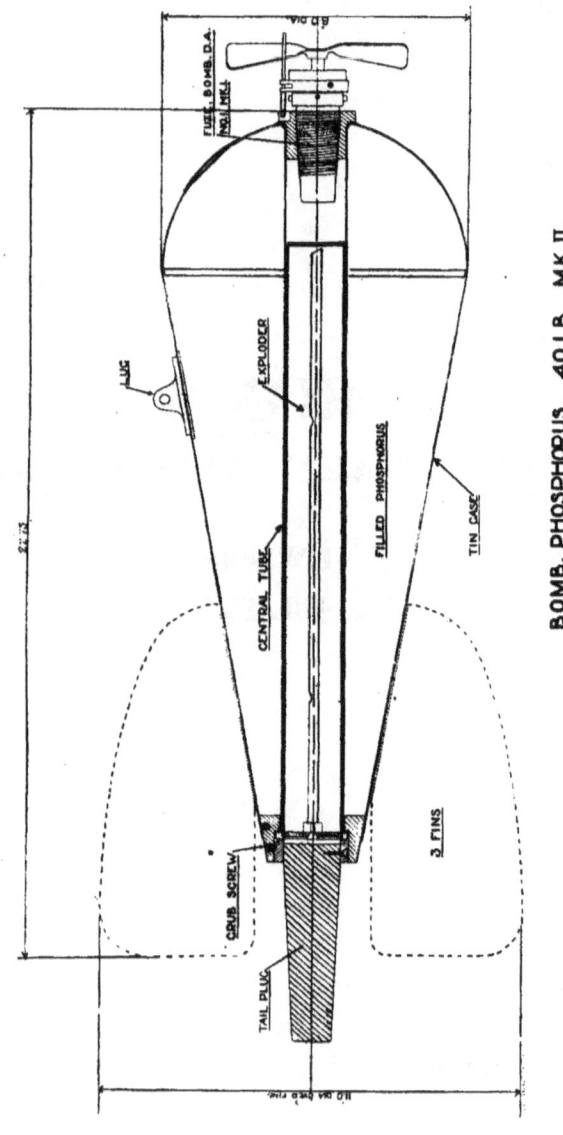

BOMB. PHOSPHORUS. 40 LB. MK II.
Fig. 1,

BOMB
INCENDIARY AND SMOKE
T.W. 40 lbs. Mk. II/L/Type B.

GENERAL DESCRIPTION.

Actual weight of bomb	40 lbs.
Weight of case	10 lbs.
Weight of charge	30 lb.
Explosive substance	Phosphorus.
Case material	Tinplate.
Thickness of case (nose, body)	All over .025 in.
Overall dimensions	1 ft. 8⅝ in. long × 8 in. mx. diameter.
How carried	Horizontally.
Type of fuse	Tail fuse (time) and nose fuse.
Construction	See diagram.

TO PREPARE FOR ACTION.

The following will be required : (A) for nose fuse, (B) for Midgeley tail fuse, (C) for special tail fuse, (D) for use with A, B, or C.

(A)
(1) 1 D.A. No. 1 Mk. I Nose fuse.
(2) 1 Special tail plug.

(B)
(1) 1 Midgeley fuse complete.
(2) 1 Special punch.

(C)
(1) 1 Special fuse.
(2) Special adapter.

(D)
Exploder—1 special for phosphorus bombs.

FUSING BOMB.

With Nose Fuse (see Leaflet 20).

(1) Before loading bomb on carrier remove tail plug and insert exploder in central tube and replace tail plug.

(2) Place bomb on carrier and remove nose plug.

(3) Load nose fuse in ordinary way, i.e., remove safety pin, safety collar and striker spindle, screw fuse into bomb and replace striker spindle, safety collar and safety pin. See that red line on vane spindle is flush with face of pressure plate. Wire safety collar to carrier.

(4) Just before leaving ground, remove safety pin from fuse.

With Special Tail Fuse (Fig. 2).

(1) Remove tail plug.

(2) Insert exploder in central tube.

(3) Untie cord becket on fuse and test vane for spinning.

(4) Screw special tail fuse and adapter into bomb.

(5) Place bomb on carrier.

(6) Just before leaving ground, remove safety pin from fuse.

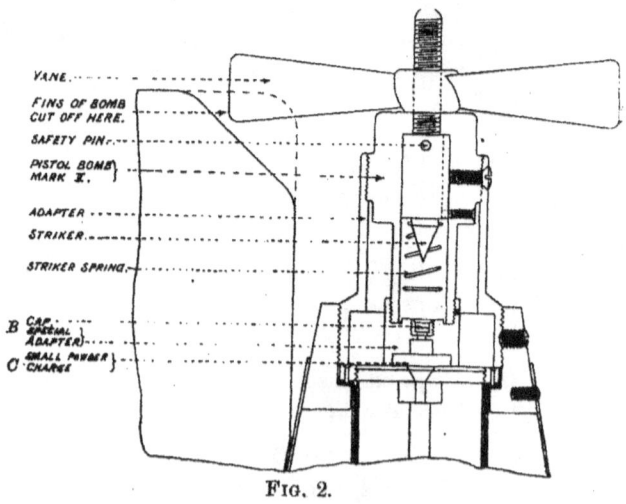

FIG. 2.

Midgeley Fuse (see Page 9, Fig. 4).

(NOTE.—This fuse must be very carefully handled.
(For description see Page 9.)

(1) Remove tail plug.

(2) Insert exploder in central tube.

(3) Punch Midgeley fuse to time required.

(4) Screw fuse into bomb, seeing that trigger is in line with bomb lug.

(5) Place bomb on carrier.

(6) Insert string of trigger under safety clip.   (For description of safety device see Fig. 3 and Page 11.)

(7) Just before leaving ground remove safety pin from fuse.

ACTION OF FUSE AND SAFETY DEVICE.

D.A. Fuse, or Special Tail Fuse.

On carrier the vane of nose fuse is held from rotating by the vane stop on safety collar, that of the tail fuse by a stop on the carrier.

On release the nose fuse works in the usual manner (see Leaflet 20). In the case of the Special Tail Fuse the striker on impact hits cap B, which sets off a small powder charge C, which in its turn fires the exploder D, and so sets off bomb (see Fig. 2).

(These two types of fuse are used for smoke production. When they are used, the bombs should be released at regular intervals flying across the wind. In this way an even distribution of smoke over the ground is obtained.)

Midgeley Fuse.

For action of this fuse see Page 9, Fig. 4.

LOADING BOMB ON CARRIER.

The 40 lb. phosphorus bombs are carried in the two outside positions on the 4-20 lb. C.F.S. carrier. For the Midgeley fuse a special safety device is added to this carrier (see Fig. 3).

(NOTE.—These bombs must not be carried with Midgeley fuse unless the safety device is fitted (see Fig. 3).

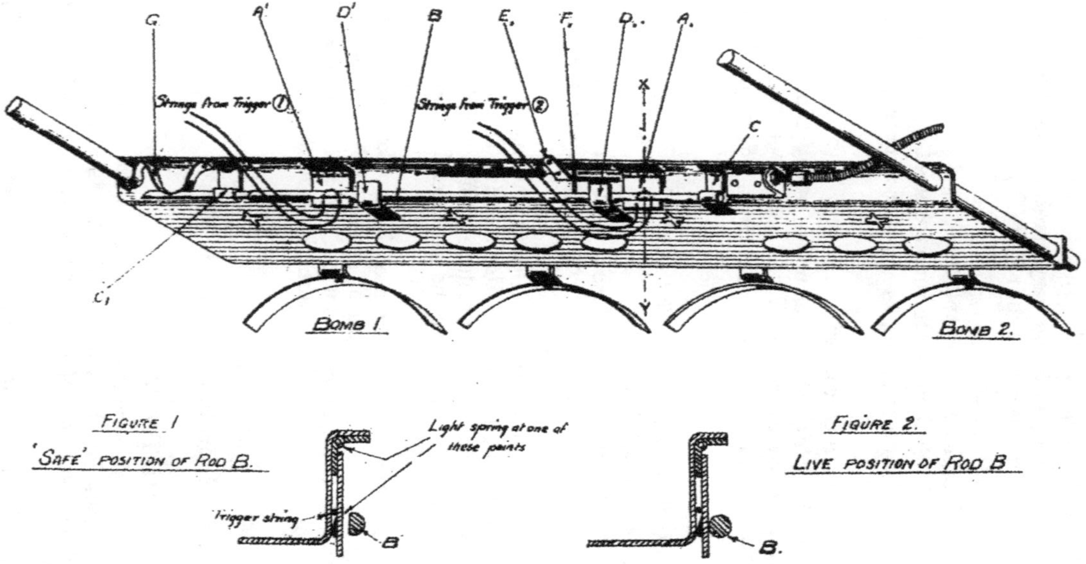

FIGURE 1
'SAFE' POSITION OF ROD B.

FIGURE 2.
LIVE POSITION OF ROD B.

SAFETY DEVICE FOR 40 LB. PHOSPHORUS BOMB
FIG. 3.

The position of the bombs when loaded is such that they are released by the third and fourth pulls of the release handle. On this account the first two pulls should be taken on the ground, *and the safety device then be reset before leaving the ground.*

The bombs must be securely housed on the carrier and not be free to move in the horizontal or vertical planes. This is obtained by the adjustment of the nose and tail pieces provided on the carrier.

Before the bombs are fused they should be dropped at least once to test the carrier. If the carrier is functioning correctly, the bombs are to be reloaded on carrier, having first been made live by the insertion of the exploder and the screwing of fuse into position.

UNLOADING BOMB.

Nose Fuse.

(1) Remove nose fuse in usual manner (i.e., remove safety collar and striker spindle, unscrew fuse and replace striker spindle, safety collar and safety pin.)

(2) Replace fuse in its tin and replace nose plug.

(3) Drop bomb off carrier.

(4) Remove tail plug and gently shake out exploder, putting it back in its tin. Replace tail plug.

Special Tail Fuse (see Fig. 2).

(1) Replace safety pin in fuse.
(2) Drop bomb off carrier.
(3) Unscrew fuse and adapter, replacing them in their tins.
(4) Gently shake out exploder and replace it in its tin.
(5) Replace tail plug.

Midgeley Fuse (see Fig. 4).

(1) Replace safety pin.
(2) Remove string from safety device.
(3) Remove bomb from carrier.
(4) Unscrew fuse and replace it in its tin.
(5) Gently shake out exploder and replace it in its tin.
(6) Replace exploder and fuse in their tins.

II.

TARGETS ENGAGED.

With D.A. nose fuse or special fuse these bombs are used for smoke production or as beacons on the ground.

With the Midgeley fuse they are used for air bursts in the attack of kite balloons. (See further instructions at end of this leaflet.)

MIDGELEY FUSE.

General Description.

This is an adjustable time fuse used in phosphorus bombs Mks, I. and II. and T.W.R. parachute flares.

Weight complete .... 1 lb. 10 ozs.
Length .... 5⅜".
Construction .... See diagram.

Method of Loading into Bomb (see Fig. 4).

(1) Remove fuse from its tin and screw it into bomb.

(2) Punch the fuse to time required. (For times see Page 10).

This is done as follows:—Open the cover A, insert one of the special punches provided, and give it a few light blows with a hammer. If the punching has been done properly the time fuse inside should appear as in Fig. B. If punched too lightly it will be as in Fig. C, and should be punched again. The fuse should on no account be punched too hard. Finally close the cover A.

(3) Put the bomb on the carrier and push the string attached to trigger B under the stud on the special safety clip on the carrier (see Fig. 3).

(4) Just before leaving the ground pull out both safety pins HH.

Action of Fuse.

The fuse does not become live until the trigger B is pulled out of the fuse by the string C when the bomb is released from the rack.

On release the striker spring D forces the striker E on to the cap F. The flash from this lights the upper rim of safety fuse G, which burns up to the punch mark, where it flashes across to the lower rim L, and finally lights the powder charge M, which is the main charge of the T.W.R. parachute flare, and in the phosphorus bomb lights the exploder.

NOTE :—This fuse should always be used in conjunction with the special safety device for phosphorus bombs fitted to 4—20 lb. bomb rack. If this safety device is used it is

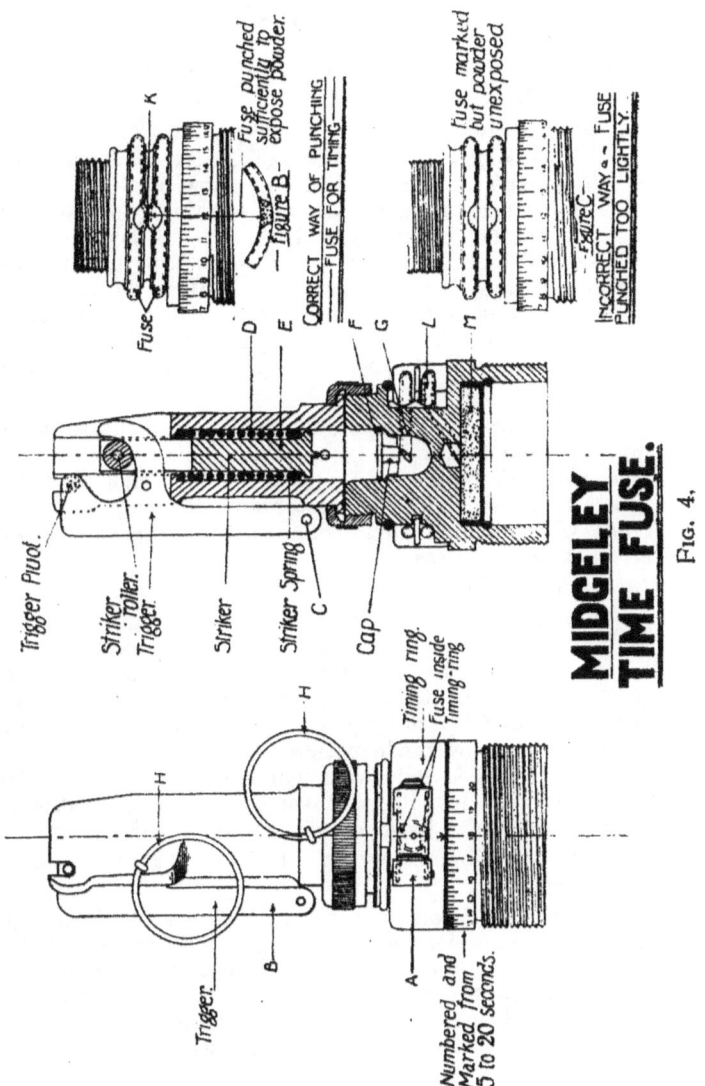

Fig. 4. MIDGELEY TIME FUSE.

impossible for the bomb to be exploded by being torn off the rack in a forced landing or crash.

METHOD OF ATTACK WITH 40 LB PHOSPHORUS BOMBS.

Accuracy Required.

These bombs may be used against kite balloons. They can be burst at any desired height below an aeroplane, and when burst spread out a shower of burning phosphorus over a circle of about 250 yards diameter. Consequently, a balloon will be hit if it is not more than 125 yards from the centre of the burning particles. It is therefore much easier to hit with these bombs than with ordinary bombs, but, at the same time, a bombsight must be used with great care in order to avoid errors greater than 125 yards.

Height of Burst.

The lumps of phosphorus slowly burn out while falling, and about half burn out while falling the first 2,000 feet from the burst. Consequently, bombs should be timed to burst about 700 feet above the target, and any bomb which is burst more than 3,000 feet above the target is practically useless.

Intervals Needed Between Bombs.

When attacking an object of known height, all bombs are set to the same fuse timing. Since each covers a circle of 250 yards diameter, it is useless to release two at the same moment, and since the aeroplane will be travelling at 40 to 50 yards per second, an interval of about 4 seconds should be made between the release of successive bombs. If this is done with four bombs, an area of about 250 × 800 yards will be covered, and thus considerable errors in range can be made without missing the target.

To Make the Bomb Burst at a Definite Distance Below an Aeroplane.

Punch the fuse at the corresponding time given in the table on the opposite page. For kite balloon and most targets it is advisable to burst the bomb 700 feet above the target, in order to allow the particles to spread out and compensate for errors in height estimation. Accordingly, Column II. is introduced, showing the height from the aeroplane to the target.

Height of aeroplane above burst. feet.	Height of aeroplane above target. feet.	Correct time of punching fuse. seconds.
400	1000	5.0
800	1500	6.6
1300	2000	8.2
1800	2500	9.6
2300	3000	11.0
2800	3500	12.1
3300	4000	13.2
3800	4500	14.2
4300	5000	15.1
4800	5500	15.9
5300	6000	16.6
5800	6500	17.2
6300	7000	17.8
6800	7500	18.2
7300	8000	18.6
7800	8500	18.9
8300	9000	19.2
8800	9500	19.4
9300	10000	19.6

PREPARATION OF THE STANDARD 20 LB. CARRIER TO TAKE THE 40 LB. PHOSPHORUS BOMBS (see Fig. 3).

The carrier should be of the *independent release* type, in which the bombs are released one at a time.

Tail Support.

As it is important to support the tail of the bomb, stirrups are issued in the cases in which the bombs are packed. These stirrups are to be securely bolted to the projecting tail pieces of the 20 lb. carrier (in the two outer positions), so that when a complete bomb is loaded in the carrier, the fuse rests on the cross-bolt of the stirrup and projects about ¾ inch beyond it.

Safety Device.

The time fuse in use with this bomb is automatically ignited when the bomb is released from the carrier. A string from the carrier to the fuse trigger pulls the latter out and retains it on the carrier as the bomb falls away. A safety device is provided to guard against the possibility of accidental firing of the bomb if it breaks away in a forced landing.

Principle of action.

Until the moment of releasing the bomb, the trigger string is only lightly held, so that, should the bomb break away for any reason without the release handle being pulled, the trigger and string will come off with the bomb and the fuse will not be ignited. The pull of the carrier lever which releases the bomb, however, also clamps the trigger string to the carrier so that the fuse is fired.

Description of Device.

The general arrangement of this device and the method of fitting to an ordinary 20 lb. carrier are shown in Fig. 3.

The string from the trigger is looped round a small button on a hinge A, which is held down by a light spring.

The sliding rod B has two bearings C and C^1 (C^1 being square to prevent rotation) and two guides D and D^1.

When the rod is in the "safe" position (as in drawing) a filed-away portion of the rod is opposite the hinges, so that, owing to the shape of the button and the lightness of the hinge spring, the trigger string very easily raises the flap and slips out without pulling the trigger. The pulling of the release lever, however, slides the rod B into the "live" position by the lever E pushing pin F, which is fixed into the rod.

When the rod is in the "live" position, the hinge is rigidly held down by the rod so that the string cannot be pulled out. The spring G is to prevent the rod from sliding when subjected to vibration.

After fitting a safety device to a carrier it should be tested in the "safe" and "live" positions with an actual fuse. In the former case, the string should slip out without pulling the trigger of the fuse (pin C having been removed from fuse), but should be held tight enough to ensure that wind and vibration will not free it. In the latter case the string should be very tightly held.

It should also be verified that the safety device does not in any way interfere with the proper working of the carrier, either by being unduly stiff or by restricting the motion of the release lever.

AIR MINISTRY,
January, 1918.

Leaflet 11a.

BOMB INCENDIARY SMOKE
T.W. 40 lbs. Mk. I/L/Type A.

GENERAL DESCRIPTION.

As for Mk. II/L/Type B., with exception that D.A. nose fuse cannot be fitted in this type.

Air Ministry,
January, 1918.

Ap.D [P.]   D.397.   2/18.

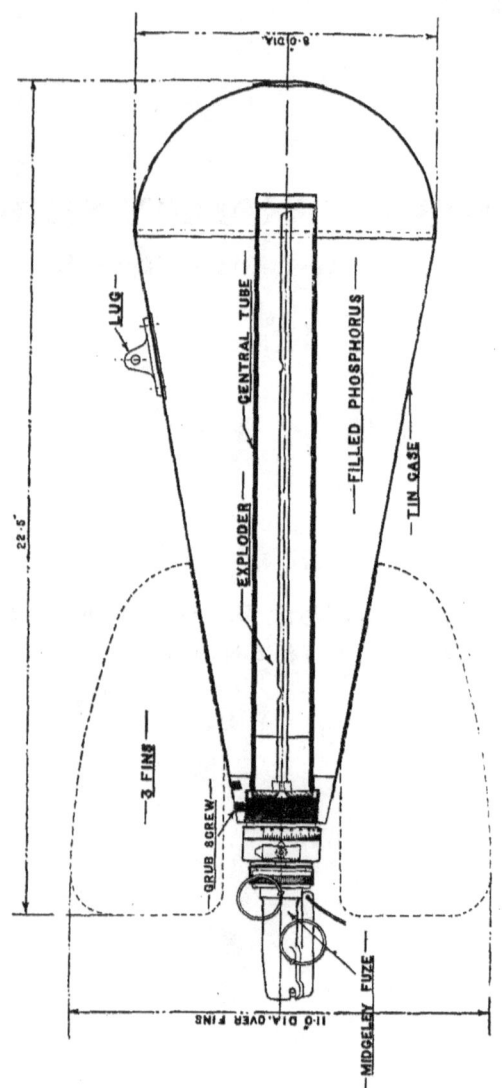

LEAFLET NO. 12.

BOMB, BABY INCENDIARY.
6½ oz. Mk. IV.

DESCRIPTION.

In principle this appliance follows that of a mortar and projectile complete.

The following is a reproduction of the notice which is fixed inside the lids of the boxes in which the bombs are issued.

INCENDIARY BOMBS.

These bombs are issued in two parts:—

(1) Bodies. (2) Cartridges. When assembling preparatory to loading the dropper-containers, *do not drop* the cartridges into the bodies—hold the body horizontally, and slide the cartridge in, but do not press it hard down, replace each cap on its own body and *press the cap home*.

The assembled bombs are to be carried in aircraft nose up—containers being loaded and handled accordingly. Spare containers may be kept loaded and ready for arming machines, and they should stand top up, but in the event of bombs being removed from the containers the cartridges are to be taken out, caps replaced on bodies, and the parts returned to their boxes.

Length of Bomb, with cartridge in place, 6″.

ACTION OF FUSE.

On impact the cartridge sets down on the striker point in the base of the body, and the functioning of the cap simultaneously ejects the cartridge, and causes ignition of the charge; the latter consists of a species of thermite, which burns with a very fierce flame, and after the flame has subsided the white hot slag residue continues the incendiary action.

> NOTE.—The clips on either side of the bomb supporting the cartridge are on impact from heights of over 30 feet, sheared, or so bent, as to allow the firing of the cap when the cartridge is set forward on the striker.

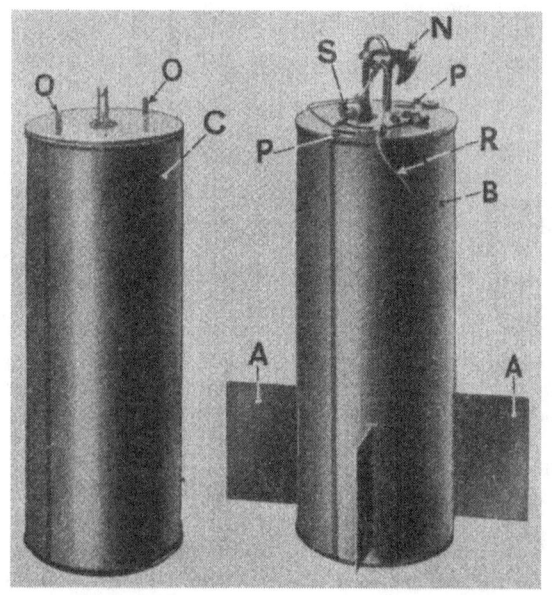

Fig. 1.

REMOVING AND REPLACING CAP OF BOMBS.

The relative fit of the body and cap should be such that the cap requires a slight effort to remove it. In doing so, it should be grasped on the dome portion and not on the vanes, otherwise the latter are liable to distortion. The body is provided with two indentations about ¼ inch above the edges of the inturned lugs. These indentations perform the function of holding the cartridge in the body after the rim of the cartridge head has passed over them; it is, therefore, best to use the vaned cap as the agent for pressing the cartridge over the indentations. This should be done with an even pressure of the fingers upon the dome portion, and not with a jerk or a blow, otherwise the inturned lugs will be bent down. With a little practice, the palm of the hand may be used direct on the cartridge end.

BOMB DROPPING AND CARRYING APPARATUS.
(See Fig. 1.)

The arrangement for carrying and dropping the bombs consists of a cylindrical case, with guide vanes, A, corresponding in size to those of either the 50 lbs. or 120 lbs. bombs (vertical carrying is only provided for).

The carrier B is so fitted that should special circumstances demand it, the bombs and carrier can be released as a complete unit, in which case the carrier would descend as a bomb, the guides A acting as tail vanes.

The bombs are protected by two walls of plating, respectively 18 and 20 gauge in thickness, and a fair degree of protection is thus afforded, but if attacked at close range by machine gun fire, it would be a precautionary measure to get rid of the load of bombs, as they are delicate to rifle fire at short range.

LOADING BOMBS INTO CARRIER. (See Fig. 1.)

The carrier B is loaded on the cartridge system, that is, it has a lining cylinder C, into which the bombs are loaded free of the external or main case B. It is intended that batches of these lining cylinders should be kept filled and in readiness for insertion in the main cases—the established number of liners may be taken as 50% in excess of cases. This practise will permit of considerable economy in the

Fig. 2.

number of " hands " required for loading. Loading should be done on a definite system, by practised "hands," whose special duty it should be to load when required. Two men should be able to assemble the bombs and maintain a stock of filled liners for an average sized station. Specially skilled men are, however, not necessarily required to insert the filled liners in the main cases, the procedure being similar to loading a machine with bombs.

FILLING LINERS. (See Figs. 2 and 3.)

Filling of Liners should be carried out in a hut, or other suitably covered space, and preferably not on a concrete floor. In fine weather it may be done in the open, but incendiary and H.E. bombs should not be stored, or handled in proximity to one another.

The illustrations accompanying these instructions demonstrate the method of loading the liners and inserting them in their cases.

Both the 112 lbs. and 50 lbs. sizes take four tiers of bombs—the former is the size illustrated.

A suitable number of bombs having been assembled, the scoop G is filled to its maximum capacity, *i.e.*, with 64 bombs, nose up. Next, the liner C having being placed in the swinging frame D, controlled and held by the lever E, the filled scoop G, which corresponds in its action to a gun rammer, is pushed in to its maximum extent; the frame is then swung over to say, 45 degs. to the vertical, and the rammer withdrawn. A tier of bombs is thus left in the liner. The withdrawal of the rammer will leave room for the insertion of four more bombs in the tier; these can readily be inserted by hand, and it is necessary that this should be done in order that the tiers pack properly one upon the other.

The process of filling the scoop and charging the liner is the same for all four tiers, the frame being swung to the horizontal before the insertion of each successive tier.

When the liner is full, the noses of the end tier should present an approximately level surface (see Fig C'), but it will be apparent in filling the scoop whether or not the bombs have been capped properly.

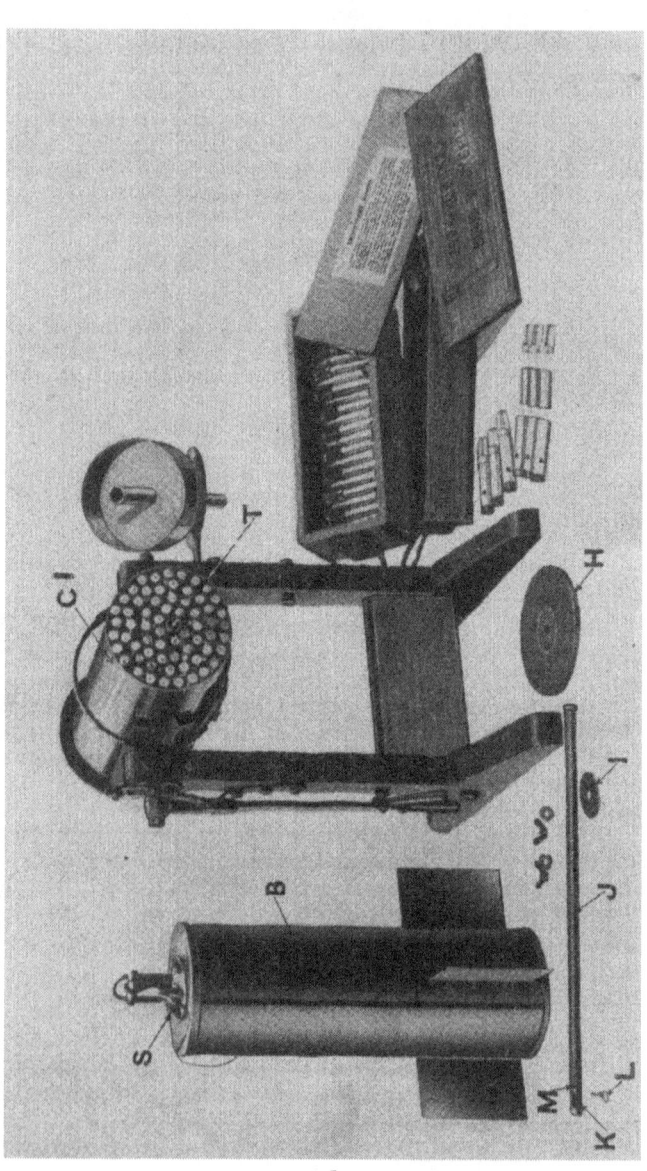

Fig 3

Now, with the frame D either horizontal or inclined, place the cap lid H over the end of the liner, slip the thick plate washer I on to the bar J, and insert the latter in the central tube T, of the filled liner C^1. The slot K in the bar should be approximately in the line with the red cross-line on the top face of the liner; then insert the ringed split pin L in the hole M in the bar J. The filled liner can now be removed from the loading frame.

LOADING LINER INTO CARRIER. (Figs. 1, 2, and 3.)

To load the filled liner C into the carrying case B, set the former vertically, and pass the latter down over the liner, keeping the red side-lines together, care being taken that the ring of the split pin L in the bar J comes upon the open side of the release mechanism on the top of the carrying case B, otherwise the split pin cannot be withdrawn after the cord R is set tight and secured.

Raise the swinging hook N to let the bar J come through the slot in the casting, and let the carrying case settle on the top of the liner; the two studs O.O. in the latter should now be in the slots P.P. Put the washers and butterfly nuts provided on the studs O.O., now reeve the cord R, so securing the swinging hook N, and clamp it by means of the nut and washers. Balloon or other strong cord should be used. The tension for a full load of bombs is approximately 8 lbs. The razor blade cutter cannot come into play except by the direct action of pulling the release cord or wire, which should be attached to the spring hook. The length of cord required after first tying the knot is approximately 10 inches. Either before or after loading a machine with the filled carriers, the split pin on the bar (now under the hook) must be withdrawn. This operation must on no account be overlooked, and an officer should satisfy himself that it is done by personal scrutiny of the carriers.

ACTION OF RELEASE GEAR (Figs. 1 and 3.)

The gear for releasing bombs from the liners is arranged so that when operated the cord R, holding down the swinging hook N, is severed. The hook N now no longer retains the bar J, which is free to slide out of the central tube M. The liner cap H falls away with the bar J, so causing the bombs to drop out of the liner.

The carrying case B and liner C may be released, if desired, as a complete unit, by operating the ordinary bomb release.

SUPPLY OF PARTS WHICH REQUIRE REPLACING.

The central bar, plate-washer, and cap lid, drop with the bombs—parts to replace are supplied in cases and crates. Knotted lengths of cord will also be issued, as it may not always be possible to secure a suitable type, should the supply of balloon cord not be available. The metal parts and cords will be supplied in the proportion of 30 to each outer case.

Spare cutters and spring hooks will also be issued in the proportion of 12 cutters and two spring hooks to each outer case.

NOTE.—Former Marks of the Baby Incendiary Bomb are not fitted with inturned lugs or indentations, as in the Mk. IV. The appearance of the nose in the Mark 1 differs from succeeding marks, but the action of the bomb is the same for all marks.
Cartridges are common to all bodies.

DIRECTIONS FOR SIGHTING.

Use an ordinary bombsight. When the sights become aligned on the target to be engaged, delay release by one second for each thousand feet of height.

OPERATIONS.

SPREAD OF BOMBS ON RELEASE.

Taking the H.P machine as a basis, the spread from one container (272 bombs) when released at approximately 5,000 ft., covers an area of approximately 30 yards by 80 yards.

The bombs provide a many-chance method of attack which is not possible with large incendiary bombs, for with the latter a direct hit must be secured upon a combustible target, and the chances are greatly against this combination being achieved. As, however, the small bombs descend in showers with a large spread, and on impact further disperse their cartridges over the target area, the chances of a successful attack are considerable. Except where roofs are unusually strong the bombs may be expected to penetrate and to eject their cartridges under the covering.

TARGETS ENGAGED.

Towns, Aerodromes, Forage, Stores, Aircraft Factories, Explosive and Chemical Works, Woods, Forests, and Crops.

> NOTE.—It is pointed out to all who may be concerned in the handling and use of these bombs, that although they are small, they contain all the essential features of a large offensive appliance. They must, therefore be treated with that respect and care which is due to such articles, observing that undue familiarity, or lack of care, may cause as much damage to our own as to enemy material. It is clearly impossible for a bomb to function spontaneously. Functioning can, therefore, only be brought about by (1) accident, or (2) by ignorance of construction ,or function; the first is liable to happen to any make of bomb, and can, in the case of this bomb, be reduced to a negligible minimum by suitable storage and care in handling. Knowledge of the bomb will entirely prevent the second.

AIR MINISTRY,
    March, 1918.

Leaflet No. 12a.

B.I. BOMB GEAR AND OPERATIONS SCHEME.

INTRODUCTORY NOTES.

Attention is drawn to the fact that the bomb itself is simply a unit in a scheme, and it bears the same relation to that scheme as does a single round of .303 to a machine gun when mounted in aircraft; the armament, therefore, requires to be thoroughly understood by those handling and using it.

The Mark IV. Body (100 per box) and the Mark IV.* Cartridge (200 per box) are the latest product, and no other pattern should be used except in cases of great urgency, in which *cartridges* from non-starred boxes may be used; *but no bodies* other than Mark IV. should be used.

The Mark IV. body is clearly distinguishable from former marks by the square holes abreast of the striker point and by the inturned lugs formed from the tin-plate body. (Figs. 5—9.)

The Mark IV.* cartridge is distinguished by the fact that it has a cannelure in the closed portion and

Errata. Leaflet No. 12A.

Page 1.—Seventh and eighth lines from bottom: For "container" and "containers" read "liner" and "liners."

pact—the percentage should be at least 95. (Recent trials show 98% on rough grass land, an inferior type of surface for the bomb.)

THE BOMB GEAR.

The containers having been charged with their filled liners, as described in Leaflet No. 12, they may be loaded into the machine in the same manner as for bombs. In the case of the Handley Page machine the skeleton slips normally for 112 lb. bombs are used. The bomb release gear should be connected up and adjusted as for bombs, this being necessary in case it is required to drop the containers complete.

If the bomb guides in some machines are found to be too restricted to allow of the containers housing freely in the bomb cells, either slue the bomb guides round on their up-

2.—Line 14: For "releasing hooks" read cutter frames."

l of the third paragraph: After "aft row"
ld "except in one case where the position of
ie third toggle rack from port will not permit
his."

connected the releas- by means s are then the *Beam Clamps* (1), clamped over the tops of b beams. These are tightened in place by means of the screwed pin (6) with thumb piece and bearing plate (7). The wires are then led to four series of release toggle racks, clamped to the cross member immediately aft of the bomb beams and spaced to fit over the lightened out portions of this member. Each toggle rack takes the four wires running from the four containers in line with it fore and aft (*see* Fig. 2), the wire to any container being on the left of the one immediately behind, in that fore and aft row.

The *Toggle Racks* (*see* Figs. 1 and 3) consist of a steel angle plate rivetted to two aluminium *Toggle Clamps* (3), with four notches to accommodate the toggles. The clamps are tightened in place by a thumb screw (6) with a bearing plate (8). The wires are threaded through holes in the toggles and clamped by means of wing nuts (12) on bolts (9). These bolts are provided with washers (10) and (11), the latter being so shaped to prevent the bolt rotating in process of clamping the wire.

It will thus be seen that the general arrangement is such that by pulling the toggles in sequence from left to right,

Leaflet No. 12a (continued).

the bombs in container starting from the forward port container, back along that fore and aft row, are first released; then the forward container next to starboard and so on.

> Page 3.—Line 8: The sentence beginning "The spring hooks," &c., should read "The spring clips attached to the cutter frames on the containers," &c.
>
> Second line from bottom: For "80 yards by 40 yards" read "75 yards by 35 yards."

cable is not so taut that the side springs in the container are being overcome by the tension. Once this adjustment has been made for any particular machine, it will be unnecessary to repeat it; the spring clips (13) will simply be attached to the releasing hooks of the new containers when reloaded.

Sighting.

Any bomb sight fitted to the machine may be employed, and adjustment carried out in the usual way. When aligned on target, release is delayed by $1\frac{1}{2}$ secs. for every 1,000 feet of height. The pull off in sequence is then commenced.

When the release of bombs takes place by other than the sighter, a simple form of signal lamp should be fitted so that the releasing operator is warned for this timing.

DISTRIBUTION OF EFFECT.

The distribution of incendiary effect depends on the manner in which releasing is carried out, and Fig. 4 shows in chart form the distribution obtained under varying timings of release. The difference of effect produced by intervals of $\frac{1}{2}$ sec., 1 sec., and 2 secs. between the pulls can readily be seen for one machine. These results can be extended, and the effect calculated of a formation of machines operating in this way.

Fig. 4 represents the result of actual experience—the area covered by one container load (272 bombs) may be accepted as 80 yards by 40 yards. In addition to its incendiary action each cartridge, during its true flaming period of approximately 14 seconds, gives an illuminating effect estimated at 14,000 C.P., so that allowing 5% for failures, one container gives an effect of 3,640,000 C.P.—absolutely blinding temporarily to personnel in the immediate vicinity.

If very close concentration of bombs is required, several containers can be emptied simultaneously by either pulling individual toggles together, or by coupling the toggles with a cord loop scheme; a fitting may eventually be provided as an addition to the present bracket to permit of this being done on a clearly defined method.

It is, therefore, necessary for the officer conducting operations of this nature to devise a scheme of operations on these lines taking into account the size and nature of the target to be engaged, the number of machines and containers to be employed. The formation may then be instructed as to the interval to be employed in releasing the bombs, and the signals for commencing release. Different targets and conditions may be suited by different formations operating in this way, and the bomb density, which it is desired to achieve, should govern the choice. This can be readily calculated on the lines of the chart given.

AIR MINISTRY,
    July, 1918.

LEAFLET No. 12A (*continued*).

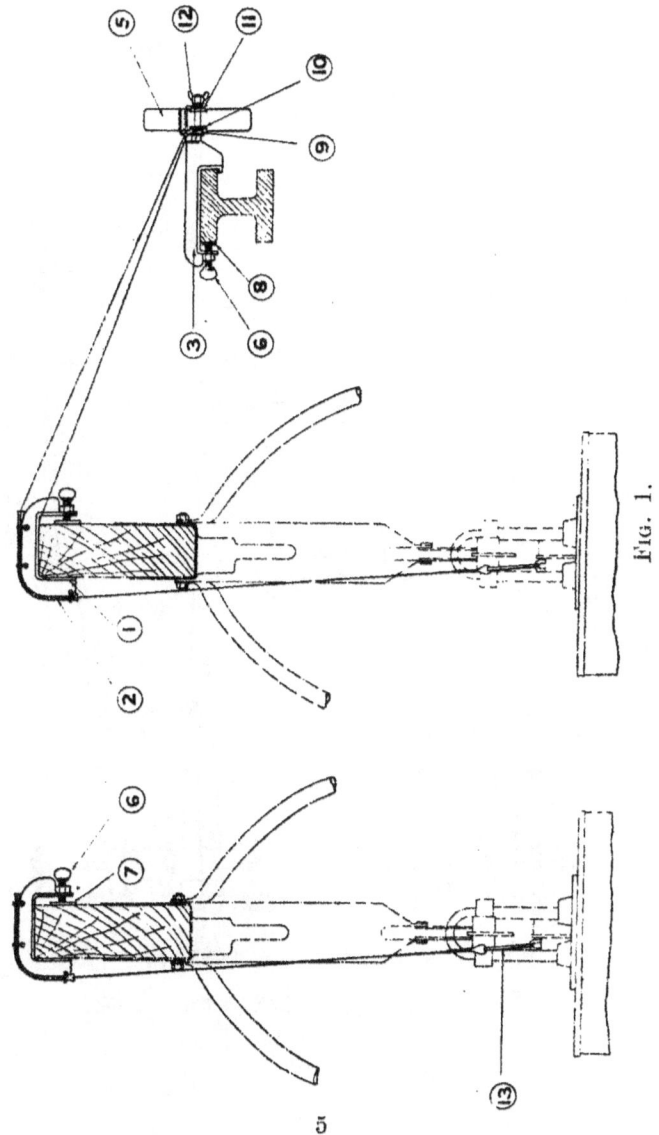

Fig. 1.

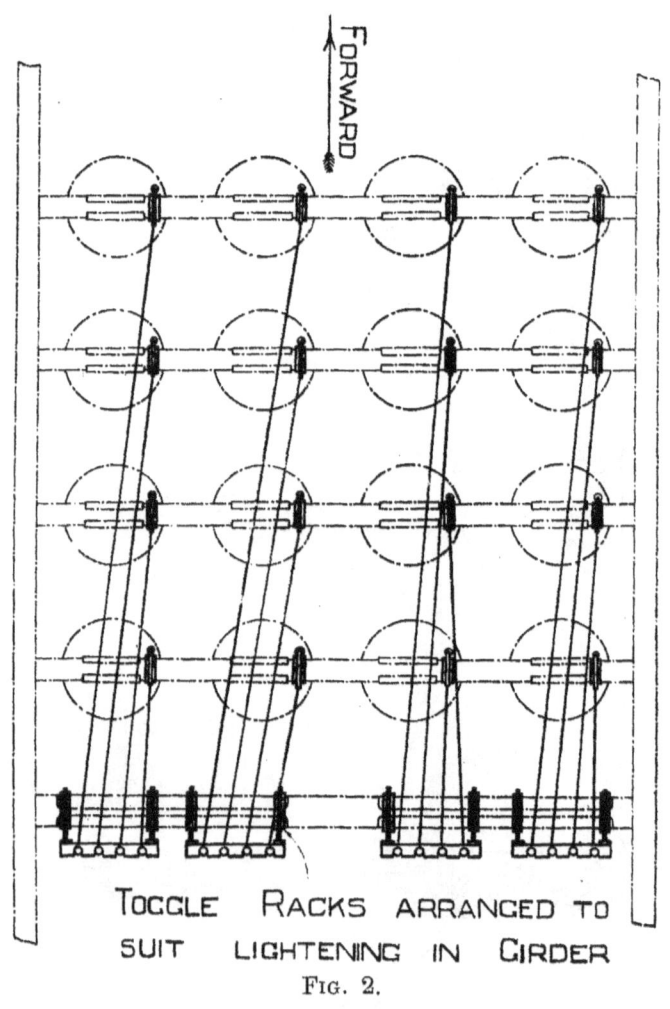

Toggle Racks arranged to suit Lightening in Girder
Fig. 2.

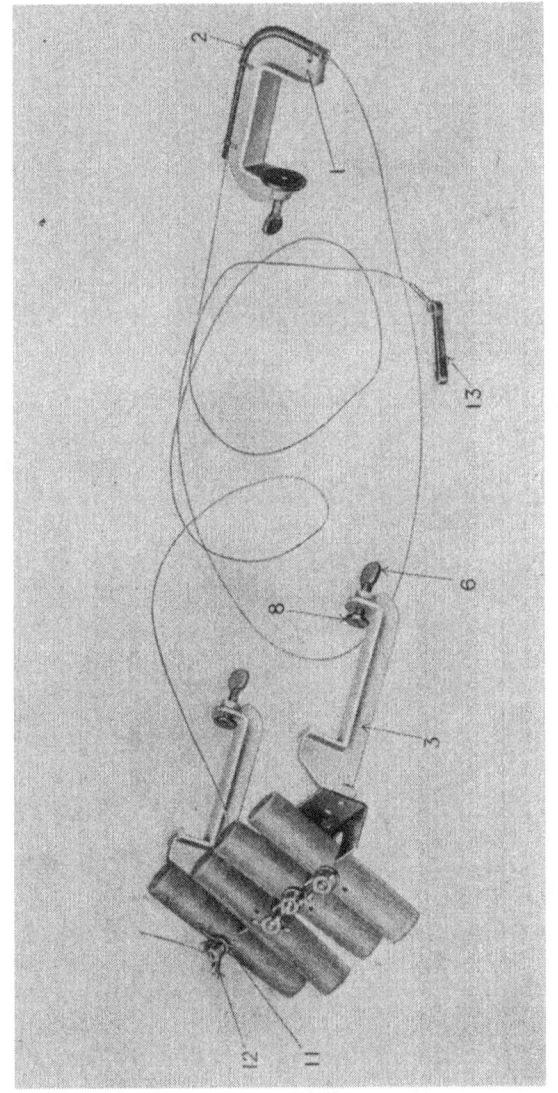

Fig. 3

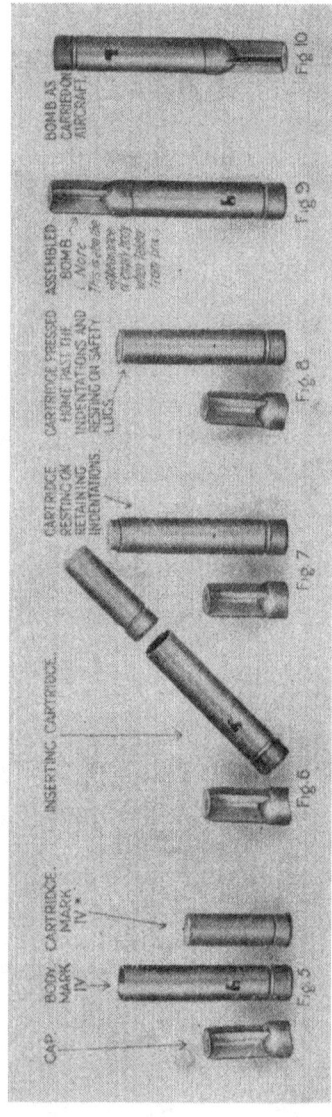

LEAFLET NO. 12A (*continued*).

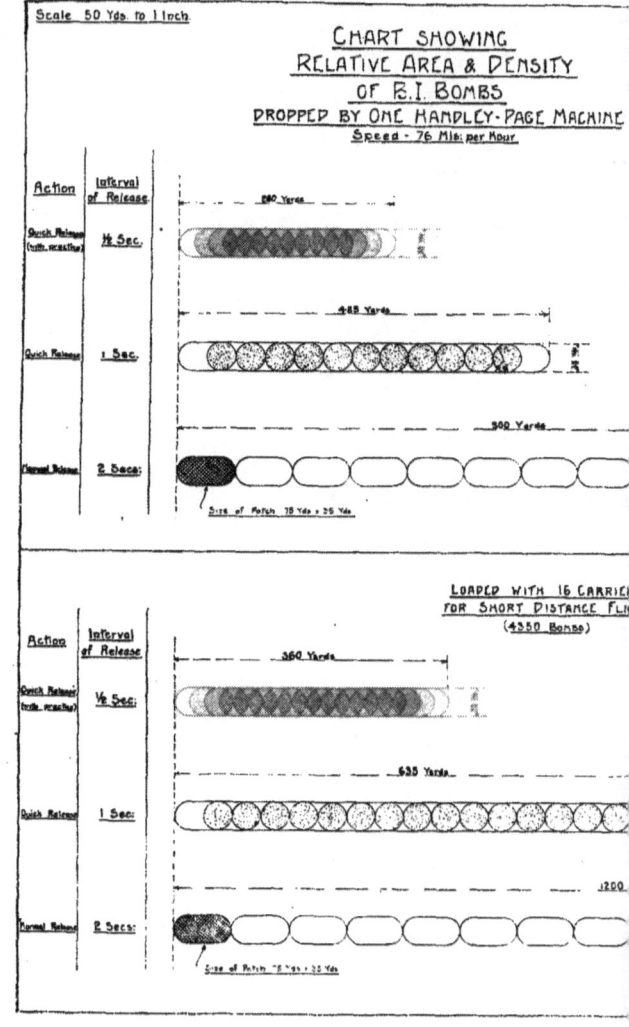

FIG. 4.

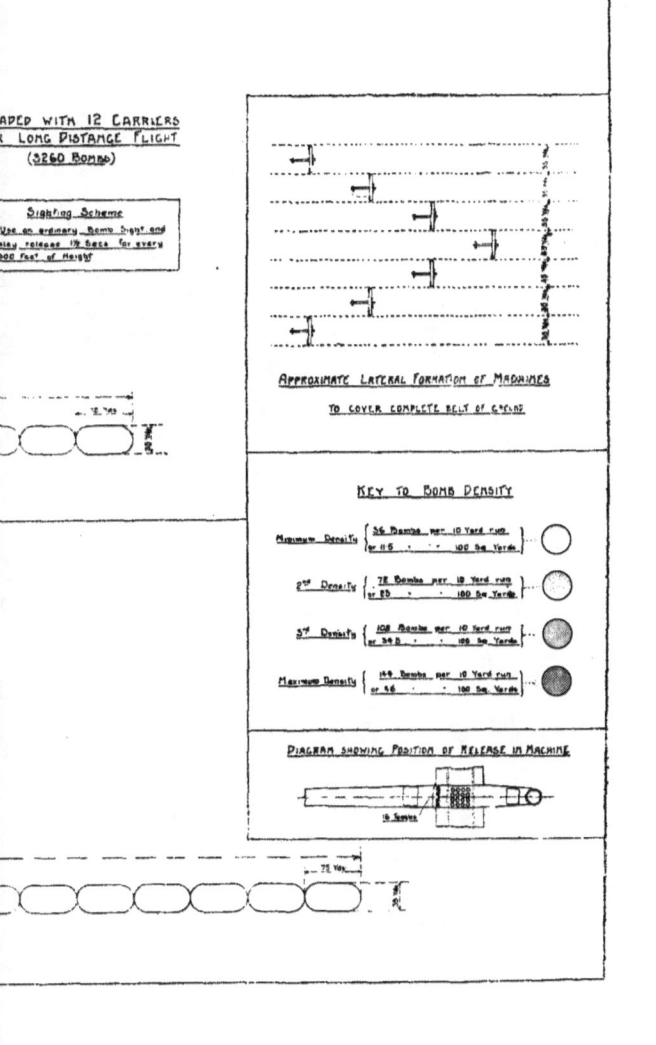

LEAFLET No. 12B.

B.1 BOMB GEAR for D.H.9 and 10 MACHINES.

In principle this gear differs from that of the Handley Page machine in that release is effected by operating the main bomb slips direct. Incidentally this method has established the fact that there is no advantage to be gained, from the safety point of view, by the ability to release the containers and bombs together (as exists with the Handley Page method).

In the D.H. type the complete container is released, and after a short drop it is brought up by a cross-bar or bolt —the cord being automatically cut before the cross-bar is reached. It has been found that the container is relieved of its weight of bombs if the cord is cut as late as $\frac{1}{4}''$ before the eye of the support bolt reaches the cross-bar.

The D.H.9 takes containers corresponding to the 50 lb. bomb—in cells for that size. The scoop number for the 50 lb. size is 33, and three more bombs are required to fill up each tier in the liner, making the total load 144.

The D.H.10 takes containers of 112 lb. size.

The single arch support bolts as supplied with the original 112 lb. containers, cannot be used with the D.H. method of release—the double arch support bolt is an essential feature, but spare support bolts of this type or complete container top mechanisms can readily be fitted to the original 112 lb. containers to adapt them for D.H.10's—their utility for Handley Page machines being unaffected by the change.

REFERRING TO ILLUSTRATIONS.

(1) Shows catch-bracket with arm—this latter is adjustable to meet the distance-of-drop conditions which exist in the D.H.9 and 10 machines—the arm is marked accordingly 9 and 10 (in the illustration the dowel pin is in 10). The casting clamps on to either type of bomb carrying

beam. The end of the cross-bar or bolt appears just behind the butterfly nut. The container top—(with double arch support bolt)—is also shown.

(2) Shows the catch-bracket in place on a bomb beam and with a container top and central bar inserted and ready for release.

At A it will be seen that a slot appears in the cutter retention spring; the metal from this slot area is turned in to form a shelf on which the cutter frame rests, so allowing the latter to engage in the hook of the arm. The retention springs of the original 112 lb. containers, previously discussed, do not possess this shelf, and when occasion arises the necessary alteration can be made from spare parts, by cutting the slot in the existing fittings and lengthening the upper tongue, or by making new retention springs.
The hook of Arm B has engaged in the cutter frame.

(3) Shows the action of release—the bar has dropped and the swinging hook C has fallen back into place.

The cross-bar or bolt is provided with a spring washer and a butterfly nut—the bolt is inserted and secured in place after the support bolt (corresponding to bomb eye-bolt) has engaged in the release slip—this it does automatically as with a bomb, and, provided Arm B (Fig. 3) is in the correct position for the type the cutter frame will also engage automatically; it is optional, however, to fit Arm B in place before or after the insertion of the support bolt.

NOTES : (1) The catch-bracket castings and fittings have been made to clear the aluminium entry-pieces on the under sides of the respective bomb beams when these entry-pieces are secured to the beams *by rivets* (which method is standard); in some cases, however, the entry-pieces are secured by *set-screws and nuts* upon which the castings are liable to foul. Where this occurs the entry-pieces should be removed, as the catch-brackets, etc., must fit snugly upon the beam plating.

(2) The cord employed for all types should always be examined before bombs are loaded, to ensure that it is in sound condition and that no deterioration has occurred.

LATER DESIGNS.

The following modifications are being introduced:—

(1) *Partition Discs*, consisting of thin circular tinned plates to be sandwiched between tiers of bombs in the liners. Three of these discs will, therefore, be issued for each liner.

(2) *Half-load Dummy Frames*, made of wood, to be inserted in lieu of tiers of bombs. This is introduced to enable the full number of shots per machine to be obtained on light load. The patch per container is thus reduced by half, but for certain types of target, half charges (136 for 112 lb. size and 72 for 50 lb. size) will be little less effective than full charges (272 and 144).

(3) *A Release Gear* on the lines of that described for D.H.9 and 10 machines is being introduced for Handley Page machines in lieu of the present gear. This will enable the bombs to be dropped from the standard release gear in the front cockpit.

AIR MINISTRY,
    August, 1918.

Leaflet No. 13.

BOMB. H.E., R.L. 112 lbs.
Mk. III. & V.
Heavy Case.
(With New Fusing Components).

GENERAL DESCRIPTION.

Actual weight of bomb ...	106 lbs.
Weight of case ...	79 lbs.
Weight of explosive ...	27 lbs.
Explosive substance ...	Amatol 80/20 (if filled Amatol 40/60 38 lbs.).
Case material ...	Cast steel.
Thickness of case ...	All over .5".
Overall dimensions ...	Bomb—29.1" long × 9" maximum diameter.
,, ,, ...	Fins—Side of square containing fins, 12.9".
How stowed ...	Vertically, nose up.
Type of fuse ...	Nose fuse and tail fuse.
Construction ...	See diagram.

TO PREPARE FOR ACTION.

The following will be required (for vertical stowage with nose and tail fuse):—

Pistol bomb, No. 3, Mk. I, or No. 5, Mk. I ... ... 1 ⎫
Adapter 1.375" (*for Mk. III only*) ... 1 ⎬ Tail Fuse.
Relay detonating 7.39", Mk. 1 or Mk. II ... ... 1 ⎪
Igniter H.E. bomb 15, 2½ or .05 sec. 1 ⎭

*Fuse, bomb, D.A., No. 9, Mk. I, with hanging eyebolt (cone thread) ... 1 ⎫ Nose Fuse
*Exploder 7.39" ... ... 1 ⎬ and Exploder
*Detonator (instantaneous) ... ... 1 ⎭ combined.
*Wood packing piece 4¾" 1

Special components not used otherwise.

FUSING BOMB.
With nose and tail fuse (new components).

1. Remove nose plug from bomb.
2. Insert 4¾" wood packing piece into central tube from nose end.

T.5.

(WITH NEW COMPONENTS)

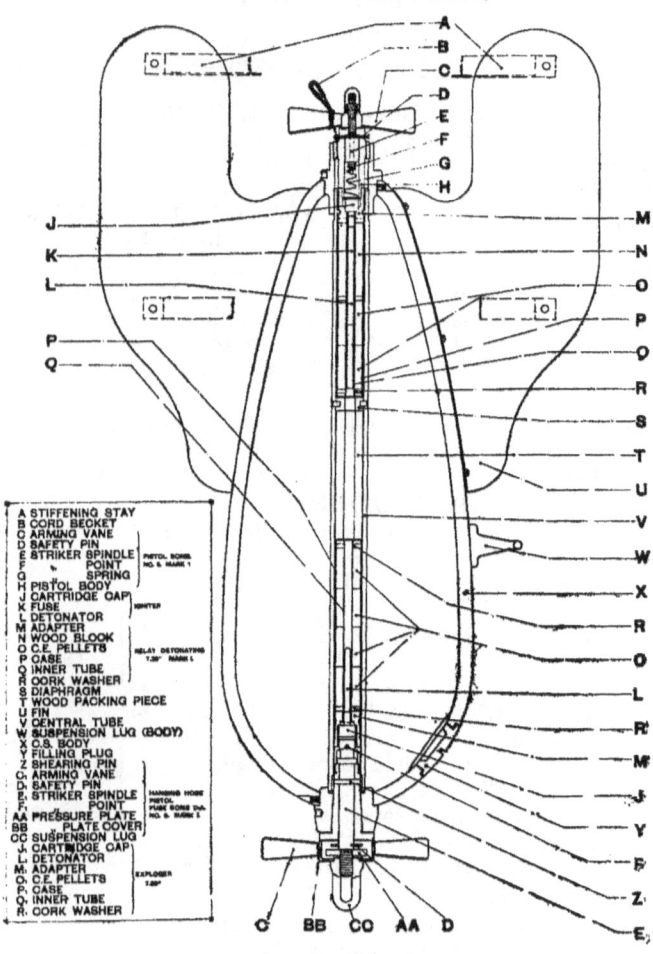

A STIFFENING STAY
B CORD BECKET
C ARMING VANE
D SAFETY PIN
E STRIKER SPINDLE
F   POINT
      SPRING   PISTOL BOMB NO. 5, MARK 1
G PISTOL BODY
J CARTRIDGE CAP
K FUSE   IGNITER
L DETONATOR
M ADAPTER
N WOOD BLOCK
O C.E. PELLETS   RELAY DETONATING 1.25" MARK 1
P CASE
Q INNER TUBE
R CORK WASHER
S DIAPHRAGM
T WOOD PACKING PIECE
U FIN
V CENTRAL TUBE
W SUSPENSION LUG (BODY)
X C.S. BODY
Y FILLING PLUG
Z SHEARING PIN
C, ARMING VANE
D, SAFETY PIN   HANGING HOSE PISTOL FUSE BOMB DIS NO. 5, MARK 1
E, STRIKER SPINDLE
F,   POINT
AA PRESSURE PLATE
BB   PLATE COVER
CC SUSPENSION LUG
J, CARTRIDGE CAP
L, DETONATOR
M, ADAPTER   EXPLODER 1.25"
O, C.E. PELLETS
P, CASE
Q, INNER TUBE
R, CORK WASHER

Leaflet No. 13 (continued).

3. Withdraw safety pin from nose pistol and test arming vanes for ease of spinning.

4. Replace safety pin.*

5. Push instantaneous detonator into exploder 7.39", and screw exploder on to nose pistol.

6. Screw nose fuse into bomb.

7. Untie cord becket from tail pistol arming vane and test vane for ease of spinning.

8. Push igniter with .05 secs. delay into relay detonating and screw relay detonating on to tail pistol.

9. Screw tail fuse into bomb and tighten grub screw.

10. Just before leaving ground remove safety pin from tail fuse.

* The safety pin will be withdrawn just before the bomb is pushed into its cell when loading up a machine.

ALTERNATIVE METHODS OF FUSING.

For fusing this bomb with tail fuse only or with the old method of fusing, see Leaflet 2.

ACTION OF FUSE AND SAFETY DEVICE.
NOSE FUSE. (See Leaflet 17.)

1. The arming vanes of the nose fuse being a fixed part carried on the pressure plate cover, can only rotate with this cover. The suspension lug is also a fixed part on the top of the pressure plate cover. The pressure plate cover and arming vanes can then only rotate when the suspension lug is free to turn. From this it is clear that when the bomb is stowed vertically no safety pin or stop on the ,carrier is required to secure the arming vanes against rotating; the suspension lug being once secured on the release slips, the arming vanes can no longer rotate. When stowed horizontally the arming vanes are to be held from rotating by a stop on the carrier.

2. On release the arming vanes are rotated by air pressure, which results in the spinning off of the pressure plate cover, so exposing the pressure plate.

3. On impact the shearing pins are sheared, and the pressure plate is driven in, so forcing the striker point on to detonator cap (Eley cap 28 bore); the cap is fired, so detonating the detonator (45 grain), which in its turn causes the detonation of the relay and exploder, so setting off the bomb.

TAIL FUSE.

1. The arming vanes of the tail pistol are prevented from rotating when the bomb is stowed vertically, by a locking arm, the fingers of which rest over one of the arming vanes. When the bomb is released this spring falls back to its normal position at the side of the bomb cell; the arming vane is then free to rotate, and spins off. When stowed horizontally the arming vane is held from rotating by a stop on the carrier. When the bomb is released the arming vane is free to spin off. On impact the bomb is checked, but the striker is free to move forward, compresses the striker spring, and fires 28 bore cap of igniter. The fuse of the igniter burns for 2.5 secs. or .05 secs., according to type, and then fires its detonator, which in its turn detonates the relay and exploder, so setting off the bomb.

LOADING BOMBS ON CARRIER.

1. *On Handley Page.* The total number of bombs to be carried, having been carefully fused, should be laid gently on the ground with safety pins in position at a convenient distance from the aeroplane on which they are to be stowed.

The release slips on the carrying gear should now be tested (see leaflet 28) before stowing the bombs. If the slips are found to be working satisfactorily the suspension hooks of all slips should now be placed open in readiness for stowing bombs.

The bombs may then be stowed in the order of the salvos from port to starboard. The safety pin in the nose fuse of each bomb should not be removed until it is actually being handled for stowing, when with the nose fuse safety pin removed, the bomb is pushed up into its cell from beneath the centre section by two or more men as required. The suspension lug on the nose fuse now engages with the suspension hook of the release slip, which it automatically closes and locks, so retaining the bomb. Before allowing the weight of the bomb to fall on the release slip the greatest care must be taken by the Officer or N.C.O. superintending the stowing to ascertain that the arm of the suspension hook is securely locked by the locking arm of the release slip. (See leaflet 28.)

The tail fuse arming vanes are now prevented from rotating by a locking arm, the fingers of which go over one of the arming vanes. The nose fuse arming vane is automatically held from rotating by the fact of its suspension lug being engaged in the release slip.

LOADING BOMB ON HORIZONTAL CARRIER.
As described in leaflet 2.

UNLOADING FROM HORIZONTAL CARRIER.
As described in leaflet 2.

UNLOADING WHEN STOWED VERTICALLY.
1. Replace safety pins in tail fuses and secure arming vanes with cord becket.
2. The weight of the bomb is taken by two or more men from below.
3. The release trigger in which the bomb being supported is engaged should now be pulled back by hand. This must be done by a man in position just behind the bomb crate within the fuselage. The release handle must not be operated in unloading bombs, since in doing so bombs other than the one being supported may be released. The bomb is now gently lowered to the ground.
4. Replace safety pins in nose fuses.
5. Unscrew and remove fuses and replace them in their tins.
6. Gently shake exploder out of central tube and replace exploder in its tin.
7. Replace nose plug in bomb.

TARGETS ENGAGED.
With Nose and Tail Fuse. Personnel, aerodromes, and road transport.
With Tail Fuse only. Material, buildings, etc.

NOTE.—The exploder 7.39" must not be confused with the relay detonating 7.39" Mk. I or Mk. II. The exploder 7.39" is similar in construction to the relay detonating 7.39", but contains 4 C.E. pellets in place of 2, and has 28 bore cap in the igniter instead of .410.

AIR MINISTRY,
March, 1918.

Leaflet No. 14.

BOMB H.E., R.L., 112 Lb., MARK VI. AND VII.
HEAVY CASE.

GENERAL DESCRIPTION.

Actual Weight of Bomb ...	116½ lbs.
Weight of firing arrangement	3½ lbs.
Weight of case	85 lbs.
Weight of explosive	28 lbs. (about).
Explosive substance	80/20 Amatol.
Case material	Mark VI. Cast Iron. (The letters C.I. are included in the mould of the 112 lb., Mark VI., to distinguish it from other Marks). Mark VII., Cast Steel.
Thickness of case	
Body	¾". { Mark VI.
Nose	1". { Mark VII., .5" all over.
Overall dimensions	
Bomb	Maximum diameter, 9" Length, 31⅝"
Fins	Side of square containing fins, 12.9".
How stowed	Vertically. nose up, or horizontally with special carrying band, nose forward.
Type of fuse	*Nose fuse (hanging type) and tail fuse.*
Construction	See diagram.

T.5. D.710.

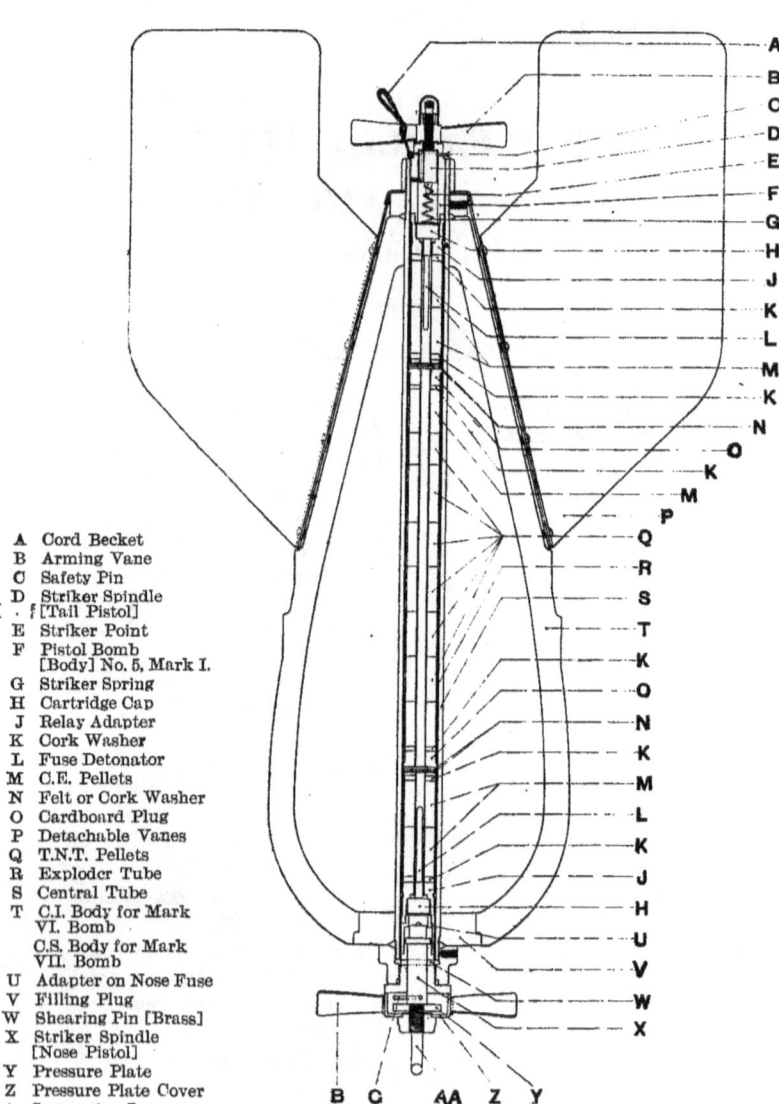

A Cord Becket
B Arming Vane
C Safety Pin
D Striker Spindle
   [Tail Pistol]
E Striker Point
F Pistol Bomb
   [Body] No. 5, Mark I.
G Striker Spring
H Cartridge Cap
J Relay Adapter
K Cork Washer
L Fuse Detonator
M C.E. Pellets
N Felt or Cork Washer
O Cardboard Plug
P Detachable Vanes
Q T.N.T. Pellets
R Exploder Tube
S Central Tube
T C.I. Body for Mark
   VI. Bomb
   C.S. Body for Mark
   VII. Bomb
U Adapter on Nose Fuse
V Filling Plug
W Shearing Pin [Brass]
X Striker Spindle
   [Nose Pistol]
Y Pressure Plate
Z Pressure Plate Cover
AA Suspension Lug

TO PREPARE FOR ACTION. (*For horizontal or vertical stowage with both nose and tail fuse.*)

The following will be required:—

*Pistol, Bomb (Tail), No. 5, Mark I. (issued complete with 4½" relay detonating and instantaneous detonator)	1
†Fuse, Bomb, D.A., No. 8, Mark I, with hanging eye bolt. (Issued complete with 4½" relay detonating and instantaneous detonator) ...	1
Exploder, Long, No. 2, Mark I or II, or Exploder, 12" paper case	1
Bomb band and lug (if for horizontal stowage)...	1

*In either case a detonator with 2½ seconds delay may be substituted; these are issued in bulk.

FUSING BOMB.

With Nose and Tail Fuse.

1. Remove nose plug from bomb.
2. Remove safety pin from nose fuse and test arming vane for ease of spinning.
3. Replace safety pin in nose fuse.
4. Screw nose fuse into nose of bomb.
5. Remove exploder from its tin and gently push it into central tube from tail end. (No detonators are required and no clearance is allowed for them. If No. 2, Mark I, exploders are used, the detonators which are issued in position at each end should be carefully removed, and subsequently be suitably stored, every care being taken to avoid accident).
6. Test arming vane of tail fuse for ease of spinning and screw in tail fuse.
7. Tighten grub screw.
8. Just before leaving the ground remove safety pin from tail fuse.

NOTE.—The safety pin in the nose fuse will be withdrawn just before the bomb is pushed up into its cell when loading up a machine.

FUSING BOMB.
With Tail Fuse Only.

Should it be thought advisable to use the bomb with tail fuse only it should be fused as directed for nose and tail fuse, with the exception that the nose fuse should first be dissembled, and its instantaneous detonator removed from the relay. This detonator may be replaced by a detonator combining a 2.5 secs. delay, or the relay can be replaced on the nose pistol with no detonator. The nose fuse in the latter case cannot function, and the effect produced will be that of tail fuse only.

ACTION OF FUSE AND SAFETY DEVICE.

NOSE FUSE (See Leaflet 17).

1. The arming vanes of the nose fuse being a fixed part carried on the pressure plate cover, can only rotate with this cover. The suspension lug is also a fixed part on the top of the pressure plate cover. The pressure plate cover and arming vanes can then only rotate when the suspension lug is free to turn. From this it is clear that when the bomb is stowed vertically, no safety pin or stop on the carrier is required to secure the arming vanes against rotating; the suspension lug being once secured on the release slips, the arming vanes can no longer rotate. When stowed horizontally the arming vanes are to be held from rotating by a stop on the carrier.

2. On release the arming vanes are rotated by air pressure, which results in the spinning off of the pressure plate cover, so exposing the pressure plate.

3. On impact the shearing pins are sheared, and the pressure plate is driven in, so forcing the striker point on to detonator cap (Eley cap, 28 bore), the cap is fired, so detonating the detonator (45 grain) which in its turn causes the detonation of the relay and exploder, so setting off the bomb.

TAIL FUSE.

1. The arming vanes of the tail pistol are prevented from rotating when the bomb is stowed vertically, by a

locking arm, the fingers of which rest over one of the arming vanes. When the bomb is released this spring falls back to its normal position at the side of the bomb cell; the arming vane is then free to rotate, and spins off.

When stowed horizontally, the arming vane is held from rotating by a stop on the carrier. When the bomb is released the arming vane is free to spin off.

On impact the bomb is checked, but the striker is free to move forward, compresses the striker spring, and fires 28 bore cap of igniter. The fuse of the igniter burns for 2.5" or functions instantaneously, according to type, and then fires its detonator, which in its turn detonates the relay and exploder, so setting off the bomb.

LOADING BOMBS ON CARRIER.

1. On Handley Page.

The total number of bombs to be carried, having been carefully fused, should be laid gently on the ground with safety pins in position at a convenient distance from the aeroplane on which they are to be stowed.

The release slips on the carrying gear should now be tested (see Leaflet 28), before stowing the bombs. If the slips are found to be working satisfactorily, the suspension hooks of all slips should now be placed open in readiness for stowing bombs.

The bombs may then be stowed in the order of the salvos, from port to starboard. The safety pin in the nose fuse of each bomb should not be removed until it is actually being handled for stowing, when, with the nose fuse safety pin removed, the bomb is pushed up into its cell from beneath the centre section by two or more men, as required. The suspension lug on the nose fuse now engages with the suspension hook of the release slip, which it automatically closes and locks, so retaining the bomb. Before allowing the weight of the bomb to fall on the release slip, the greatest care must be taken by the Officer or N.C.O. superintending the stowing, to ascertain that the arm of the suspension hook is securely locked by the locking arm of the release slip. (See Leaflet 28).

The tail fuse arming vanes are now prevented from

rotating by a locking arm, the fingers of which go over one of the arming vanes. The nose fuse arming vane is automatically held from rotating by the fact of its suspension lug being engaged in the release slip.

LOADING BOMB ON HORIZONTAL CARRIER.

The bomb must be securely housed on the carrier, and on no account be free to move either in the horizontal or vertical planes.

This object is attained by the adjustment of the nose and tail pieces. This adjustment must be repeated in the case of every bomb loaded.

Before the bomb is fused, it must be loaded on the carrier and dropped at least once, to ascertain that the carrier is functioning correctly. When this has been done, and provided the carrier is found to be working satisfactorily, the bomb is to be re-loaded on the carrier and made live by the insertion of the exploders and detonators, and the subsequent screwing of the fuses into position.

UNLOADING FROM HORIZONTAL CARRIER.

1. Replace safety pins in fuses.
2. Drop bomb off carrier.
3. Unscrew and remove fuses and replace them in their tins.
4. Gently shake exploder out of central tube and replace exploder in its tin.
5. Replace nose plug in bomb.

UNLOADING WHEN STOWED VERTICALLY.

1. Replace safety pins in tail fuses and secure arming vanes with cord becket.
2. The weight of the bomb is taken by two or more men from below.
3. The release trigger in which the bomb being supported is engaged should now be pulled back by hand. This must be done by a man in position just behind the bomb crate within the fuselage. The release handle must not be operated in unloading bombs, since in doing so bombs other than the one being supported may be released. The bomb is now gently lowered to the ground.
4. Replace safety pin in nose fuses and proceed as directed in Nos. 3, 4 and 5 for unloading from horizontal carrier.

TARGETS ENGAGED.

Nose and Tail Fuse. Personnel, aerodromes, and road transport.

Tail Fuse only. Material, Buildings, etc.

NOTE.—The exploder 7.39″ must not be confused with the relay detonating 7.39″ Mk. I. or Mk. II. The exploder 7.39″ is similar in construction to the relay detonating 7.39″, but contain 4 C.E. pellets in place of 2, and has 28 bore cap in the igniter instead of .410.

AIR MINISTRY,
March, 1918.

Leaflet No. 15.

BOMB, H.E., R.L., 50 Lb., MARK IV.

HEAVY CASE.
GENERAL DESCRIPTION.

Actual weight of fused bomb	49⅛ lbs.
Weight of case	37 lbs.
Weight of explosive	10 lbs.
Weight of firing arrangements	2⅛ lbs.
Explosive substance	80/20 Amatol.
Case material	Cast Iron.
Thickness of case	
Nose	⅝".
Body	½".
Overall dimensions	
Bomb	28¼" long by 7" maximum diameter.
Fins	Side of square containing fins, 10¼".
How carried	Vertically, nose up.
Type of fuse	Nose fuse (hanging type) *and* tail fuse.
Construction	See diagram.

TO PREPARE FOR ACTION. (*For horizontal or vertical stowage with both nose and tail fuse.*)

The following will be required:—

*Pistol, Bomb (Tail), No. 5, Mk. I (issued complete with 4½" relay detonating and instantaneous detonator) 1
*Fuse, Bomb, D.A., No. 8, Mark I, with hanging eye bolt. (Issued complete with 4½" relay detonating and instantaneous detonator) ... 1
Exploder, Long, No. 2, Mark I or II, or Exploder, 12" paper case 1
Bomb band and lug (if for horizontal stowage)... 1

In either case a detonator with 2⅕ seconds delay may be substituted; these are issued in bulk.

FUSING BOMB.
With Nose and Tail Fuse.

    1.   Remove nose plug from bomb.
    2.   Remove safety pin from nose fuse and test arming vane for ease of spinning.
    3.   Replace safety pin in nose fuse.
    4.   Screw nose fuse into nose of bomb.
    5.   Remove exploder from its tin and gently push it into central tube from tail end. (No detonators are required and no clearance is allowed for them. If No. 2, Mark I, exploders are used, the detonators which are issued in position at each end should be carefully removed, and subsequently be suitably stored, every care being taken to avoid accident).
    6.   Test arming vane of tail fuse for ease of spinning and screw in tail fuse.
    7.   Tighten grub screw.
    8.   Just before leaving the ground remove safety pin from tail fuse.

        NOTE.—The safety pin in the nose fuse will be withdrawn just before the bomb is pushed up into its cell when loading up a machine.

FUSING BOMB.
With Tail Fuse Only.

    Should it be thought advisable to use the bomb with tail fuse only it should be fused as directed for nose and tail fuse, with the exception that the nose fuse should first be dissembled, and its instantaneous detonator removed from the relay. This detonator may be replaced by a detonator combining a 2.5 secs. delay, or the relay can be replaced on the nose pistol with no detonator. The nose fuse in the latter case cannot function, and the effect produced will be that of tail fuse only.

        NOTE.—Owing to its design it is considered advisable only to drop this bomb when fitted with nose and tail fuse.

ACTION OF FUSE AND SAFETY DEVICE.

NOSE FUSE. (*See Leaflet 17*).

    1.   The arming vanes of the nose fuse being a fixed part carried on the pressure plate cover, can only rotate with this cover. The suspension lug is also a fixed part on

the top of the pressure plate cover. The pressure plate cover and arming vanes can then only rotate when the suspension lug is free to turn. From this it is clear that when the bomb is stowed vertically, no safety pin or stop on the carrier is required to secure the arming vanes against rotating; the suspension lug being once secured on the release slips, the arming vanes can no longer rotate. When stowed horizontally the arming vanes are to be held from rotating by a stop on the carrier.

2. On release the arming vanes are rotated by air pressure, which results in the spinning off of the pressure plate cover, so exposing the pressure plate.

3. On impact the shearing pins are sheared, and the pressure plate is driven in, so forcing the striker point on to detonator cap (Eley cap, 28 bore); the cap is fired, so detonating the detonator (45 grain) which in its turn causes the detonation of the relay and exploder, so setting off the bomb.

TAIL FUSE.

1. The arming vanes of the tail pistol are prevented from rotating when the bomb is stowed vertically, by a leaf spring in compression, resting against the pistol body. When the bomb is released this spring falls back to its normal position at the side of the bomb cell; the arming vane is then free to rotate, and spins off.

When stowed horizontally, the arming vane is held from rotating by a stop on the carrier. When the bomb is released the arming vane is free to spin off.

On impact the bomb is checked, but the striker is free to move forward, compresses the striker spring, and fires 28 bore cap of igniter. The fuse of the igniter burns for 2.5 or functions instantaneously, according to type, and then fires its detonator, which in its turn detonates the relay and exploder, so setting off the bomb.

LOADING BOMB ON CARRIER.

(*Gledhill Bomb Gear*).

The bombs to be stowed should be carefully fused and gently laid on the ground with safety pins in position, at a convenient distance from the machine on which the bombs are to be carried.

The release gear having been tested for its proper functioning (see leaflet 27) the release handle is to be placed in the free position. This having been done the bombs should be systematically stowed in order, from port to starboard. The safety pins in the nose fuses should only be removed as the bombs are actually handled for stowing. The bomb with the safety pin of the nose fuse removed is then pushed up into its cell until the lug on the nose fuse engages with the suspension hook of the release slip, which it then automatically closes and locks, and the bomb is retained in position on the carrier. The greatest care should be taken to ascertain that the release has locked effectively before leaving the bomb unsupported on the slip.

The tail pistol arming vane is now prevented from rotating by a leaf spring in compression resting against the pistol body.

The nose pistol is automatically held from rotating by the fact of its suspension lug being engaged in the hook of release slip.

LOADING BOMB ON HORIZONTAL CARRIER.

The bomb must be securely housed on the carrier, and on no account be free to move either in the horizontal or vertical planes.

This object is attained by the adjustment of the nose and tail pieces. This adjustment must be repeated in the case of every bomb loaded.

Before the bomb is fused, it must be loaded on the carrier and dropped at least once, to ascertain that the carrier is functioning correctly. When this has been done, and provided the carrier is found to be working satisfactorily, the bomb is to be re-loaded on the carrier and made live by the insertion of the exploders and detonators, and the subsequent screwing of the fuses into position.

UNLOADING FROM HORIZONTAL CARRIER.

1. Replace safety pins in fuses.
2. Drop bomb off carrier.
3. Unscrew and remove fuses and replace them in their tins.
4. Gently shake exploder out of central tube, replace exploder in its tin.
5. Replace nose plug in bomb.

UNLOADING WHEN STOWED VERTICALLY.

1. Replace safety pins in tail fuses and secure arming vanes with cord becket.
2. The weight of the bombs are taken by two or more men from below, *care being taken that the bombs forming the salvos to be released are the bombs being supported*. The release is then operated (great care must be taken that not more than one salvo of bombs is released). The bombs are then gently lowered to the ground.
3. Replace safety pins in nose fuses.
4. Proceed as directed in Nos. 3, 4 and 5 for unloading from horizontal carriers.

TARGETS ENGAGED.

With Nose and Tail Fuse. Personnel, aerodromes, and road transport.

> NOTE.—The exploder 7.39″ has been incorrectly referred to in Leaflet 19 as a relay detonating 7.39″ Mk. II. The exploder 7.39″ is similar in construction to the relay detonating 7.39″, but contains 4 C.E. pellets in place of 2.

AIR MINISTRY,
    March, 1918.

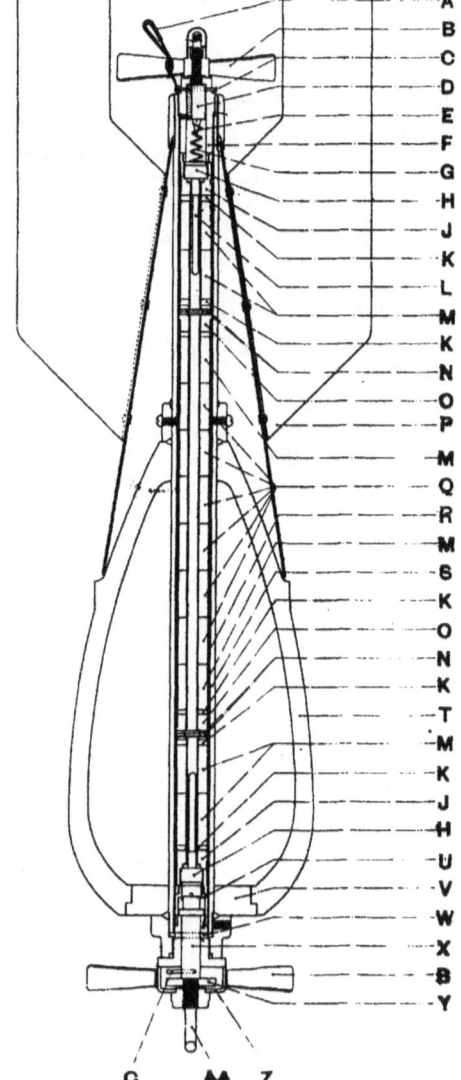

A Cord Becket
B Arming Vane
C Safety Pin
D Striker Spindle [Tail Pistol]
E Striker Point
F Pistol Bomb [Body] No. 5, Mark I.
G Striker Spring
H Cartridge Cap
J Relay Adapter
K Cork Washer
L Fuse Detonator
M C.E. Pellets
N Felt or Cork Washer
O Cardboard Plug
P Detachable Vanes
Q T.N.T. Pellets
R Exploder Tube
S Central Tube
T C.I. Body
U Adapter on Nose Fuse
V Filling Plug
W Shearing Pin [Brass]
X Striker Spindle [Nose Pistol]
Y Pressure Plate
Z Pressure Plate Cover
AA Suspension Lug

Leaflet 15a.

SPECIAL NOTE.

(Ref. Leaflets 13, 14, 15, and 17.)

The detonators for the 112 lb. Bombs Marks VI. and VII. and the 50 lb. Bomb Mark IV referred to in above leaflets, are issued in two varieties, instantaneous, and delay of $2\frac{1}{2}$ secs.

The *DELAY* detonator has the following features which distinguish it from the instantaneous:—

1. The top of the cartridge cap is covered with a thin paper washer coated with Pettman cement, and has four gas escape holes.
2. It has one cannelure in the brass sleeve below cap box.
3. It is approximately $\frac{1}{4}''$ longer.

Air Ministry,

July, 1918.

Note:—Since the first issue of this leaflet, Service names have been assigned for these two detonators, as follows:—

Detonator, Aerial Bomb, No. 4, Mark I. (instantaneous); and

Detonator, Aerial Bomb, No. 5, Mark I. (2.5 secs. delay).

September, 1918.

Leaflet 15b.

Supplementary Leaflet.

(Additional to Nos. 14 and 15).

The 112 lb. Bomb, Mark VII., is issued with the following items which have not been detailed in the above leaflets: —

Plug Nose, 1.05", Mark I.

Plug Bomb Tail, No. 7, Mark I.

Bolt Eye Slinging Bomb, $\frac{1}{2}$", Mark I.

Both these plugs are prepared for receiving the eye bolt in case it is necessary to drop the bomb with one of the fuses only. They also have a stem to make them equivalent in length to the fuse they replace.

The 50 lb., Mark IV. and the 112 lb., Mark VI. bombs are issued with a short plug:—

Plug Bomb Tail, No. 5, Mark I.

both in the nose and tail socket, and no eyebolt slinging. This is due to the fact that these bombs are of cast iron, and must be used with both nose and tail fuses. The long plug and eyebolt are therefore unnecessary. The 112 lb. Bomb, Mark VII., being of cast steel, may be dropped with either nose or tail fuse.

Where the long plugs and eyebolt have previously been issued for the cast iron bombs, they should be kept spare in view of possible changes.

Air Ministry,
May, 1918.

LEAFLET No. 15c

Supplementary Leaflet.

(Additional to Leaflets Nos. 14 and 15.)

REF.: BOMBS H.E., R.L., 112 LB., MARK VI. AND VII.,
AND 50 LB., MARK IV.

When using EXPLODER, H.E. BOMB, 12.75", No. 2, MARKS I. OR II., with these bombs, it has been incorrectly stated that Detonators, H.E. Bomb, Marks I. or II., are not necessary.

This is not the case; the exploders should always have their corresponding Detonators, H.E. Bomb, 56 grs. In the case of the Mark I. Exploder they are not to be removed, and in the case of the Mark II. Exploder they are to be screwed into the ends before inserting in the bomb.

When using EXPLODER, H.E. BOMB, 12.22", No. 9, MARK I. (Paper Exploder), a flanged Detonator will be employed in addition, details of which will be circulated later.

NOTE:—Service name for the flanged detonator is as follows:—
Detonator, H.E. Bomb, 5 grs., No. 1, Mark I/A/.

Cancelled

AIR MINISTRY,
June, 1918.

Leaflet No. 15d.

FLANGED DETONATOR H.E. BOMB, 45 GRAINS.

The diagram shows details of the above detonator, which will be used in *Exploder H.E. Bomb 12.22" No. 9 Mark I*. (Paper Exploder). (*See* Leaflet No. 15c.) Two detonators will be issued per exploder, one being inserted at each end when assembling fusing components.

In construction it has the same tube and filling as the Detonator Aerial Bomb No. 4 Mark I., with a brass flange instead of the 28 bore cap. A card wad is pressed down on the surface of the fulminate and the mouth of the tube is closed by a tinfoil protecting disc.

This exploder and detonator will only be employed at present with Bombs H.E. R.L. 112 lbs. Marks VI. and VII. and 50 lbs. Mark IV. (*See* Leaflets No. 14 and 15.)

Air Ministry,
July, 1918.

FLANGED DETONATOR, H.E. BOMB, 45 GRAINS.

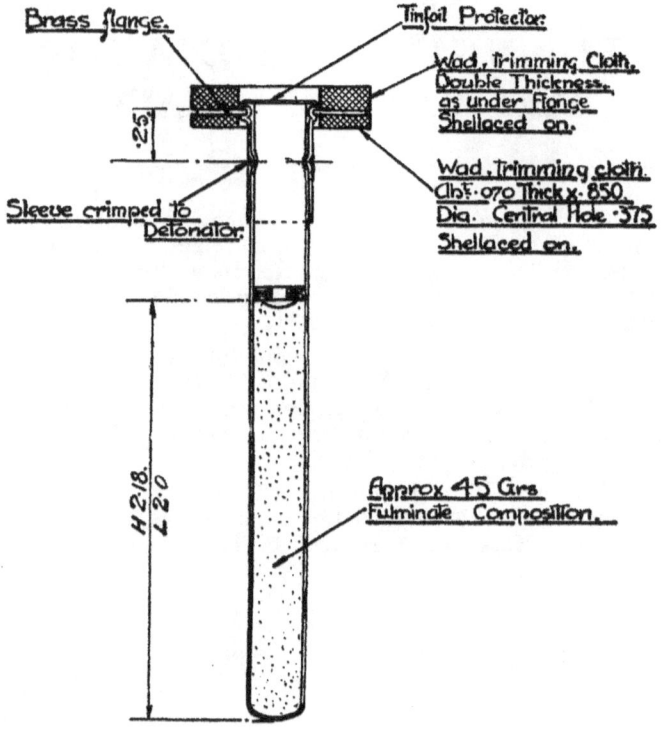

Leaflet No. 16.

EXPLODER Long No. 1.

(Mk. I./C/) with one detonator. 77 gr. Mk. I.

Weight, Complete.—11 ozs.

Overall Dimensions.—12·6 inches long × ·95 inches diameter.

Explosive Substance.—2 Tetryl pellets at detonator end and 7 TNT. pellets.

Detonators.—1 77 gr. Mk. I (this detonator is stuck in with shellac, or sometimes only pushed in).

Used in.—R.L. 16 lb. Bomb.

Issued in tins, sometimes with, sometimes without, detonator in position.

Construction.—See Diagram.

Method of Loading Into Bomb.

Push in from tail end, detonator last.

Note:—

The 77 gr. detonator is a percussion detonator, being directly struck by the striker of the bomb pistol and not fired by a flash, as in the 56 gr. detonator Mk. 1 or Mk. 11.

A Mk. 11 exploder of this type, with screw in 56 gr. detonator is in existence, but not in general use.

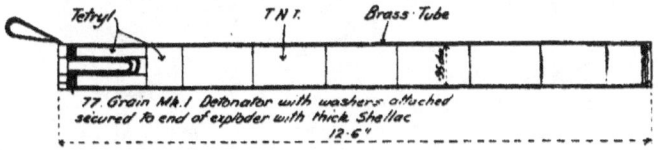

AIR MINISTRY,
January, 1918.

Leaflet No. 17.

Standard Nose Fuse.

FUSE BOMB D.A. No. 8, MK. I., WITH HANGING EYEBOLT.

FOR CONSTRUCTION, SEE DIAGRAM (FIG. I.).

This fuse is issued as a complete unit. It consists of a hanging nose pistol, a 4.5 inch relay detonating and an instantaneous detonator, or a detonator combining a 2.5 second delay, as required. If delay action is required, the instantaneous detonator, with which the fuse is issued, must be removed and the detonator combining the 2.5 second delay must be substituted.

ACTION OF FUSE AND SAFETY DEVICE.

    1. The arming vanes of the nose fuse being a fixed part carried on the pressure plate cover, can only rotate with this cover. The suspension lug is also a fixed part on the top of the pressure plate cover. The pressure plate cover and arming vanes can then only rotate when the suspension lug is free to turn. From this it is clear that when the bomb is stowed vertically, no safety pin or stop on the carrier is required to secure the arming vanes against rotating; the suspension lug being once secured on the release slips, the arming vanes can no longer rotate. When stowed horizontally, the arming vanes are to be held from rotating by a stop on the carrier.

    2. On release, the arming vanes are rotated by air pressure, which results in the spinning off of the pressure plate cover, so exposing the pressure plate.

    3. On impact, the shearing pins are sheared, and the pressure plate is driven in, so forcing the striker point on to detonator cap (Eley cap, 28 bore); the cap is fired, so detonating the detonator (45 grain), which, in its turn, causes the detonation of the relay and exploder, so setting off the bomb.

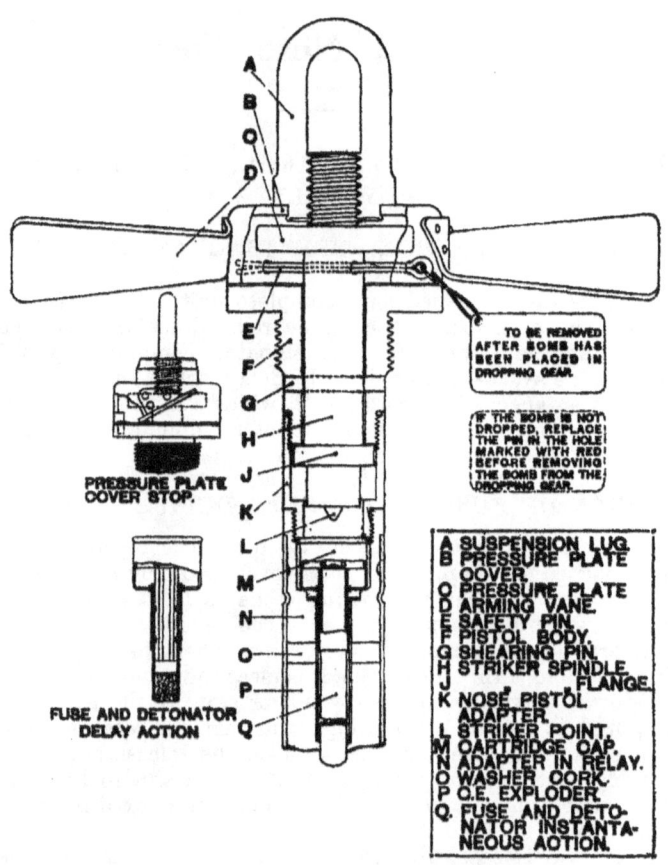

Fig. 1. Fuse, Bomb, D.A., No. 8, with Hanging Eyebolt (Parallel Thread).

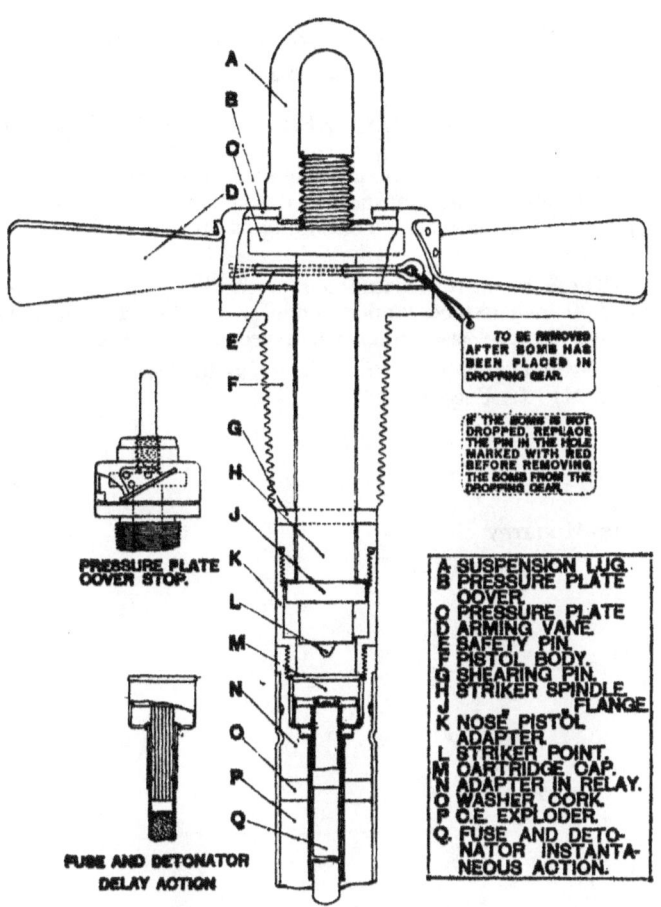

Fig. 2. Fuse, Bomb, D.A., No. 9, with Hanging Eyebolt (Taper Thread).

FUSE BOMB D.A. No. 9, MK. I., WITH HANGING EYEBOLT (TAPER THREAD).

USED ONLY IN BOMBS H.E., R.L. 112 LB., MK. III. AND V.

FOR CONSTRUCTION, SEE DIAGRAM (FIG. 2).

This fuse consists of a hanging nose pistol, a 7.39 inch exploder and an instantaneous detonator, which may be replaced by a detonator combining a 2.5 second delay, if desired.

These three fuse components, the hanging nose pistol, the 7.39 inch exploder and detonator are issued separately, and will require assembling when preparing to fuse a bomb.

Action of fuse and safety device as for Fuse Bomb D.A. No. 8, Mk. I., Page 1.

AIR MINISTRY,
March, 1918.

LEAFLET NO. 18.

(A third issue is being prepared. It must be taken at present in conjunction with 19A and 19B.)

(Second issue. To cancel issue of January, 1918.)

EXPLODERS.

EXPLODER NO. 2 MK. I/L AND EXPLODER NO. 2, MK. II/L.

Weight Complete.—11 ozs.

Overall Dimensions.—12.8 inches × .95 inch diameter.

Explosive Substance.—4 Tetryl pellets (2 at each end) and 5 T.N.T. pellets.

Detonators.—2—56-gr. In. Mk. I, stuck in with shellac, and in Mk. II screwed in.

Used in Bomb H.E.—R.L. 112-lb. Mk. III and upward.
,, ,, R.L. 100-lb. and 65-lb.
,, ,, R.L. 50-lb.
,, ,, R.L. 250-lb.
,, ,, R.F.C. 230-lb. Mk. I and upwards
,, ,, 520-lb. and 550-lb. Mk. I/N.

Construction.—See diagrams.

METHOD OF LOADING EXPLODER.

WITH EXPLODER NO. 2 MARK I/L.

(1) Remove exploder with detonators attached from its tin.

(2) Push it into bomb from nose or tail end as required.

METHOD OF ACTION.

The flash from the fuse sets off the detonator at one end of exploder which fires the exploder and the bomb.

UNLOADING.

Remove exploder from bomb by shaking gently and replace exploder in its tin.

WITH EXPLODER NO. 2 MARK II.

(1) Remove exploder and detonators from their tins and screw detonators into exploder.

(2) Push exploder into bomb from nose or tail end as required.

METHOD OF ACTION.

The flash from the fuse sets off the detonator at one end of exploder which fires the exploder and the bomb.

UNLOADING.

(1) Remove exploder from bomb by shaking gently.

(2) Unscrew detonators from the exploder and replace them and exploder in their tins.

NEW 12" PAPER EXPLODER. (EXPLODER H.E. BOMB 12.22" No. 9, MARK I.)

Weight $6\frac{1}{2}$ ozs.

This exploder is designed for use in conjunction with the new form of fusing used in the 112 lb. bombs Mark VI, and 50 lb. bomb Mark IV. A flanged detonator will be issued for this exploder, details of which will be circulated later.

This exploder may be used to replace earlier Marks of 12" exploders when used in conjunction with new fusing only. These exploders will not be issued for use in the Tropics or Mediterranean.

RELAY DETONATING H.E. BOMB 7.39" MARK III.

Weight $6\frac{1}{2}$ ozs.

This relay detonating (sometimes called 7.39" Exploder) is a modification of the Relay Detonating 7.39". Mk. I and II. The dissimilarity between the two lies in the fact that the Mark III contains 4 C.E. pellets in place of two as in Mks. I and II, and in addition the Mk. III has included in its design an adapter to fit the 28 bore cap of the detonator used in the new D.A. fuse No. 8 and No. 9 (with hanging eyebolt), whilst the adapter in the 7.39" Relay Mks. I. and II. is designed to fit the .410 cap of the igniter used in the common Stokes' assemblage.

Will only be used in bomb with a diaphragm in central tubes. (See Supplementary Leaflets 18A and 19A.)

AIR MINISTRY.

May, 1918.

EXPLODERS.

EXPLODER, H.E. BOMB, 12.75", No. 2, MK. II/L.

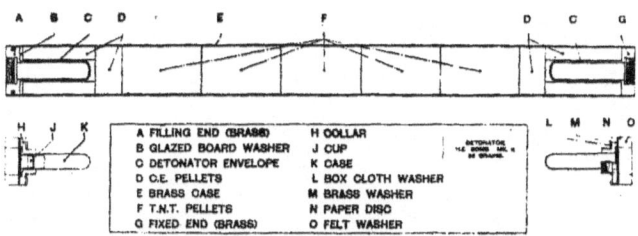

A FILLING END (BRASS)
B GLAZED BOARD WASHER
C DETONATOR ENVELOPE
D C.E. PELLETS
E BRASS CASE
F T.N.T. PELLETS
G FIXED END (BRASS)
H COLLAR
J CUP
K CASE
L BOX CLOTH WASHER
M BRASS WASHER
N PAPER DISC
O FELT WASHER

EXPLODER, H.E. BOMB, 12.75", No. 2, MK. I/L.

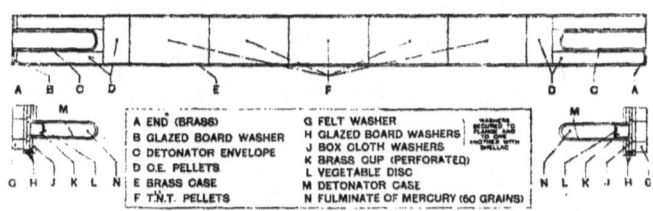

A END (BRASS)
B GLAZED BOARD WASHER
C DETONATOR ENVELOPE
D C.E. PELLETS
E BRASS CASE
F T.N.T. PELLETS
G FELT WASHER
H GLAZED BOARD WASHERS
J BOX CLOTH WASHERS
K BRASS CUP (PERFORATED)
L VEGETABLE DISC
M DETONATOR CASE
N FULMINATE OF MERCURY (60 GRAINS)

H.E. BOMB, 12.22", No. 9, MK. I. (PAPER EXPLODER).

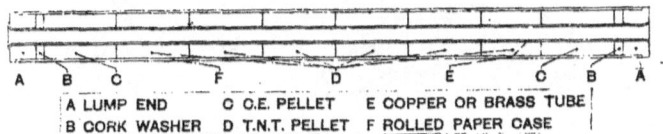

A LUMP END
B CORK WASHER
C C.E. PELLET
D T.N.T. PELLET
E COPPER OR BRASS TUBE
F ROLLED PAPER CASE

RELAY DETONATING H.E. BOMB, 7.39", MK. III.
("EXPLODER 7.39"").

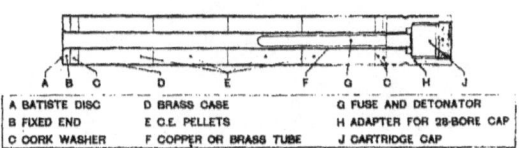

A BATISTE DISC
B FIXED END
C CORK WASHER
D BRASS CASE
E C.E. PELLETS
F COPPER OR BRASS TUBE
G FUSE AND DETONATOR
H ADAPTER FOR 28-BORE CAP
J CARTRIDGE CAP

LEAFLET NO. 19.

(Second issue to cancel issue of Jan., 1918.)
(A third issue is being prepared. It must be taken at present in conjunction with 19A and 19B.)

TAIL-FUSES.

STOKES' ASSEMBLAGE. (FUSE, BOMB, TAIL No. 18 WITH DETONATOR.)

The following components, when assembled, constitute Stokes' Assemblage (see Fig. 1).
(1) Pistol bomb No. 5, Mk. I. (See Fig. 2).
(2) Relay detonating Mk. I. or Mk. II.
(3) Igniter (with delay action as required 15 sec., 2.5 sec. or .05 sec.).
(4) Pistol Adapter 1.375" (for use with Bomb H.E. R.I, 112 lbs., Mk. III. only).

Weight Complete.—1 lb. 1 oz.

Construction.—See diagram.

METHOD OF LOADING INTO BOMB.

(1) Untie cord becket from pistol vane and test vane for ease of spinning.

(2) If using 112 lb. bomb, Mk. III, screw adapter on to bomb pistol and tighten grub screw.

(3) Select igniter required; these are manufactured with delay action as follows:—
        15 secs.—Blue.
        2.5 secs.—Green.
        .05 secs.—White.

(4) Push igniter into relay detonating, and screw pistol on to relay.

(5) Screw fuse into tail of bomb and tighten grub screw.

(6) Just before leaving ground pull out safety pin.

SAFETY DEVICES AND METHOD OF ACTION (*See Fig. 1*).

On the carrier the vane B is held from rotating by a stop on the carrier. When the bomb is released the vane B is free to rotate, and spins off.

The striker F is then supported by the striker spring G.

On impact the bomb is checked, but the striker being free to move forward, compresses the striker spring, and fires the cap J of the igniter. This cap fires the length of Fuse M which in its turn fires a number 8 detonator R. This detonator fires the 56 grain detonator in the exploder, and so fires the bomb.

UNLOADING.

(1) Insert safety pin in pistol and loosen grub screw.

(2) Unscrew fuse from bomb.

(3) Dissemble the fuse replacing pistol, relay detonating and igniter in their respective boxes.

FUSE BOMB, TAIL No. 3 OR No. 4.

These fuses consist of a Pistol Bomb No. 1, Mk. II. screwed into a No. 3 or No. 4 magazine.

These fuses are now used only in the 250 lb. Naval Bomb and are not illustrated.

The No. 3 fuse has a delay of .25 secs., the No. 4 a delay of about .025 secs.

NOTE ON TAIL FUSE NOMENCLATURE.

As a certain number of old pattern pistols and fuses are still extant, and to prevent confusion, the following summary of the different types is given:—

PISTOLS BOMB.

Ob. No. 1.	Mark. 1.	
Ob. No. 1.	Mark. II.	All 24 threads to the inch on body, and sharp pointed strikers.
Ob. No. 1.	Mark III.	
Ob. No. 1.	Mark IV.	
Ob. No. 2.	Mark I.	1″ diameter body, 14 threads to inch. Other details as No. I Mk. IV.

Ob. No. 3.	Mark I	Same as No. 2 Mark I, but threaded internally to take screwed gland for use with early type of Stokes' 15 sec. delay; blunt striker.
No. 4.	Mark I.	Same as No. 1 Mark IV., except that striker point is blunted for use against the anvil cap of the cartridge head in Stokes Assemblage. Also a left hand creep spring is fitted instead of a right handed one, in order to prevent it catching when screwing into the relay detonating.
No. 5.	Mark. I	Same as No. 3 Mark I, except for differences given in previous case for use in Stokes' Assemblage.
No. 6.		For Bomb Incendiary and Smoke Mk.II/L. (See Leaflet 11.)

NOTE.—Ob.=Obsolescent.

Ob. Fuse, Bomb, Tail No. 14.	No. 3 Pistol and Detonating Relay without detonator.
Fuse, Bomb, Tail No. 15.	No. 6 Pistol, fixing screw and adapter (See Leaflet 11, there called " Special Tail Fuse ").
Fuse Bomb Tail No. 18. [This is " Stokes Assemblage " without detonator. See above.]	No. 5 Pistol and Detonating Relay, without detonator.

AIR MINISTRY.

May, 1918.

STOKE'S ASSEMBLAGE

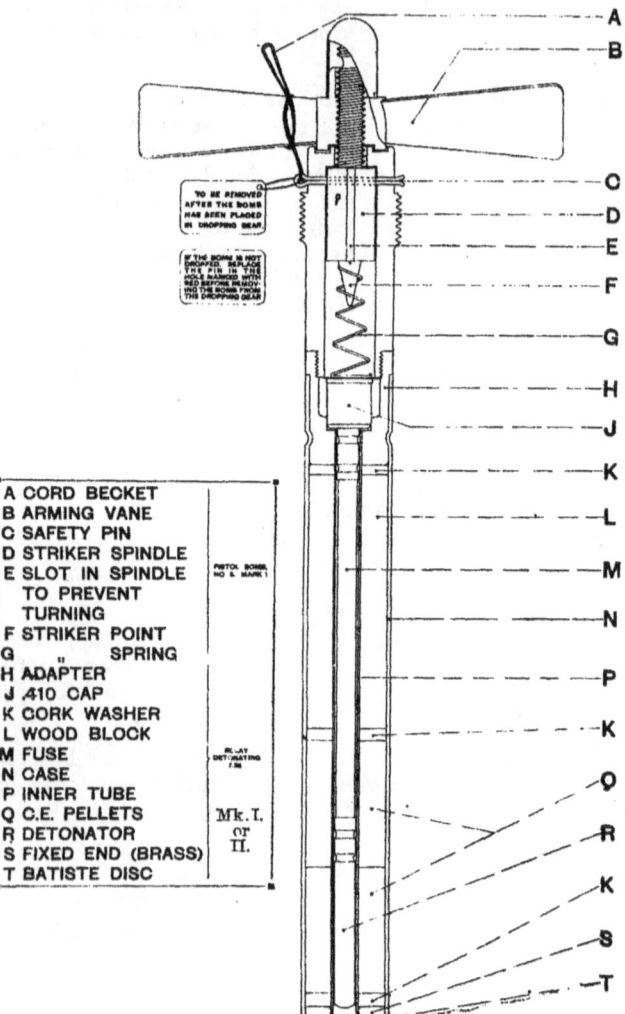

FIG. 1.

LEAFLET No. 19A. SUPPLEMENTARY TO LEAFLET 19.

SUPPLEMENTARY NOTE ON RELAYS AND DETONATORS.

Cases having occurred of indescriminate interchanging of fusing components where failures inevitably followed, the following notes are intended to give detailed instructions on these points.

(I.) *Detonators, Aerial Bomb No. 4, Mark I* (instantaneous) and *Detonators, Aerial Bomb No. 5, Mark I* (2.5 sec. delay) are the new short 45 gr. detonators with 28 bore cap, as distinct from:—

Detonators Aerial Bomb, Mark II with .05 sec., 2.5 sec., and 15 sec. delay; commonly called "igniters" with .410 cap, as used in Stokes Assemblage.

(II.) The Detonators, Aerial Bomb, No. 4., Mark I and No. 5, Mark I, may only be used with:—

Relay Detonating H.E. Bomb, 7.39", Mark III. (commonly referred to as " Exploder 7.39"), or

Relay Detonating H.E. Bomb 4.5", Mark I/L., and on no account may these detonators be used with:—

Relay Detonating H.E. Bomb, Marks I. or II., as a failure is bound to occur.

This is owing to the fact that the Mark III. relay detonating 7.39" has four C.E. pellets in place of the two C.E. pellets and wood block of the Marks I. and II.

To give prominence to this important distinction, it was originally named the " Exploder 7.39". It will be seen that the longer Detonator, Aerial Bomb, Mark II, reaches the two C.E. pellets of the Relays, Detonating 7.39" Marks I. and II., whereas the shorter Detonator, Aerial Bomb, No. 4, Mark I. and No. 5, Mark I., will not do so, its end being adjacent to the wood block and thus incapable of detonating the relay. Where, however, as in the Mark III., Relay Detonating 7.39", with four pellets, there are two C.E. pellets adjacent to this short detonator, it is capable of functioning.

(III.) *Detonators Aerial Bomb, Mark II* (.05 sec. delay) are being ultimately replaced by Detonators Aerial Bomb No. 4, Mark I. (instantaneous), but so long as they are issued, may be employed with Relay Detonating H.E Bomb 7.39",

Marks I., II., or III. The alternative No. 4, Mark I, however, can only be used with the Mark III., 7.39″ Relay Detonating or Mark I/L 4.5″ Relay Detonating.

(IV.) *Detonators Aerial Bomb, Mark II* with 2.5 sec. delay, must not be used under any circumstances. They are to be returned to Store.

(V.) For present replacement of *Detonators Aerial Bomb, Mark II* with 2.5 sec. delay, Detonators, Aerial Bomb No. 5, Mark I. (with 2.5 sec. delay), will be issued and can then only be employed with Relay Detonating H.E. Bomb 7.39″ Mark III., or Relay Detonating H.E. Bomb, 4.5″, Mark I/L, as explained above.

(VI.) *Detonators Aerial Bomb, Mark II* (15 sec. delay), will continue to be used when this length of delay is necessary, and may be employed with Relay Detonating H.E. Bomb 7.39″, Marks I., II., or III. They will be modified later to have a 28-bore cap, instead of the .410.

(VII.) *Pistol, Bomb, No. 3, Mark I.* with screwed gland, must have this gland removed before being used in any tail assemblage in bombs for sea use. (Vide A.T.O. No. 246).

(VIII.) Special note should be taken of difference between—

Detonators, Aerial Bomb, for the various *Relays Detonating* mentioned above and—

Detonators H.E. Bomb, for various *Exploders* in use. (Thus, one must be careful to note that the commonly called " Detonators 56 grs., Marks I. and II." are liable to be confused with the others, unless the words " H.E. Bomb " are always added after " Detonators ". They should always be referred to as " Detonators H.E. Bomb, 56 grs., Marks I. or II ". . Similarly, " Detonators, H.E. Bomb, 60 grs., No. 2, Mark I/C ").

APPLICATION TO BOMBS.

The following particular references may therefore be made to individual bombs:—

(I.) 230 LB. BOMB, H.E., R.F.C., MARKS I. OR III.

Tail Fuse A.
(1) *Pistol Bomb No. 5, Mark I*, or *Pistol Bomb No. 3, Mark I* (with gland removed for sea use).
(2) *Relay Detonating*, H.E. Bomb, 7.39″, Marks I or II., and
(3) *Detonator, Aerial Bomb*, Mark II (.05 sec.. or 15 sec. delay).

Leaflet No. 19a (continued).

(Detonators Aerial Bomb, No. 4, Mark I, or No. 5, Mark I., must on no account be used in " A " assemblage).

Tail Fuse. (1) *Pistol Bomb* (as for A).
         (2) *Relay Detonating* H.E. Bomb, 7.39″, Mark III. (only). (Sometimes called " Exploder 7.39″), and

or   B.   (3) *Detonator Aerial Bomb*, Mark II. (.05 sec., or 15 sec. delay), or
         (3) *Detonator Aerial Bomb*, No. 4, Mark I. (instantaneous), or
         (3) *Detonator Aerial Bomb*, No. 5, Mark I., 2.5 sec. delay.

Variations can only be made as stated within either assemblage A or B. No other combinations must on any account be employed.

Assemblage A will be recognised as the commonly known Stokes Assemblage."

(II.) BOMB, H.E., 112 LB., MARKS III. AND V.

(*a*) Horizontal stowage, with nose and tail fuse, or vertical stowage with tail fuse only.

A or B Assemblage as detailed for 230 lb. bomb, may be employed for the Tail Fuse, together with—

Vertical Stowage tail fuse only.
    Exploder, H.E. Bomb, 12.75″, No. 2, Marks I/L or II/L.
    2. Detonators, H.E. Bomb, 56 grs., Marks I or II., Plug, Fuse/Hole, special No. 3c, Mark II/Bolt eye, bomb slinging ½″, Mark I.

Horizontal Stowage Nose and Tail Fuse
    Fuse, Bomb, D.A. No. 1 Mark 1. With the above instead of Plug, Fuse/Hole.

Mark III bomb requires in addition—
    Adapter 1.375″ for Pistol.
  Bomb of above.

See Leaflet No. 25.

(*b*) Vertical Stowage with Nose and Tail Fuse.

Assemblage " A " or " B " for Tail Fuse, together with—
> Fuse, Bomb D.A. No. 9. Mark I.
> Relay Detonating H.E. Bomb 7.39". Mark III.
> Detonator, Aerial Bomb, No. 4. Mark I. (instantaneous).
> Wood Packing Piece 4¾".

(Leaflet No. 25.)

(III.) *Bomb, H.E., 112 lb., Marks VI. and VII.*, and—
(IV.) *Bomb, H.E., 50 lb., Mark IV.*

As previously detailed in Leaflets 14 and 15. The 7.39" Relay Detonating is not employed.

(V.) *Bomb, H.E., R.L., 250 lbs., Mark I.*

When the alternative method of fusing for seaplanes is employed (See Leaflet No. 25) the following may be used—

Assemblage " A " or " B " for Tail Fuse as detailed above for 230 lb. bomb together with—
> *Exploder*, 7.2", No. 8, Mark I, with two Detonators.
> H.E. Bomb, 60 grs., No. 2, Mark I/C.
> Exploder, 12.6", No. 8, Mark I, with two Detonators.
> H.E. Bomb, 60 grs., No. 2, Mark I/C.
> and, Fuse Bomb, D.A. No. 1, Mark I.

Leaflet No. 19b.

NOMENCLATURE.

The following table gives in parallel columns the correct service nomenclature and the names by which some of the principal fusing components are commonly known. The correct service names, as given here, cancel previous names in these leaflets which differ, and should be taken into use.

DETONATORS.

Correct Service Nomenclature.	Popular Names.	Remarks
Detonator, H.E. Bomb, 56 grs. No. 1, Mark I.	Detonator, 56 grs, Mark I.	For Exploder H.E. Bomb 12.75" No. 2, Mark I/L.
No. 1, Mark II.	Detonator, 56 grs, Mark II.	For Exploder H.E. Bomb 12.75" No. 2, Mk. II/L.
Detonator, Aerial Bomb. Mark II., with .05 secs. 2.5 secs. or 15 secs delay.	Igniter.	.410 cap with instantaneous or safety fuse, as used in Stokes Assemblage.
Detonator, Aerial Bomb. 2.5 secs. delay 5, Mark I.	New 45 grain detonators, or igniters, 28 bore cap (Described in Leaflet No. 17).	28 bore cap. For new fusing components. (See Leaflets 13, 14, 15 and 17).
Detonator, Aerial Bomb. Instantaneous, No. 4, Mark I.	Ditto.	Ditto.

T.5. D.770

RELAYS.

Correct Service Nomenclature.	Popular Names.	Remarks.
Relay Detonating, H.E. Bomb. 7.39" Mark I..	Relay detonating, 7.39", Mark I.	*Two* C.E. pellets and wood block, copper sleeve.
Mark II.	Mark II.	*Two* C.E. pellets and wood block. Sleeve (other than copper).
Mark III.	7.39" Exploder.	*Four* C.E. pellets, For Detonators, Aerial Bomb No. 5, Mark I. and No. 4, Mark I. (See Leaflets 13, 14, 15, and 17).
4.5" Mark I/L.	Relay Detonating, 4.5"	See Leaflets above.

FUSES.

Fuse, Bomb D.A. No. 7. Mark I/L.	Cooper Fuse.	
Fuse, Bomb, Tail, No. 14.	Early Stokes' Assemblage without igniter. No. 3 Pistol.	No. 3 Pistol, with Relay Detonating 7.39", Marks I, or II. without detonator, aerial bomb.
Fuse, Bomb, Tail, No. 18.	Stokes' Assemblage, without igniter.	No. 5, Pistol with Relay Detonating 7.39" Marks I. or II. without detonator, aerial bomb.

EXPLODERS.

Correct Service Nomenclature.	Popular Names.	Remarks.
Exploder, H.E. Bomb, 12.75". No. 2, Mark I./L.	Exploder, Long No. 2, Mark I.	With Detonators H.E. Bomb 56 grs., Mark I., in place (Leaflet 18)
Exploder, H.E. Bomb, 12.75". No. 2, Mark II./L.	Exploder, Long No. 2, Mark II.	Detonators H.E. Bomb 56 grs., Mark II. to be screwed into place for use.
*Exploder, H.E. Bomb, 12.22". No. 9, Mark I.	*Paper Exploder.	See Leaflets 13, 14 and 15.

A revised issue of Leaflet No. 19 on Tail Fuses has been issued, which gives a summary of the standard nomenclature for Pistols, Bomb.

Special note should be taken of the difference between "Detonators H.E. Bomb" and "Detonators, Aerial Bomb."

*An additional flanged detonator will be issued for use with this exploder, details of which will be circulated shortly.

Air Ministry.
June, 1918.

Leaflet No. 20.

FUSE BOMB. D.A. No. 1.

Mark I.

Weight Complete.—1 lb. 1 oz.
Construction.—*See* diagram.

This is at present the standard nose fuse, used in all nose fuse bombs except the Cooper bomb, R.L. 50 lb. Mk. IV and upwards, and 112 lb. Mk. VI and upwards.

Method of Loading into Bomb.

(1) Remove safety pin and safety collar.

(2) Test striker spindle for ease of spinning, and then remove it.

(3) Screw fuse home into nose of bomb and replace striker spindle, safety collar and safety pin.

See that red line on striker spindle is flush with face of pressure plate and that short end of vane stop on safety collar engages in castellation on nose of bomb.

(4) Wire safety collar to bomb carrier.

(5) Just before leaving the ground pull out safety pin.

Safety Device and Method of Action.

On the carrier the vane of the fuse is held from rotating by means of the long end of the vane stop. On release, the vane and striker spindle are free to rotate, and are spun round by the air pressure. At the end of its travel the striker on the striker spindle obtrudes beyond the striker holder. On impact the blow comes on the vane and pressure plate, the shearing pins are sheared and the striker is forced on to the cap, the detonation of which sets off the C.E. (composition, exploding) in the chamber of the fuse body and so sets off the bomb.

In unloading the following method must be adopted.

(1) Remove safety collar and striker spindle.

(2) Remove fuse from bomb.

(3) Replace striker spindle, safety collar, and safety pin in fuse and put fuse back in its tin.

Air Ministry,
January, 1918.

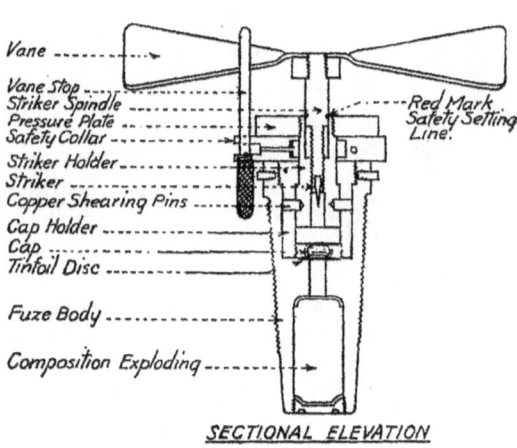

SECTIONAL ELEVATION

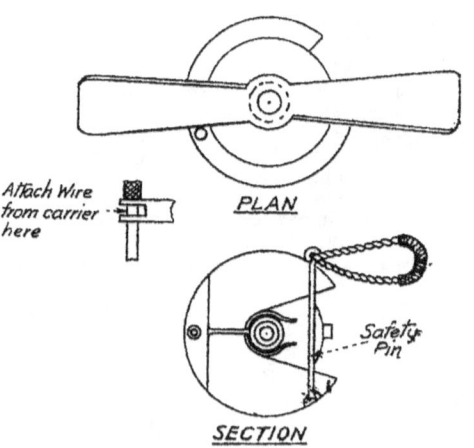

PLAN

SECTION

LEAFLET 21.

HOLTS WING TIP FLARES.

Weight complete (per pair)   8¾ to 9 ozs.
Method of firing .... Electrical.
Construction .... See diagram.
How issued .... In tins containing 1 flare each.
How carried .... On the wing tips or tail booms in special holder.

LOADING.

Before loading them in the holder it is essential to short the leads from the accumulators to the holders to see that there is a spark and so ensure there being sufficient current to fire the flare. When this has been done the flares should be clipped into their holders and wired up to the terminals at top of the flare holder.

NOTE.—These flares are carried on night flying machines, for assistance to pilot in case of forced landings. The flares are made in two types, white and red. The latter are most suitable for use in mists, as their fog piercing effects are better than the white, whilst their illumination on clear nights is approximately equal to the white.

These flares should not be kept on machines for extended periods as they are liable to be affected by damp.

AIR MINISTRY.

January, 1918.

Ap.D. [P.]   D.396.   2/18.

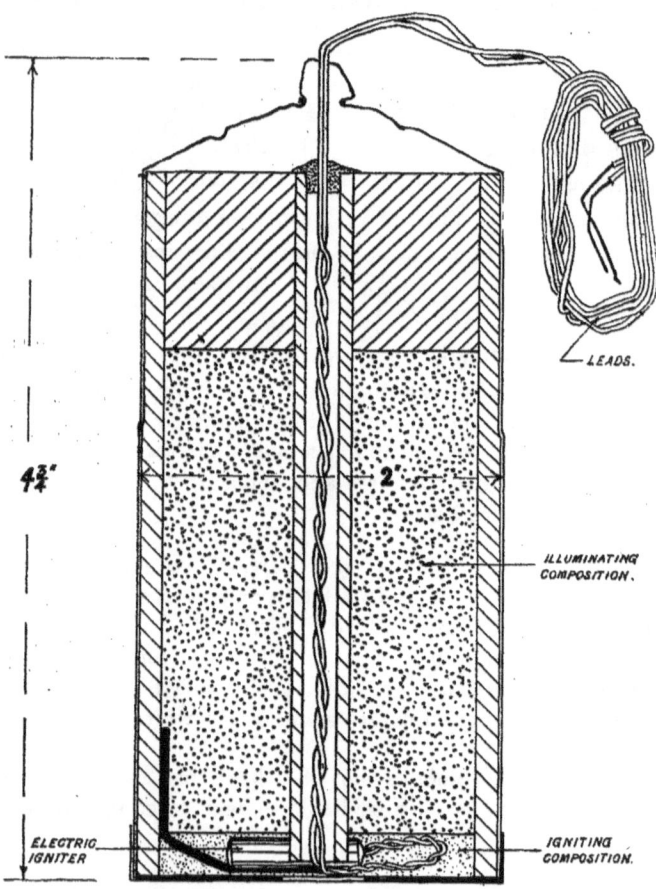

HOLT WING TIP FLARE.

Leaflet 22.

MICHELIN PARACHUTE FLARE.

Weight, complete	23 lbs. 10 ozs.
Weight of case and parachute	5 lbs. 10 ozs.
Weight of candle	18 lbs.
Illuminating element	One flare candle.
Case material	Tin.
Overall dimensions	3 ft. 2 in. long × 4½ in. diameter.
How carried	Horizontally on special carrier.
Type of fuse	Special nose fuse.
Time of burning	7 to 11 minutes.
Construction	See diagram.

ACTION OF FUSE AND SAFETY DEVICE (see Fig. 1).

On the carrier the vane of the fuse (B) is held from rotating by a stop on the carrier.

On release the vane is spun round by the air pressure, and after about 7 seconds the friction igniter (C) lights the composition (D), which fires the charge (E) and lights the flare candle (F).

The candle and parachute (G) are projected from the case and the parachute opens.

LOADING FLARE ON CARRIER (see Fig. 2).

(1) Push the studs AA on flare simultaneously upwards into the holes AA on carrier. The flare will now be automatically retained by the operation of a spring and scissors device, contained beneath the plates shown in Fig. 1 at A.

(2) The flare should now be released to ascertain if the carrier is functioning correctly. If the carrier is working satisfactorily, replace the flare.

Ap.D.(P.) D395. 2/18

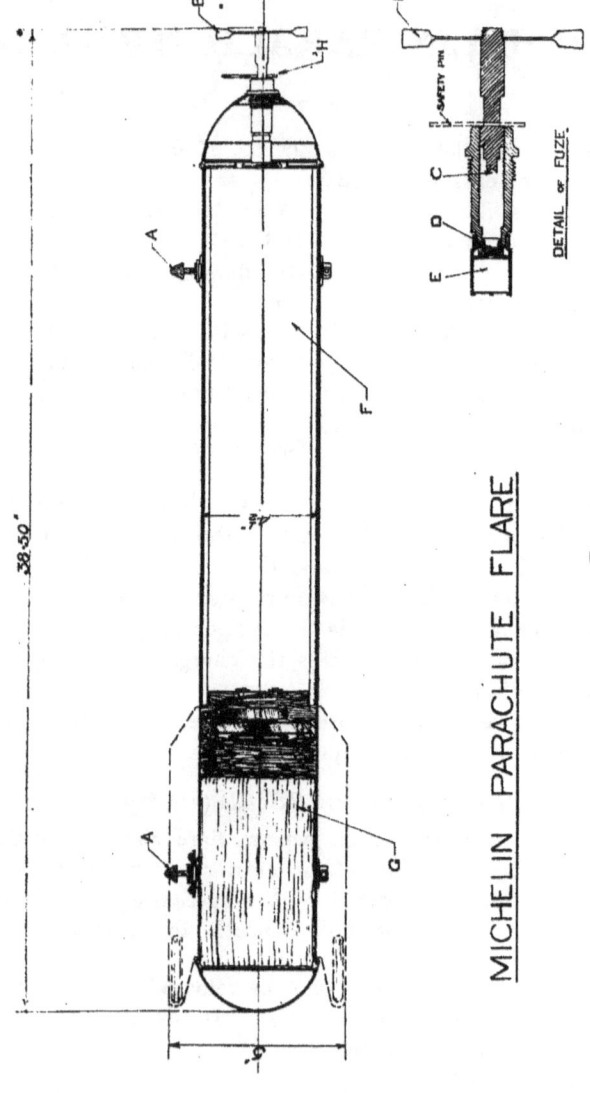

MICHELIN PARACHUTE FLARE

Fig. 1.

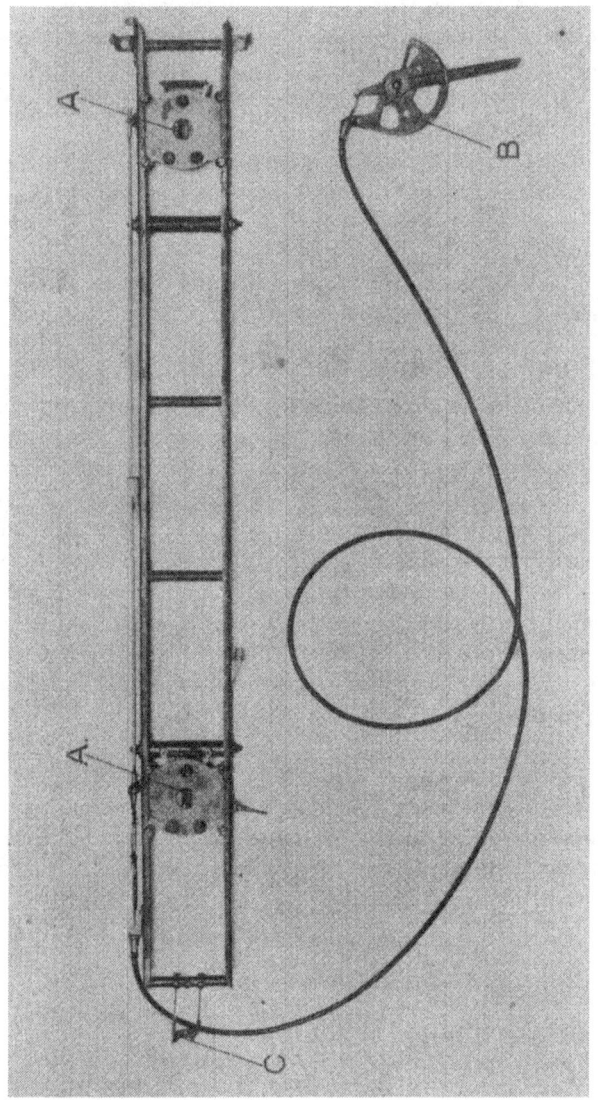

FIG. 2.

(3) Ascertain that the clip C on the carrier fits over the flats on the vane spindle of the fuse, so preventing its rotation.

(4) Just before leaving the ground remove the safety pin H (see Fig. 1).

NOTE.—Special care should be taken not to knock the vane of the fuse, as this would prevent it working.

UNLOADING.

Replace safety pin H in fuse and release flare from carrier.

ACTION OF MICHELIN FLARE CARRIER (*see Fig. 2*).

On depressing the release handle B, the arms of a spring and scissors device contained at both ends of the carrier at AA are separated by the rotation of a cam pivoted between the arms of the scissors. This action results in the release of the flare, which is, when loaded on the carrier, retained by the arms of the scissors gripping the two studs on the flare (see Fig. 1 AA) whose upper portions are cones, with grooves running round their respective bases in which the arms of the scissors are held by means of a spring, so securing the flare on the carrier except at such times as the release handle is operated.

FITTING.

There is at present no standard fitting for mounting this type of carrier on machines. The carrier may, however, be mounted in any way convenient, affording sufficient security. It is easily wired into position as required.

AIR MINISTRY,
January, 1918.

Leaflet No. 23.

T.W.R. PARACHUTE FLARE.

Weight complete.—15 lbs. 4 ozs.
Weight of case and parachute.—6 lbs. 4 ozs.
Weight of candles.—9 lbs.
Illuminating element.—4 flare candles.
Case material.—Tin.
Overall dimensions.—2 ft. 6 in. long by $4\frac{1}{8}$ in. diameter.
How carried.—Horizontally on 4-20 lb. bomb carrier.
Type of fuse.—Midgeley fuse.
Time of burning.—3-4 minutes.
Construction.—See diagram.

To Prepare for Action.

The following will be required:—

1 Midgeley Fuse complete.

Fusing Flare.

1. Unscrew base plug on flare.

2. Screw on Midgeley Fuse.

3. Punch fuse to time required.

4. Place flare on carrier.

5. Insert string attached to trigger under safety clip on carrier. This should be done with utmost care, making positive that the string attached to trigger is actually pushed past, and

clear of the button and spring clip of safety device. Care must be taken that the string is not drawn tight when the bomb is in position, but allowed about two inches of play or sag so that any slight movement of the bomb tail in the vertical plane will not withdraw the string from safety device, so causing the bomb, when released, to fall unarmed.

6. Just before the machine leaves ground remove safety pins.

Action of Fuse and Safety Device.

For full instructions, *see* 40 lb. phosphorous bombs, Leaflet 11.

Loading Flare on Carrier (4–20 lb. carrier).

The flares must be securely housed on the carrier and not be free to move in the horizontal or vertical planes. This is obtained by the adjustment of the nose and tail pieces provided on the carrier.

Before the flares are fused they should be released at least once to test the carrier. If the carrier is functioning correctly the flares are to be reloaded on the carrier having first been made live by the screwing of fuse into position. Care must be taken that the safety device is working correctly, this is the case when the string loops inserted under the clips of the safety device are free to pull out should the bomb be accidentally torn off the machine in a crash (*see* Leaflet 11).

Unloading.

1. Replace safety pins.
2. Remove string from safety device.
3. Remove bomb from carrier.
4. Unscrew fuse and replace it in its box.

Operating Flare.

The following table gives the times at which the fuse should be punched for various heights of the aeroplane. These times should result in the flare bursting 2,000 ft. above the ground.

Height of machine above ground.	Punched Time.
2,500 feet	5 seconds.
3,000 "	7 "
3,500 "	9 "
4,000 "	11 "
4,500 "	13 "
5,000 "	15 "
5,500 "	17½ "
6,000 "	19½ "

AIR MINISTRY,
January, 1918.

4

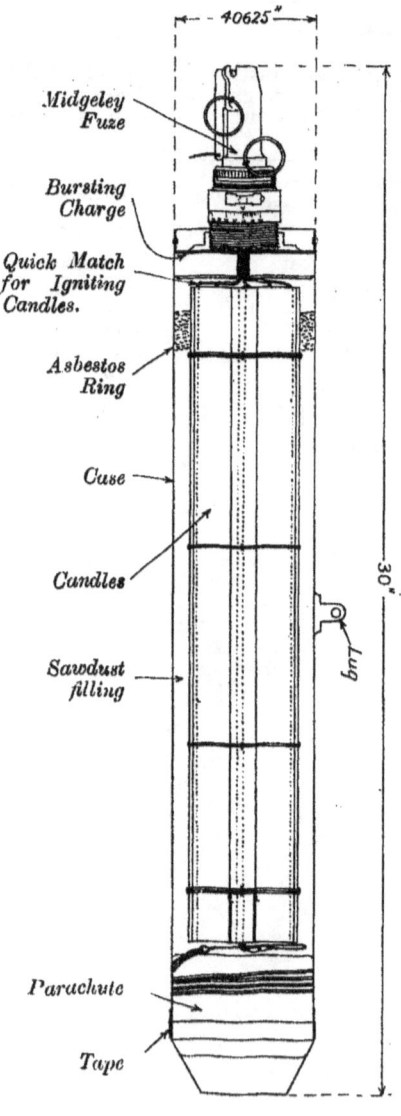

Leaflet No. 24.

VERY CARTRIDGES.

Supplied in three colours:—White, Red, Green.

Dimensions.—$3\frac{1}{4}$ inches long × $1\frac{1}{2}$ inches diameter.

Weight.—4 to 6 ozs., according to colour.

Construction.—*See* diagram.

These cartridges are used as signals and are fired from the $1\frac{1}{2}$-inch Very Pistol (No. 2, Mk. 1). In order to facilitate distinguishing between the colours in the dark the rim of the cartridge is milled differently for each colour. The milling is:—

RED	Milled all round.
WHITE	Milled half way round.
GREEN	No milling.

AIR MINISTRY,
January, 1918.

[OVER

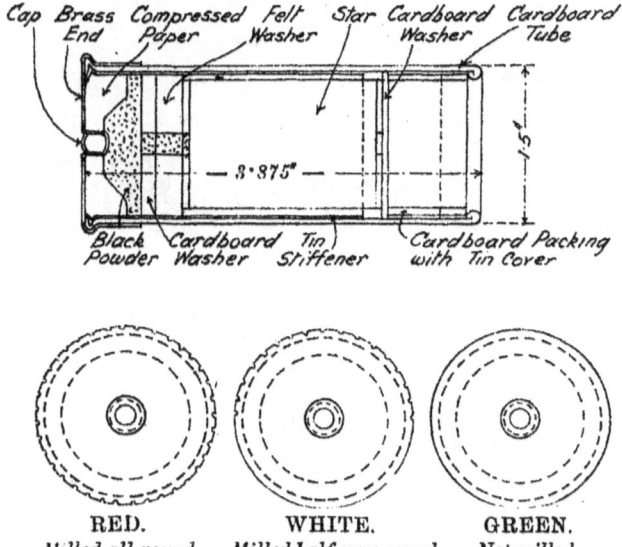

RED.
Milled all round.

WHITE.
Milled half way round.

GREEN.
Not milled.

Leaflet No. 25.

H.E. Bomb Components.

Bomb Type.	Components.		Remarks.
Bomb, H.E., 112 lb., Mk. III. and V. (For horizontal stowage with nose and tail fuses or vertical stowage with tail fuse only.)	Pistol, bomb, No. 3 Mk. 1. or No. 5 Mk. I.	1	Used with nose fuse against personnel, aerodromes and road transport; with tail fuse against material buildings, etc. Are stowed horizontally externally. May be stowed vertically with special hanging nose plug.
	Adaptor, 1.375" (for Mk. III. only)	1	} Tail fuse.
	Relay, detonating, 7.39", Mks. I. or II.	1	
	Igniter, H.E. Bomb, 15 secs., 2¼ secs., or .05 secs.	1	
	Fuse, bomb, D.A. No. 1, Mk. I	1	Nose fuse.
	Exploder, long, No. 2, Mk. I. or II.	1	} Exploder.
	Detonator, H.E. bomb, 56 gr., Mk. I. or II	2	
	Plug, fuse hole (nose), tapped ¼", Whitworth	1	To replace nose fuse for vertical stowage.
	Eye bolt, bomb, slinging	1	
Bomb, H.E. 112 lb., Mk. III. and V. (For vertical stowage with nose and tail fuse.)	Pistol, bomb, No. 3 Mk. 1. or No. 5 Mk. I.	1	} Tail fuse.
	Adaptor, 1.375" (for Mk. III. only)	1	
	Relay, detonating, 7.39" Mks. I. or II.	1	
	Igniter, H.E. bomb, 15, 2½ or .05 secs.	1	
	*Fuse, bomb, D.A., No. 9 Mk. I., with hanging eye bolt	1	} Nose fuse and Exploder combined.
	*Exploder, 7.39"	1	
	*Igniter, with 28 bore cap and detonator (instantaneous)	1	With hanging nose pistol stowed internally on H.P. machines.
	*Wood packing piece, 4¾"		
	*Special components not used otherwise.		

Bomb Type.	Components.		Remarks.
Bomb, H.E., 112 lbs., Mk. VI. and VII. and Bomb, H.E., 50 lbs., Mk. IV. (For horizontal or vertical stowage with both nose and tail fuse.)	*Pistol, bomb, No. 5, Mk. I. (issued complete with 4¼" relay detonating and instantaneous detonator)	1 Tail fuse.	Mk. VI., being of cast iron, may break up on impact, and should for this reason be fused with nose and tail fuse, except for special purposes when tail fuse may be used alone.
	*Fuse, bomb, D.A., No. 8 Mk. I., with hanging eye bolt (complete, with 4¼" relay detonating and instantaneous detonator)	1 Nose fuse.	
	Exploder, long, No. 2 Mk. I. or II., or Exploder, 12", paper case	1 Exploder.	
	Bomb band and lug (if for horizontal stowage)	1	
	*In either case a detonator with a 2.5 second delay may be substituted; these are issued in bulk.		
H.E., R.F.C., 230 lbs.	Pistol, bomb, No. 3 Mk. I. or No. 5 Mk. I.	1 ⎱ Tail fuse	Used against buildings, railways and roads, and when fitted with nose cap against submarines. Effective man killing radius of action about 30 yards.
	Relay, detonating, 7.39", Mks. I. or II.	1 ⎰	
	Igniter, 15" and 2.5" or .05" as required	1 ⎫	
	2 Exploders, No. 2 Mk. I. or II.	2 ⎬ Exploder.	
	Detonators, H.E. bomb, 56 gr., Mk. I. or II., according to Mark of exploder used	⎭	
Bomb, H.E., R.L., 250 lbs., Mk. I.	Tail fuse, No. 3 or No. 4 (complete with pistol bomb, Mk. II., and magazine No. 3 or 4.)	1 Tail fuse.	Used against personnel, aerodromes and transport, fitted with nose fuse. Fitted with tail fuse it may be used against buildings.
	Bomb fuse, D.A., No. 1 Mk. I.	1 Nose fuse.	
	Exploder, long, No. 2 Mk. I. or II.	1 ⎫	
	Detonator, H.E. bomb, 56 gr., Mk. I. or II., according to Mark of exploder used	2 ⎬ Exploder.	
	Relay, 12"	1 Relay.	

Bomb Type.	Components.		Remarks.
Bomb, H.E.R.L., 250 lbs., Mk. I. Alternative method of fusing which may be used by R.N.A.S.	Pistol bomb tail, No. 4 Mk. I. Exploder, 7.39". Igniter, H.E. bomb, 15 secs, 2.5 secs. or .05 secs. Exploder, 7.2", No. 8 Mk. I., 60 gr. detonators Exploder, 12.6", No. 8 Mk. I., 60 gr. detonators Fuse, bomb, D.A., No. 1 Mk. I.	1 } Tail fuse. 1 1 1 } Exploder. - Nose fuse.	This form of fusing is intended only for use with Seaplanes, and will not be made use of for land purposes.
Bomb, H.E., R.A.F., 336 lbs.	Bomb fuse, D.A., No. 1 Mk. I. Exploder, No. 4 Mk. I/L. Two 60 gr. detonators, No. 2 Mk. I/C, for R.A.F. bombs	1 Nose fuse. 1 } Exploder. 2	Used against Railway Stations, Workshops and Aerodromes. Although this bomb is capable of being fitted with a tail fuse it has become customary not to do this, owing to its unreliable action in this bomb.
Bomb, H.E., Cooper, 20 lbs.	1 Cooper bomb detonator. (The Cooper nose fuse is issued in position on the bomb, protected by a special nose cap.)	1 Detonator.	Used against personnel and aerodromes.

Air Ministry, March, 1918.

LEAFLET No. 26.

BOMB CARRIERS.

Diagrams and instructions for the 112 lb., 230 lb and 4—20 lb. Mark I carriers are included in this leaflet.

Further instructions and diagrams dealing with the later types of carriers as shown below will be issued shortly.

NOMENCLATURE OF BOMB CARRIERS.

The following nomenclature for carriers is now in use :—

CARRIER.	NAME.
R.F.C. Pattern.	
4—20 lb. bombs.	Carrier 4—20 lb., Mark I.
1—112 lb. with sleeve release slip (obsol.).	Carrier 112 lb. Single Mark I.
1—112 lb. with skeleton release slip.	Carrier 112 lb. Single Mark II.
2—112 lb. with sleeve release slip (obsol.).	Carrier 112 lb. Twin Mark I.
2—112 lb. with skeleton release slip.	Carrier 112 lb. Twin Mark II.
1—230 lb. with sleeve release slip (obsol.).	Carrier 230 lb. Single Mark I.
1—230 lb. with skeleton release slip.	Carrier 230 lb. Single Mark II.
2—230 lb. with sleeve release slip (obsol.).	Carrier 230 lb. Twin Mark I.
2—230 lb. with skeleton release slip.	Carrier 230 lb. Twin Mark II.
R.N.A.S. Pattern.	
1—50/180 skeleton tubular carrier.	Carrier Skeleton Tubular 112 lb. Mark V. (F).
1—230 lb skeleton tubular carrier.	Carrier Skeleton Tubular 230 lb. Mark IV. (F).
1—520/550 lb. skeleton tubular carrier.	Carrier Skeleton Tubular 520 lb. Mark II. (F.).

The (F) after the Mark for bomb carriers for Seaplanes indicates that Fusing Devices are fitted.

Flare Carriers. (See Leaflet 22.)
    Michelin Flare Carrier
        (French Release).   Carrier Flare Michelin Mk. I.
    Michelin Flare Carrier
        (Gibbons Release).   Carrier Flare Michelin Mk. II.

NOTES ON MAINTENANCE OF GEARS.

(1) The first essential in the care of carriers is to keep every part absolutely free from from rust, the utmost care being observed in keeping the carrying mechanism, whether of the sleeve or slip pattern, free of dirt, rust, or other foreign matter.

(2) To maintain the gears in good sound working order, they should periodically be painted over with a mixture of P.924 non-freezing oil and graphite.

(3) The fusing rods in the tubes of the skeleton gears should receive occasional drops of non-freezing oil to ensure their working smoothly. Care should also be taken to see that the springs in front of the fusing rods are operating correctly.

(4) All uncovered Bowden wires should be kept coated with a non-freezing mixture throughout their length to ensure their correct functioning.

(5) Release gears should be regularly tested twice a week, and any adjustment found necessary should be executed without delay.

(6) It is only with strict compliance with these rules that the risk of bombs hanging up on carriers can be reduced to a minimum.

(7) In the case of seaplanes, the slip should be thoroughly cleaned and re-coated with non-freezing mixture after each patrol.

20 lb. CARRIER.

WEIGHT OF CARRIER, 9 lbs.

The following bombs may be loaded on to this carrier:—

Bomb, H.E., Cooper, 20 lbs.
Bomb, H.E., Hales, 20 lbs.
Bomb, H.E., R.L., 16 lbs.
Bomb, Incendiary Carcass, Mark II.
Bomb, Incendiary Phosphorus, 40 lbs.*
Bomb Incendiary R.L., Mark III.
T.W.R. Parachute Flare.

Each carrier is fitted to take four bombs.

DESCRIPTION OF THE CARRIER (See Fig. 1).

All the bombs mentioned above are fitted with lugs, which support the weight of the bombs in the carrier. The bombs are held by nose and tail steadies.

The parts of the carrier may easily be identified from the following list and figures:—

L, lugs for attaching carrier to rib.
SSSS, slots through which lugs on bombs project.
TTTT, triggers supporting bombs.
HHHH, catches holding triggers in position.
K, sliding bar with projections MMMM and ratchet Z.
N, lever connected by Bowden wire to release J.
Q, Q1, brackets for supporting Bowden cable.
W, large pawl pivoted on N.
B, small pawl pivoted on corner and provided with spring to make it engage with ratchet.
R, return spring for re-setting K.
J, release toggle.

In this case several modifications have to be made in the carrier, and only two bombs may be loaded. (Leaflet 11, page 7, Fig. 3.)

20LB BOMB CARRIER.

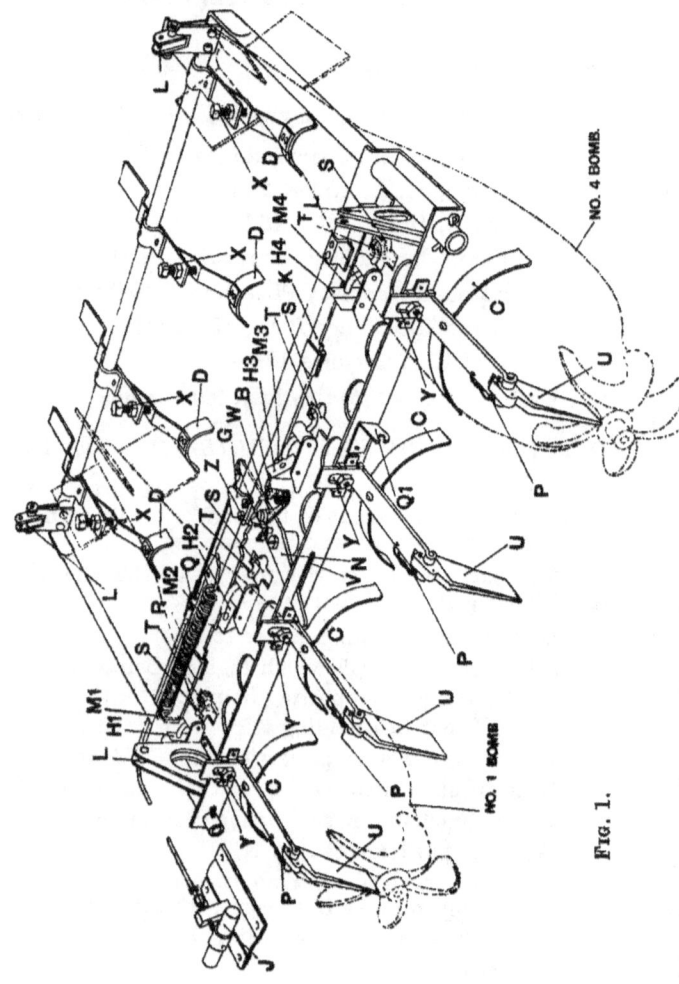

Fig. 1.

Leaflet No. 26 (continued).

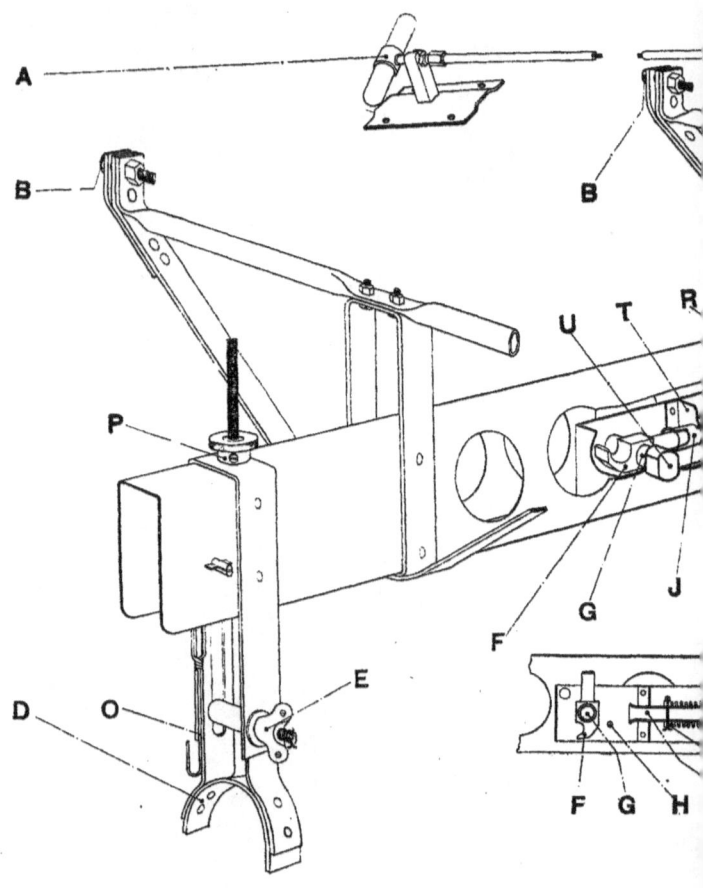

**VIEW SHEWING TRIGGER "F"
RELEASED BY TRIGGER SLEEVE "J."
THUS ALLOWING BOMB TO FALL.**

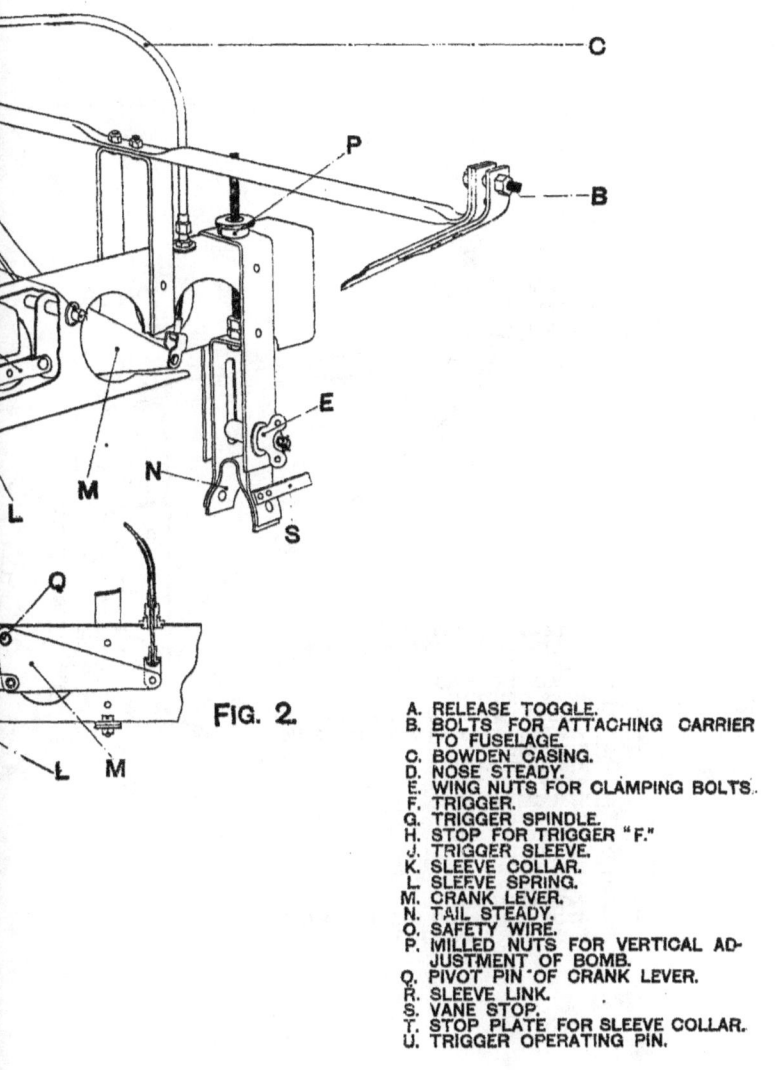

FIG. 2.

A. RELEASE TOGGLE.
B. BOLTS FOR ATTACHING CARRIER TO FUSELAGE.
C. BOWDEN CASING.
D. NOSE STEADY.
E. WING NUTS FOR CLAMPING BOLTS.
F. TRIGGER.
G. TRIGGER SPINDLE.
H. STOP FOR TRIGGER "F."
J. TRIGGER SLEEVE.
K. SLEEVE COLLAR.
L. SLEEVE SPRING.
M. CRANK LEVER.
N. TAIL STEADY.
O. SAFETY WIRE.
P. MILLED NUTS FOR VERTICAL ADJUSTMENT OF BOMB.
Q. PIVOT PIN OF CRANK LEVER.
R. SLEEVE LINK.
S. VANE STOP.
T. STOP PLATE FOR SLEEVE COLLAR.
U. TRIGGER OPERATING PIN.

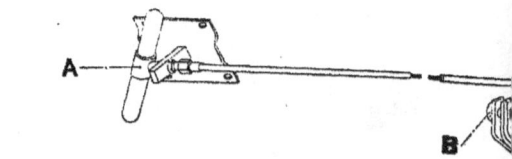

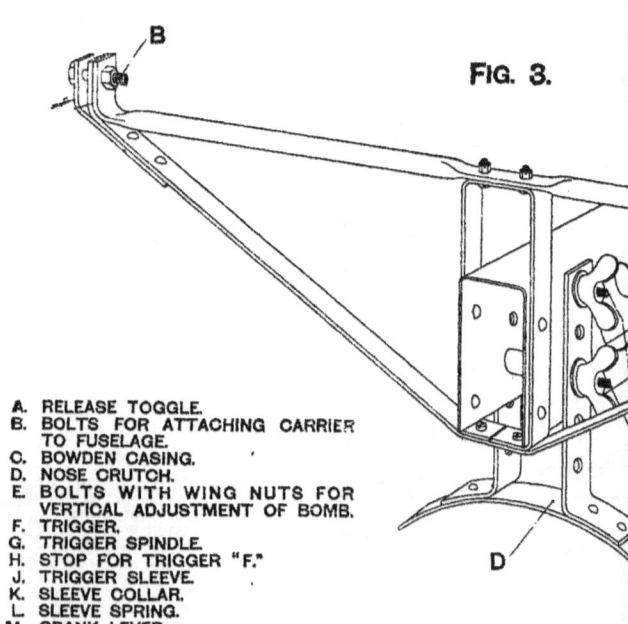

FIG. 3.

A. RELEASE TOGGLE.
B. BOLTS FOR ATTACHING CARRIER TO FUSELAGE.
C. BOWDEN CASING.
D. NOSE CRUTCH.
E. BOLTS WITH WING NUTS FOR VERTICAL ADJUSTMENT OF BOMB.
F. TRIGGER.
G. TRIGGER SPINDLE.
H. STOP FOR TRIGGER "F."
J. TRIGGER SLEEVE.
K. SLEEVE COLLAR.
L. SLEEVE SPRING.
M. CRANK LEVER.
N. TAIL STEADY.
O. VANE STOP.
P. INDICATOR PIN.
Q. STOP PLATE FOR SLEEVE COLLAR.
R. SLOT FOR INDICATOR PIN.

FIG. 3A.

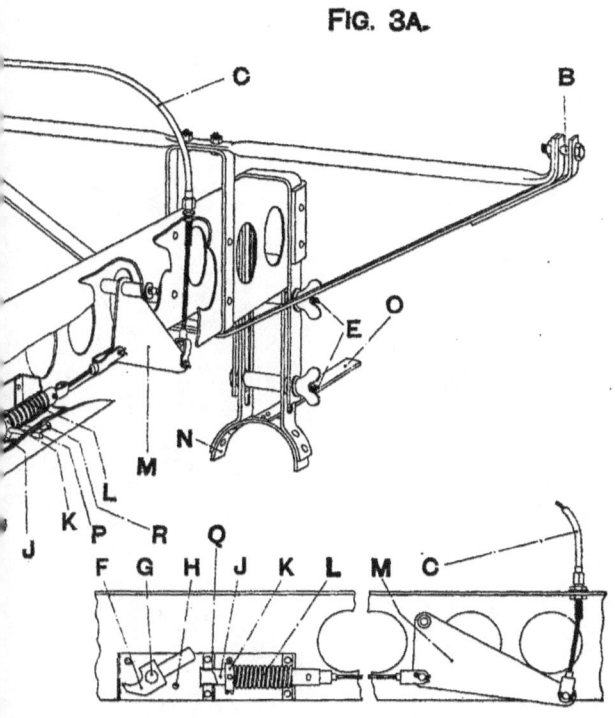

VIEW SHEWING TRIGGER "F" RELEASED
BY TRIGGER SLEEVE "J,"
THUS ALLOWING BOMB TO FALL.

Leaflet No. 26 (continued).

    PPPP, pins for fixing UUUU.
    G, bracket for attaching cable for salvo release.
    CCCC, nose clips adjusted by slots YYYY.
    UUUU, prongs for locking Cooper fan.
    DDDD, tail clips adjusted by XXXX.
    Two Cooper bombs shown dotted.

MECHANISM.

On pulling the release handle (J), the lever (N) rotates through the full extent of the slot (V) and the large pawl (W), which is pivoted on (N), engages in ratchet (Z), and pushes the bar (K) over to the left through $\frac{1}{2}$ inch so that the projection (M_2) knocks over catch (H_2), thus freeing trigger (T_2) and releasing No. 2 bomb. The small pawl (B) holds the ratchet (Z) forward when release handle (J) returns to its normal position. The next time (J) is pulled No. 3 bomb is released. The third and fourth pulls release No. 4 and No. 1 bombs.

A modified release, with a different type of ratchet, and without the small pawl (B), is in use. With this all four bombs are released successively, but by a single pull.

The Bowden release wire is attached through the bracket (Q) to one end of lever (N) when carrier is fitted to left hand plane.

A spare bracket (Q 1) on the front of the carrier is provided to get a direct pull when the carrier is fitted to a right hand plane.

To release bombs in " Salvo " the Bowden wire is attached to the bracket (G).

ADJUSTMENT OF CABLES.

The cables should be adjusted so that the lever (N), Fig. 1, can be moved through its complete range of motion, as limited by the slot (V) on the carrier. When the handle is in the normal position the lever should be right back against one end of the slot, and the cable just slack. When the handle is pulled up the lever should move round until it comes against the other end of the slot. It is most important that the lever (N) should move the complete length of the slot (V) when the handle is worked.

In fitting cables it is very important to see that they are not led round sharp corners, but are taken as straight as possible from the carrier to the handle, with only gentle bends. All bends in the cable make the handle much stiffer to pull. Should the cable be much too long it should be shortened, and not looped up to take up the excessive length.

The cables always stretch a little when first used, and may want a little adjustment occasionally. Also, the adjustment of the cable is different if the cable be straight, or has several bends in it, so that the final adjustment should always be done when the carrier is fixed on the aeroplane, and after the cables are fixed in their places. Long loops of loose cable should be tied down, and not allowed to blow about in the wind.

LOADING ON BOMBS.

First see that the sliding bar (K), Fig. 1, is back in its normal position, by releasing the pawls (W. and B.) of the ratchet, when it will fly back by a spring. Raise the end of the trigger (T), so that the hooked end projects down through the bottom of the carrier. Put this through the lug on the bomb, and return the trigger to its normal position, when its end can be secured by the catch (H). While the bomb is being loaded the screw (X) on the tail adjustment should be screwed up to the top. After the bomb is secured on the trigger, the nose support (Y) is laid down as low as it will go, and locked by a nut. The tail steady is then screwed down until the bomb is just held firmly, all excessive pressure being carefully avoided.

When loading the bomb, care should be taken to see that the lug is quite free in the slot (I), so that there is no chance of it sticking. Occasionally it may be found that some bombs have lugs which are wider than the standard width ($\frac{1}{4}$ inch), in which cases they should be filed down.

    The Carcass Incendiary bomb is fused before it is placed on the carrier. (For instructions in fusing and loading this bomb see leaflet No. 5.) The 20 lbs. Cooper should, however, be placed on the carrier before it is made live by the insertion of its detonator. (For instructions in fusing and loading see leaflet 10.)

Before leaving the ground, a pilot should invariably satisfy himself that the following points have not been neglected in loading up his bombs:—

1. Ascertain that the safety vanes have been tested for ease of spinning. (This should have been done before the bomb was placed on the carrier, or made live by the insertion of exploder or detonator).

2. The safety vanes are prevented from rotating while the bomb is on the carrier.

3. That the bombs are securely housed, and not free to move in the horizontal or vertical planes.

4. That the safety pins are removed just before leaving the ground, or in the case of the 20 lbs. Cooper, that the wire securing the arming vane is removed.

NOTE.—Bombs should only be loaded in the presence of an experienced officer or N.C.O. Detonators and other fusing components should be inserted by an officer or N.C.O.

CARRIER 112 lb. SINGLE Mk. I.

WEIGHT, 11 LBS.

A drawing of this carrier is shown in Fig. 2. There are no safety devices for making the fuse "live" or safe while in flight, and the bomb when released is always dropped "live."

A Bowden wire connects the release gear to the release toggle. The latter is of the type shown in Fig. 2, and is mounted inside the fuselage.

The release gear consists of a trigger and sleeve, and differs from the release in the obsolete 100 lb. carrier in that between the Bowden wire and the sleeve a lever (M), pivotted on the pin (Q) and connected to the sleeve by the link (R), serves to increase the leverage of the pull.

A wire (O) at the forward end of the carrier is used for attaching to safety collar of the D.A. No. 1 Mark I. fuse. This is done after the bomb is fused in the carrier, the safety collar being drawn off when the bomb is released.

Adjustable nose and tail steadies (D) and (N) are provided.

A bar (S) is fixed to the tail steady to act as a vane stop should a tail fuse be employed.

ADJUSTMENT OF CABLES.

The cable operating the release mechanism should be adjusted so that it is just slack when the handle is "down," and the sleeve (J) (Fig. 2) "home" as far as it will go over the end of the trigger (F).

When the release handle is pulled up and the sleeve is pulled to the end of its travel in the opposite direction the handle should still have another $\frac{1}{4}$ in. to $\frac{1}{2}$ in. motion possible.

LOADING ON BOMBS.

The bombs for this carrier should always be loaded on to the carrier before their fusing components are inserted, as these can easily be put in afterwards.

It will generally be found most convenient for one mechanic to sit on the ground under the carrier, with the bomb resting on his knees. He can then, by raising his knees, bring the bomb up so that the lug engages with the trigger (F). The release handle is during this time held up. As soon as the bomb is raised so high that the trigger can be brought back until it engages with the sleeve (J), the release handle is lowered, and the bomb is then secure on the carrier. The carrier should then be examined to see that the sleeve (J) is "home," *i.e.*, that the collar (K) on it is up against the plate (T).

The bomb should now be released to make sure that the carrier is functioning correctly. If the bomb falls satisfactorily it should be reloaded as previously directed, and now, when secure on the carrier, and the fusing components inserted, the nose and tail steadies (D) and (N) are screwed down by the milled nuts (PP).

These steadies should be screwed down until the bomb obtains no play; undue pressure should not, however, be exerted.

When this adjustment has been made the steadies (D) and (N) are locked by the wing nuts (EE). These can be further secured if desired by running a locking wire through a hole in the wings of this nut, and through the main part of the carrier.

The bomb should now be carefully inspected to see that all is in order.

In case the lugs on the bombs should not be of standard size, it is advisable always to inspect the bomb to see (1) that the lug is not so narrow that there is a possibility of it jamming on the trigger; (2) that it is not so wide that there is a possibility of it jamming on the sides of the carrier.

The bomb should not be fused until it is finally secured on the carrier.

Carriers, 230 lb. Single. Mark I.

WEIGHT, 14 LBS.

A drawing of this is shown in Fig. 3.

It will be seen that the release gear is almost identical with that of the 112 lb. carrier just described.

With these carriers special care has to be taken to see that the sleeve (F) has gone home after the bomb has been loaded on to the carrier. When this is the case the collar on the sleeve is close up against the distance plate (Q), inside the framework of the carrier. Care should be taken with these carriers to see that this is the case before the pilot is allowed to leave the ground. In the 230 lb. carrier an indicator pin (P) has been attached to the collar on the sleeve. This pin projects through a longitudinal slot (R). When the release toggle is pulled, prior to loading a bomb, the indicator pin will slide to the right (see Fig. 3A). The lug on the bomb is now hooked on to the trigger, and when the trigger handle is horizontal the release is allowed to slide home. If the release goes home satisfactorily the indicator pin (P) will travel forwards to the left hand end of the slot (as viewed in Fig. 3).

The brackets for steadying the 230 lb. bomb consist of a nose crutch, which presses over the upper portion of the body of the bomb about 6" in front of the lug.

The pointed steel nose of the bomb projects about 16" beyond this nose crutch.

The tail steady for the bomb is rather like that used on 112 lb. carriers, though it is adjusted by hand instead of milled nuts and tightened in position by wing nuts on the side of the bracket.

The fan on the tail pistol is locked by the projecting bar (O) fixed, as shown, to the tail steady.

The directions given in the case of the 112 lb. carrier apply in the case of the 230 lb. carrier, as regards loading the bomb on to the machine.

AIR MINISTRY,
May, 1918.

LEAFLET 26A. (Supplementary to Leaflet No. 26).

BOMB CARRIERS.

CARRIER 112 LB. TWIN MARK I.

This consists of two single carriers braced together fore and aft by frameworks of tubular members, with four suspension extensions drilled for the suspension bolts. The extensions are spaced at the standard distance of 21″, and are bolted to steel ribs under the fuselage or planes. The release is of the sleeve type; and loading instruction apply as for the Single Carrier Mark I. (See Fig. 4.)

CARRIER 112 LB. SINGLE MARK II. (Fig 5.)

DESCRIPTION.

This carrier is designed to replace the Mark I., and differs mainly in having a skeleton release slip (1). It is of channel form, and has adjustable tail and nose steadies, (2) and (3) respectively. These differ from the Mark I. in not having the screw and milled head for adjusting, but are pushed down by hand and are tightened with wing nuts (4).

The slip is bolted to the carrier by two bolts (5).

The release wire (16) is attached to the trigger (6) and passes thence over a pulley (7), being prevented from disengaging by the pin (8). It passes thence through a bracket (9) in the top of the channel through a Bowden casing (10) to the release toggle (17). A pin is provided at forward end of the carrier, which carries a wire hook (11) for attaching to safety collar of fuse, when Fuse D.A. No. 1 Mark I., is employed.

When it is required to sling the 112 lb. Marks VI. and VII. horizontally, a special band with suspension lug is issued for the bomb, and the above carrier will then require vane stops on nose and tail steadies. These are not shown in the figure, but will be fitted when issued.

A *Safety Spring* (12) is provided, which is soldered to the release wire at one end and connected to a special eye (13) on the slip suspension bolt. It is adjusted to allow about

1 inch of slack in the cable when the suspension hook is home. The exact adjustment of this amount of slack is not so important for this gear, as it is in the case of a salvo release (see Leaflet No. 28), but too much will make an awkward pull for the operator, and too little will, of course, reduce the safety margin.

Bolts (14) are provided for attaching the carrier to ribs on the machine.

LOADING ON BOMBS.

The bombs should be loaded on the carrier before being fused.

The loading can best be carried out by two men facing each other; one supporting the bomb at the nose end, and the other at the fins. In the case of larger bombs two more men are required, one on each side, to lift the bomb by means of a rod or lath placed approximately under the centre of gravity of the bomb.

The carrier is first prepared for loading by unscrewing the wing nuts on nose and tail steadies and pushing the latter up to the limit of their travel. Next, the suspension hook of the release slip should be freed by pulling back the trigger.

The bomb should then be raised, keeping it approximately horizontal, till its lug engages the suspension hook, when it may be pushed home. The trigger should go home automatically over the arm of the suspension hook by the action of its spring.

Care should be taken to see that the trigger is home over the arm of the suspension hook, both when the bomb is loaded and before the machine leaves the ground. It is not sufficient to feel the hook go home.

The bomb should now be released to ensure that the lug of the bomb is not jammed in any way in the release slip.

Reload the bomb on the carrier and insert the fusing components. Remove safety pins from the fuses, and attach hook to safety collar in the case of the D.A. No. 1 Mark I. Fuse.

Push down nose and tail steadies till firmly engaging the bomb. This should be done by hand and no undue force applied and no other implements used. Tighten the wing nuts.

Examine the bomb and release slip and ensure that it is securely housed, by attempting to shake the bomb sharply.

Examine the safety spring and see that a bight of the right amount exists in the release wire.

CARRIER 112 LB. TWIN MARK II.

This consists of two single carriers with skeleton slips braced together in the same manner as described above for the Twin Mark I.

Loading instructions apply as for the single carrier.

CARRIER 230 LB. SINGLE MARK II.

(For 230 lb., 250 lb., or 336 lb. bombs.)

DESCRIPTION.

This carrier differs from the Mark I. in very much the same way as the corresponding 112 lb. Mark II. differs from the Mark I. It has a skeleton release slip (1) of heavier construction, and the safety spring (12) is connected to an eye on the slip itself. (See Fig. 6.) The nose crutch (3) is of curved channel form, and has two adjusting screws (18), with milled heads passing through bosses in the crutch and steady the bomb laterally.

The figure illustrates a form of crutch which will be replaced, when these carriers are issued, by one of channel section to give greater strength.

The release wire (16) is attached to the trigger (6) and passes thence over a pulley (7), being prevented from disengaging by the pin (8). It passes thence through a bracket (9) in the top of the channel, through a Bowden casing (10) to the release toggle (17).

The tail steady (2) is shown in the figure in position for the 230 lb. bomb. When it is required to use the carrier for the 250 lb. bomb, the steady is removed by taking off wing nuts and bolts (4) and fitted to forward guide (19).

When required for the 336 lb. bomb, the tail steady (2) is reversed in the 230 lb. position, so as to allow the vane stop (15) to clear the opening in the vane fairing of this bomb.

The wire hook (11) is provided at the forward end for attaching to safety collar of the fuse when carrying the 250 lb. bomb with Fuse D.A. No. 1 Mark I.

The carrier is attached to ribs on the machine by bolts (14).

LOADING ON BOMBS.

Instructions apply as for the 112 lb. carrier, except for screwing down steadying screws of nose crutch instead of pushing down nose steady. This should be done after the tail steady is pushed down.

CARRIER 230 LB. TWIN MARK II.

This consists of two single carriers with skeleton slips braced together as for the other twin carriers described. (See Fig. 7.)

Reference letters for Fig 7 correspond with numerals of Fig 6 (the single carrier) as follows:—

A is pin for wire hook (11).
B is forward guide (19) for 250 lb. bomb.
C is pulley (7) for release wire.
D is safety spring (12).
E is bracket (9).
F are adjusting screws (18) for nose crutch.
G is nose crutch (3).
H are wing nuts (4) for tail steadies.
K is vane stop (15) for tail fuse.
L indicates position of suspension bolts (14) for attaching carrier to the ribs of machine.

AIR MINISTRY,
    June, 1918.

Leaflet No. 26a (continued).

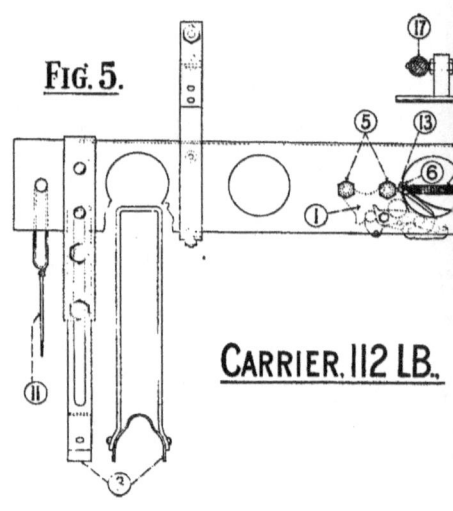

Fig. 5.

CARRIER, 112 LB.

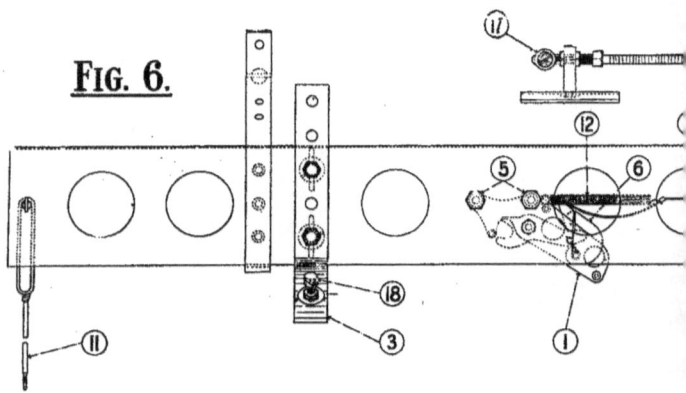

Fig. 6.

CARRIER, 230 LB

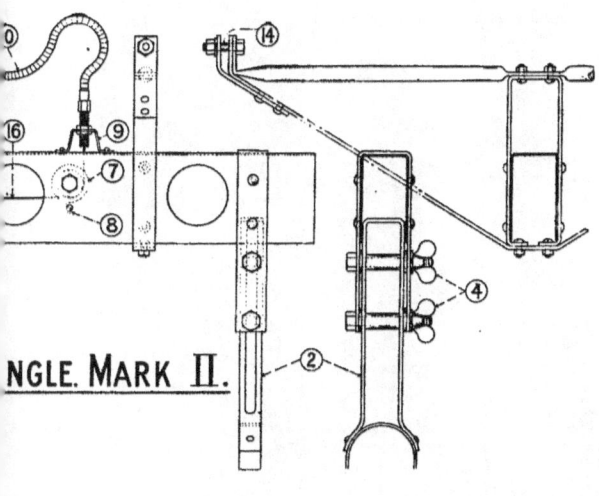

NGLE. MARK II.

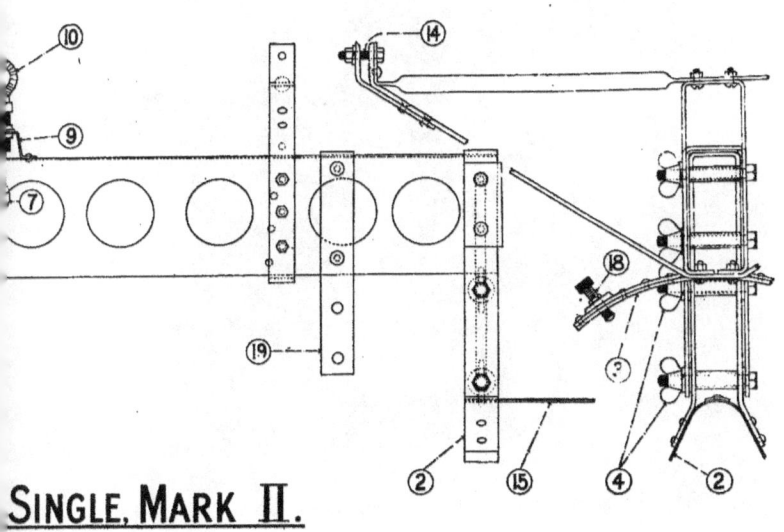

SINGLE, MARK II.

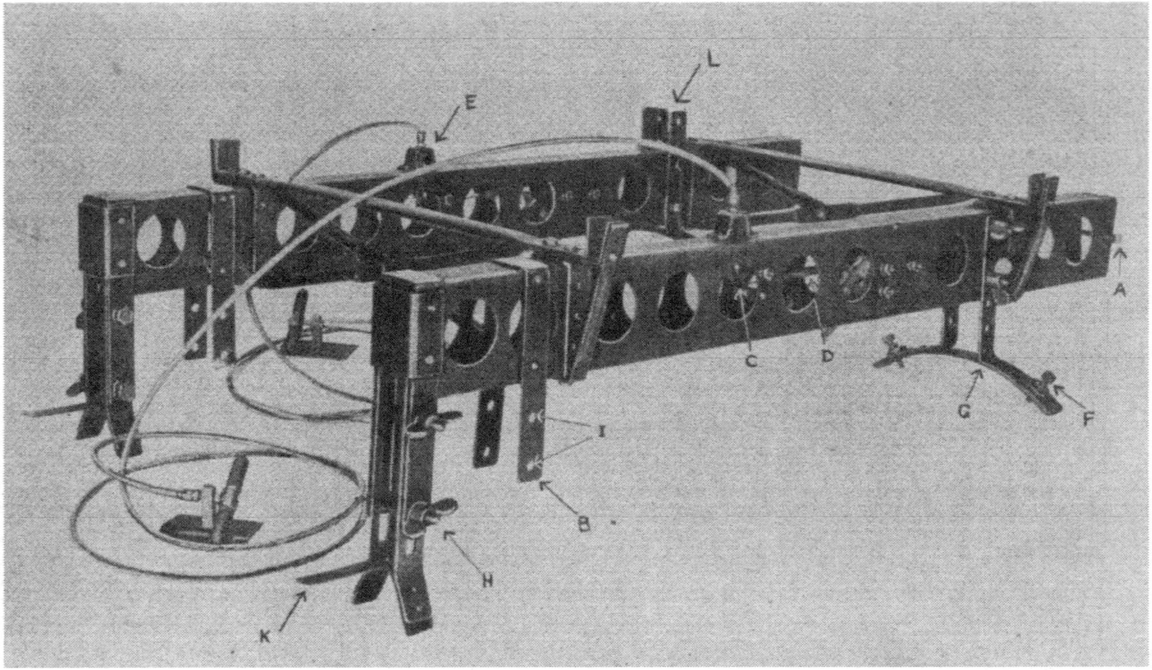

Fig. 7

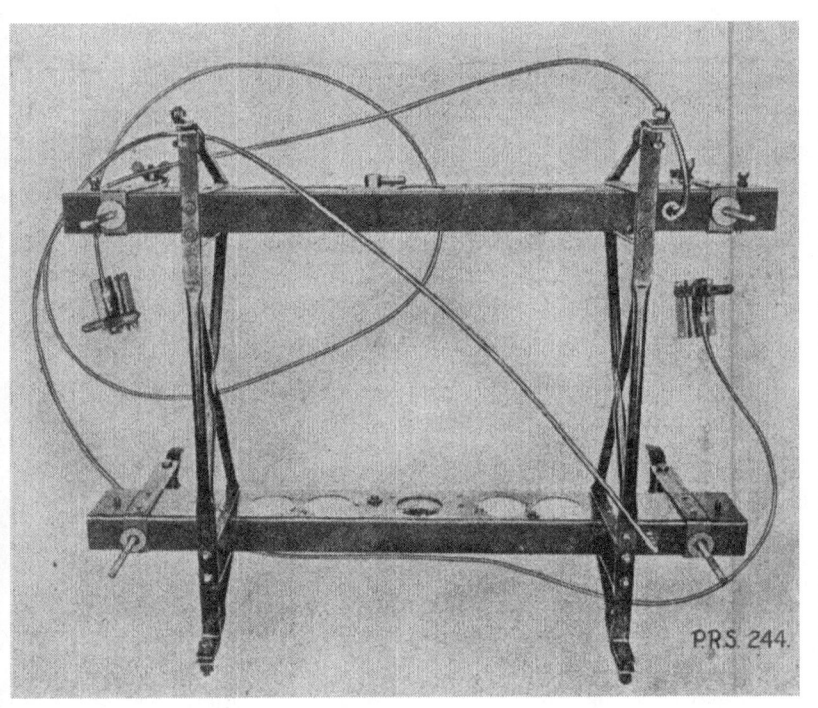

Fig. 4.

Leaflet No. 26b.

BOMB CARRIERS.

Two different types of carrier are now in use—the R.N.A.S. type and the "W.O." type. The latter have been described in Leaflets No. 26 and 26a. The following are described below:—

Carrier Skeleton Tubular 112 lb. Mark V. (F) (one 50 lb., 65 lb., 100 lb., or 112 lb. bomb).

Carrier Skeleton Tubular 230 lb. Mark IV. (F) (one 230 lb. or 250 lb. bomb).

Carrier Skeleton Tubular 520 lb. Mark II. (F) (one 520 lb. or 550 lb. bomb).

The (F) after the Mark for bomb carriers for seaplanes indicates that fusing devices are fitted.

The skeleton carriers, of the tubular type, vary only in dimensions, with the exception of the 230 lb. bomb size, which has no nose fusing arrangement, and the nose fork is replaced by a crutch which fits over the body of the bomb.

All skeleton carriers are fitted with a fusing arrangement which is to be used on airships, flying boats, seaplanes and ship aeroplanes.

Land machines will in future not be fitted with fuse control.

DESCRIPTION OF THE CARRIERS.

CARRIER SKELETON TUBULAR 112 lb. MARK V. (F) (Fig. 3).

This carrier consists of a tube (1), to which are attached at either end struts (2) and (3), and in the centre the release slip (15). Fitted inside the tube is the fusing rod (16), which enables the pilot to drop the bomb—

(i.) With the tail fuse only alive.
(ii.) With both fuses alive.
(iii.) With both fuses safe.

Each of the end struts consists of an outside streamline steel sheath (2) and (3), bent over at its upper end where it abuts against the tube. The struts are held against the tube by clips (12), tightened round the tube by bolts and nuts, which are prevented from coming loose by spring washers. The clips (12) also serve to steady the carrier when mounted on a machine.

Sliding in these steel sheaths are the end forks (4) and (5), fixed in any position by the clamping bolts (9). The wooden distance pieces (6) between the end forks prevent distortion of the sheath and fork when tightening the wing nuts. These nuts are prevented from coming loose by spring washers. The end forks fit over the fuses of the bomb and stay it fore and aft. Eye nuts (8) attached to a screwed eye-bolts (7) passing through the metal sheath provide attachments for staying wires or struts for holding the bomb carrier laterally.

In the centre is the slip for holding and releasing the bomb. This consists of two plates, between which is pivoted a hook interlinking with the trigger. The trigger is forced by the spring to abut against the inner end of the hook. In the released position of the slip, ready for a bomb shackle to be fitted in the carrier, the projecting lower end of the hook hangs downwards, and the upper end rests against the bolt attaching the slip to the tube. As the bomb is pushed into position the upper end of the shackle presses up the spur of the hook and the upper end of the hook presses against the trigger until it slides into the groove in the the trigger, which instantly, by the action of the spring, moves forward, locking the hook in position. It is impossible for the hook to release itself, owing to the abutting surfaces of hook and trigger being circular about the pivot of the trigger.

The bomb shackle is released by pulling the trigger by a wire or other attachment to the hole provided.

(*See* Leaflet No. 28, where this slip is illustrated.)

At either end of the bomb are fitted the fusing wires (*see* Fig. 5) to prevent the bomb becoming alive in the event of its being dropped by accident. These are held in the tube by horizontal pins (19), forming part of the fusing rod (16). These horizontal pins normally do not engage with the upper eye-end of the fusing wires. By pulling the fusing rod operating lever (not shown on the drawing, as this is fitted beside the pilot's or passenger's seat) back to the first position the pin at the tail-end of the fusing rod engages with the eye-end of the tail fusing wire. If the bomb were now dropped the rear fuse only would be made live, as only the rear fusing wire would be removed. By pulling back the operating lever to the full extent both pins engage with the fusing wires; then the bomb when dropped leaves both fusing wires behind, thus making both fuses live.

In addition to the pins on the fusing wires, bars (26) are rivetted to the nose and tail forks of the bomb carrier to prevent the fuse-arming vanes from turning as long as the bomb is in the carrier.

These fixed bars form the fuse vane locking arrangement for land machines, on which fusing wires are no longer used.

The above description applies equally to Figs. 1, 2 and 3 given for Marks I., III., V. The latter, which will now be taken into use, also has a pulley (28) for the fusing wire mounted at one end. This end can either be for nose or tail of the bomb and the arrangements are shown for fusing from either end (*see* Fig. 3). A pulley (29) is also mounted on the same end bracket as the other pulley, to provide a guide for the release wire. The end pulley bracket (11) has a bush (30) which acts as a stop for the fusing slide; this stop is provided for at the other end by the internal portion of the end cap (10). The fusing slides are fitted with eyes (31) as for the Mark IV.

The following marks are obsolescent and will be replaced by the Mark V. described above.

Mark I. is the original type, in which the stroke of the fusing rod is $\frac{5}{8}$ inch, the fusing rod guides are cross shape in section, and the tail-end strut is full in way of the fusing wire adjusting screw. (*See* Fig. 1.)

Mark II. differs from Mark I. in that the stroke of the fusing rod is one inch, the fusing rod guides are box shaped, and the tail-end strut is cut away to give access to the fusing wires adjusting screw. The object of the box-sectioned fusing rod guide is to enable the loop of the fusing wire to project further up past the fusing pin than was possible in the Mark I.

Mark III. is the same as Mark II. except that the tube is slightly longer and the fusing gear is pulled from the forward end. This Mark will be used chiefly in airships. (*See* Fig. 2.)

Mark IV. is arranged to fuse from both front and rear. It has eyes for fusing slide instead of flats and split pins of previous types. The fusing slides are prevented from turning within the tube by indentations instead of set screws.

CARRIER SKELETON TUBULAR 230 lb. MARK IV. (F).

This carrier (Fig. 4) is similar to the 112 lb. in general features, except that the nose crutch (3) is of the shape shown. This crutch has two steady screws (6) which steady the bomb laterally. The fusing rod (17) and fusing slides (10) are of the usual pattern, and a fuse wire pulley (32) is fitted as for previous carrier. It can be fused from both point and rear, and the arrangements for doing so are shown. The tail strut (2) and the end fork (8) are of usual pattern, and an arming vane stop (34) is provided for it. An additional pulley (33) is mounted on the end pulley bracket for the release wire.

Marks I.—III. are obsolescent and will be replaced by the Mark IV. described above. The following traces the developments:—

Mark I.—As for Mark I. 112 lb. carrier.

Mark II.—As for Mark II. 112 lb. carrier.

Mark III.—In addition is arranged to fuse from both front and rear. The fusing slides are prevented from turning in the tube by indentations in the side of the tube instead of set screws of the previous Marks.

Mark IV.—As for Mark V. 112 lb. carrier; has the pulleys for fusing and release wires, and hooks and eyes for fusing slide attachments instead of flats and split pins.

CARRIER SKELETON TUBULAR 520 lb. MARK II. (F).

This is similar to the Mark V. 112 lb. and the Mark IV. 230 lb. carriers, having all the new features embodied in them as described above. The following Mark is obsolescent, and will be replaced by the Mark II.

Mark I.—As for Mark I. 112 lb. and 230 lb. carriers.

FITTING THE BOMB CARRIER TO A MACHINE.

In all cases the weight of the bomb must be taken by attachments from the central or supporting clip. It is not intended that the steadying clips be used for supporting the weight of the bomb.

The supporting clips can be attached to the aeroplane either by suspending wires passing through the holes in the lugs or by a clip with suitable lugs bolted through the holes provided. In some cases it may be convenient to fit a cross bar or tube in or under the fuselage or planes, to which the supporting clips may be attached.

The steadying clips are to be used for staying the ends of the bomb gear and must on no account be used for taking the weight of the bomb. Suitable steel brackets and clips or cross members in or under the fuselage or planes are to be provided on the aeroplane for taking these clips.

It is of the utmost importance that all clips or brackets that are subjected to stresses due to the bomb's weight should be free from welds or brazing. The stresses must invariably be transmitted to the machine through unwelded metal.

To stay the bombs laterally wires must be fixed to the eye-nuts on the sides of the end struts and led to suitable clips or eye-bolts on the planes or fuselage, the wires being made taut by the usual turnbuckles. Care must be taken that these wires do not foul the vanes of the bomb. In some cases it will be found more convenient to stay the bombs laterally by means of small struts attached by the eye-bolts on the end struts of the gear, instead of wires, in which case stays would be required on one side only.

FITTING GROUPS OF CARRIERS IN MACHINES.

Where two or more bombs are fitted to the machine, the carriers should, if possible, be placed one behind the other, to diminish head resistance if exposed to the air. If the carriers are disposed parallel to one another the outside one should be stayed laterally by wires to the eye-nuts, the inside eye-nuts being used for cross bracing-wires. The inside eye-bolts only need be used if struts are employed.

When two or more bombs are arranged in line ahead the fusing arrangements will be simplified if all the bombs in the line are fused together. This is done by removing the tail piece of the front tube and the nose piece of the tube directly behind it, and so to the end of the line, and taking out the release springs of all but the foremost gear. Fig. 2a shows the connecting link, which should be about 12 W.G. steel wire. On the front end of this link there is fixed a small coupling sweated on, of such size as will suit the coupling nut of the front fusing rod; on the back end of the link there is a small jaw-piece with split pin for taking the eye on the forward end of the back fusing rod. To prevent water getting into the tubes, a thin sheet-iron clip is bolted over the gap between the tubes. The distance between the tubes should be such as to enable the fuse of a rear bomb to clear the vane stays of the bomb in front of it when falling. An exception may be made in the case of seaplanes, carrying bombs without nose fuses; in this case the two tubes can be butted one against the other.

FITTING UP THE FUSING GEAR.

The end of each fusing rod has a Bowden wire union attached to it. Into this must be fitted a nipple with the operating wire attached to it.

The other end of the Bowden cable is attached to the fusing lever, and the latter is conveniently fixed for operation close to the pilot's or observer's seat. It is a simple lever working in a quadrant which has three notches:—

(1) Safe.

(2) Fusing tail fuse only.

(3) Fusing both tail and nose fuse.

When the lever is in the middle notch a wire loop (*see* Fig. 5) inserted in the slot at the tail end of the carrier should be caught by the fusing pin at that slot; when the fusing lever is hard over, wire loops inserted at both slots should be caught.

The wire used for operating the fusing gear should be Bowden No. 51, this is the standard wire supplied from Store.

FITTING THE BOMB RELEASE WIRE.

In every case it is necessary to fit a safety spring to the releasing gear. This is illustrated in Figs. 5 and 6, previous Leaflet No. 26a. The wire used should not be thicker than Bowden No. 51, which is supplied from Stores. To prevent the bomb being accidently released the safety spring keeps a bight of about one inch in the release wire, so that the spring must be extended by about this amount before the trigger begins to move. A nipple is provided on the spring, and this is sweated on to the wire as shown on the sketch.

Bowden outer casing is no longer used for either fusing or release wires.

The bare wires are led through copper bell-mouthed fairleads and round brass pulleys, where turns of more than 15° are necessary.

To prevent any accidental release of the bombs the wires both fusing and release should have fairleads or pulleys fitted about every nine inches along their length where they are exposed outside the fuselage or planes and in the cockpits where they are liable to be touched by the crew.

In most machines there is a certain distance between the point where the wires leave the gears and the point where they enter the fuselage or hull. If this distance is more than six inches and no spar or strut is available along which the wires can be led, they should be enclosed in a thin gauge steel tube sufficiently large in bore to take all the wires without touching or deflecting them. All wires should be fitted with an adjustable coupling or, if this is not available, with a turnbuckle to facilitate adjustment. Adjustable couplings for Bowden 51 wire are obtainable from Stores.

Vaseline, grease or ordinary oil must not be used for lubricating Bowden wire. Nothing but a mixture of non-freezing oil (obtainable from Stores), and powdered graphite is to be used. A convenient mixture is five parts by weight of the former to four of the latter.

METHOD OF FIXING THE BOMB IN THE CARRIER
(For bomb with tail fuse only).

The forks in the end struts must be adjusted to suit the bomb. They should be left slightly short, so that the bomb shackle can easily fit into the slip. The slip must be in the released position. The tail fusing wire must be fitted into the tube and hang from the fusing pin. Small brass guides (32), Fig. 3, are fitted to enable the loop of the fusing wire to go easily into the slot cut for it and to hold it in the correct position. The bomb is then lifted into position, the shackle pushed home in the slip, which will lock itself in position. Simultaneously the fusing wire spring clip must be fitted over the tail fuse body, then the end forks of the carrier are pulled down to abut tightly against the nose plug and tail fuses. When this is done the wing nuts on the clamping bolts must be screwed up tight. The screws on the fore crutch of 230 lb. bomb carrier should rarely require adjusting.

METHOD OF RELEASING THE BOMB.

The bomb can be released either by a lever or a toggle pulling on the operating wire fastened to the upper end of the trigger.

A release toggle which will shortly be in service is shown in Fig. 6. The toggle bracket is fitted with a pulley which enables the release wire to be led off at an angle with the direction of the pull, in machines where this is found convenient.

The bombs can be released safe, that is, with both fusing wires on. By pulling back the fusing lever to the first position the tail fusing wire only is pulled off the bomb when it is dropped, and by pulling back the lever to the full extent both fusing wires are removed.

BOMB RELEASING IN SALVOS.

The introduction of the practice for dropping bombs in salvos has made it necessary to fit special apparatus for releasing.

At present three gears, designated Marks I., III. and IV., are being issued.

Mark I. consists of four rocking levers operated by fingers projecting from a central spindle which is rotated through 90° by a hand lever. The projecting arms of the rocking levers are bored to take the ends of the Bowden wires. The arms extend beyond the wire attachments for convenience in cocking. The stroke of the levers is two inches. (Fig. 7). Mark II. is obsolete.

Leaflet No. 26b (continued).

Mark III.—The framework of this gear consists of an upper and a lower channel between which the split rocking levers are placed. These hinge on pins through the lower channel, and their free forked ends slide in slots in the upper channel. (Fig. 8).

A longitudinal slotted plate inside the upper channel forms in it a double groove, along which a small travelling block is pulled by means of a Bowden wire fastened to it. This block, catchiing on the end of the first lever pulls it over until the circular motion of the end of the lever enables the travelling block to override it and engage with the second lever, and so on. The release wires are fastened to small swivelling blocks on the sides of the levers.

The operating wire can either be pulled straight through the end of the gear or, by means of an adjustable pulley on the end, pulled in any convenient direction. Another wire is attached to the travelling block to pull it in the opposite direction for cocking.

Mark IV. is similar to Mark I., but has a shorter stroke and releases 16 bombs. A full description is given in Leaflet No. 28, " Bomb Gear in Handley Page Machine."

One feature of all these salvo gears, as contrasted with the toggle release, is the definite and unadjustable travel of the release wire. As a result it may easily happen that the stroke of the release wire is different from that necessary to stretch the safety spring and pull over the trigger of the bomb gear. Referring to Fig. 9, A is the stroke of the release gear, B is the stroke of the trigger, plus the length of the wire in the safety bight. B can be made anything more than the stroke of the trigger by sweating the nipple of the safety spring in a suitable position. B must not be greater than A or the bomb will not release. To allow for any inaccuracy in fixing the length of the bight, a tension spring is introduced into the release wire. When the trigger of the bomb gear release slip has come up against the stop the wire still tends to travel to the full extent of the rocking lever's stroke, *viz.*, A; the tension spring is introduced to allow it to do so. When this spring has extended an amount C (B+C being=A) the operating pin or block of the release gear slides over the lever, which is pulled back by the safety spring, and the releasing of the next bomb commences.

In some machines the release mechanism is in an awkward position for sweating in the ends of the wires. To get over this the wire should be cut in two and the terminal nipples sweated on; the wire is joined by the adjustable coupling. This coupling should be arranged in the most accessible position possible.

The adjustable coupling, the tension spring, and the safety spring should be arranged in the order shown in Fig. 9, and must only be fitted on a straight run of the wire.

With these gears Bowden casing is not to be used. The releasing wires must be led round pulleys where the angle of bend exceeds 15° and through small bell-mouthed copper fairleads where the angle is less than this amount.

The greatest care must be taken to see that the adjusting couplings, safety spring and nipples and tension springs have sufficient travel, otherwise if there is any obstruction to their movement a jam will occur.

New patterns of salvo releasing gear are being developed, particulars of these will be issued when they are available.

PNEUMATIC RELEASING GEAR.

A device for dropping bombs by compressed air is undergoing trials and will shortly be in service and it will be described fully in a separate paper when issued.

INSTRUCTIONS FOR FITTING GEAR FOR HANGING BOMBS VERTICALLY.

When a machine has to carry bombs vertically stowed—and this is by far the best method of stowage and can be employed for bombs of 50 lb., 65 lb., 100 lb., 112 lb., 230 lb., and 250 lb.—overhead girders must be fitted above the bomb cells to take the weight of the bombs.

Clips for hanging the slips must be free from welds or brazing.

Hanging of bombs.—The bombs are suspended from the nose, and for this purpose G.S. plugs are used, bored and tapped, as shown in Fig. 10. Eyebolts can be had from Stores when required, as " Bolts, Eye, bomb slinging, $\frac{1}{2}''$, Mark I," and prepared plugs are also issued now as " Plugs, Fuse-hole, Special No. 11, Mark II."

This applies to the 65 lb. Mark I., 100 lb. Mark I., 112 lb. Marks III. and V., and 250 lb. Mark I., with the standard fuse hole for Fuse Bomb D.A. No. 1 Mark I.

This method is now being superseded by the introduction of Hanging Nose Fuse D.A. No. 8, which is used in the 50 lb. Mark IV., 112 lb. Marks VI. and V.II., and Fuse Bomb D.A. No. 9 for the 112 lb. Marks III. and V. (new fusing). (*See* Leaflets Nos. 13, 14, 15, and 17 and Supplements.)

The 230 lb. Bomb Mark III. is also prepared for slinging by the nose. (*See* Leaflet No. 7a.)

RELEASING GEAR.

This will be exactly as for horizontally stowed bombs, the remarks about safety springs, fairleads and pulleys applying equally to each case.

FUSING ARRANGEMENTS.

In seaplanes with vertical stowage, to render the fuse live there is fitted to the side of the bomb cell a small bracket in which slides a fusing rod of U shape, which is kept in the " safe " position by means of a spring. There is a small cell in this fusing bracket, which takes the loop of the fusing wire. This wire (Fusing Wire for Vertical Stowage, Mark II.), can be obtained on demand from Store. When fixed in position the wire is horizontal. (Fig. 11).

The end of the loop should be flush with the outside of the wood forming the cell, and the loop itself should be bent downwards about ¼ inch to facilitate its leaving the cell if the bomb is to fall safe. On the end of the fusing wire are two fingers, which passing on either side of the fuse vane, prevent the latter from turning.

The sleeve nut for adjusting the length of the wire is liable to slacken; this will be prevented if the wire is bent just outside the nut.

It is absolutely necessary to keep the vane of the fuse in line with the fusing wire, otherwise the latter will lock on and probably render the vane inoperative.

The above fusing arrangements apply to airships, seaplanes and ship aeroplanes.

Land machines as stated above, will in future not be fitted with any fusing arrangements. In this case a spring locking arm is fitted near the bottom of the cell to prevent the tail arming vane from turning. (*See* Fig. 12.)

This locking arm consists of an arm hinged at the side of the cell where it is clear of the bomb fins and the body of the bomb when falling. At the end of the arm is a U, which fits under the tail arming vane and prevents the latter from turning when the bomb is in the cell, the U being pressed up against the underside of the vane by a spring on the hinge pin of the arm.

When the bomb is released and has left the cell the locking arm folds up against the side of the cell.

The locking arms must be held down when inserting the bomb into the cell, and then lifted up and placed under a blade of the arming vane when the bomb is in position.

An alternative arrangement of locking the tail arming vane on land machines is shown on Fig. 13.

This consists of a strip of spring steel with its upper end bolted to the side of the cell and its lower end passing through the arming vane.

The bomb when falling presses the strip sideways out of the way.

To facilitate the insertion of bombs into the cell, a catch is provided to hold the lower end of the locking strip against the side of the cell.

R.F.C. BOMB CARRIERS.

These are in all cases fastened to the machine by means of T section ribs. A special rib is made for each type of machine.

The ribs are fixed to the machine 21" apart, and have holes bored in them to suit all the carriers which the machine is likely to take. Thus a machine capable of taking a bomb load of, say, 460 lb. bombs would have to take one twin 230 lb. carrier, or two twin 112 lb. carriers, and probably four four-series 20 lb. carriers.

(*See* Leaflets No. 26 and 26a for detailed description, also for " Notes on Maintenance of Gears ").

AIR MINISTRY,
    June, 1918.

Leaflet No. 26b (continued).

CARRIER SKELETON

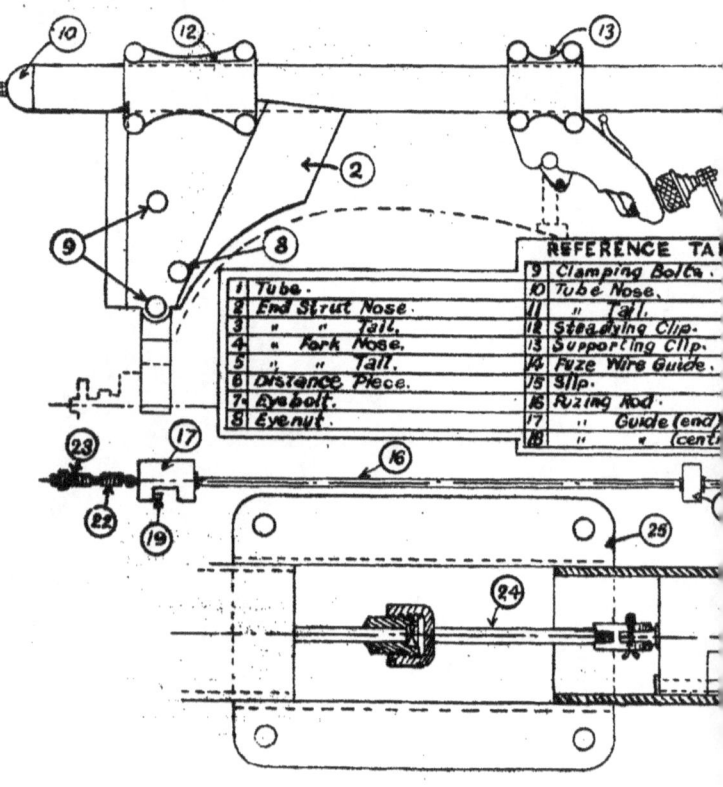

	REFERENCE TA...
1 Tube.	9 Clamping Bolts.
2 End Strut Nose.	10 Tube Nose.
3 " " Tail.	11 " Tail.
4 " Fork Nose.	12 Steadying Clip.
5 " " Tail.	13 Supporting Clip.
6 Distance Piece.	14 Fuze Wire Guide.
7 Eyebolt.	15 Slip.
8 Eyenut.	16 Fuzing Rod.
	17 " Guide (end)
	18 " " (centre)

TUBULAR 112 L.B. MARK.I.(F).

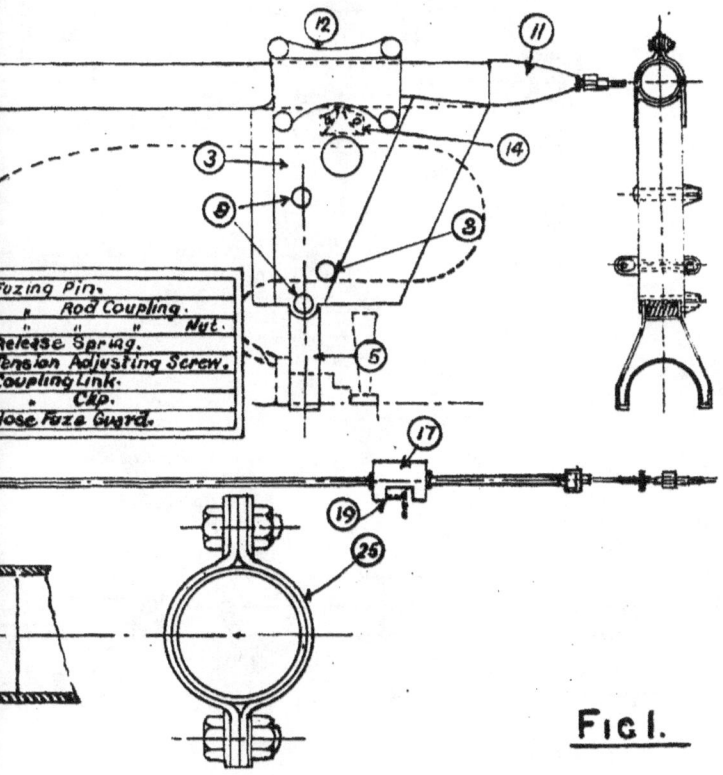

Fuzing Pin.
" Rod Coupling.
" " " Nut.
Release Spring.
Tension Adjusting Screw.
Coupling Link.
Clip.
Nose Fuze Guard.

Fig 1.

CARRIER SKELETON TUBULAR

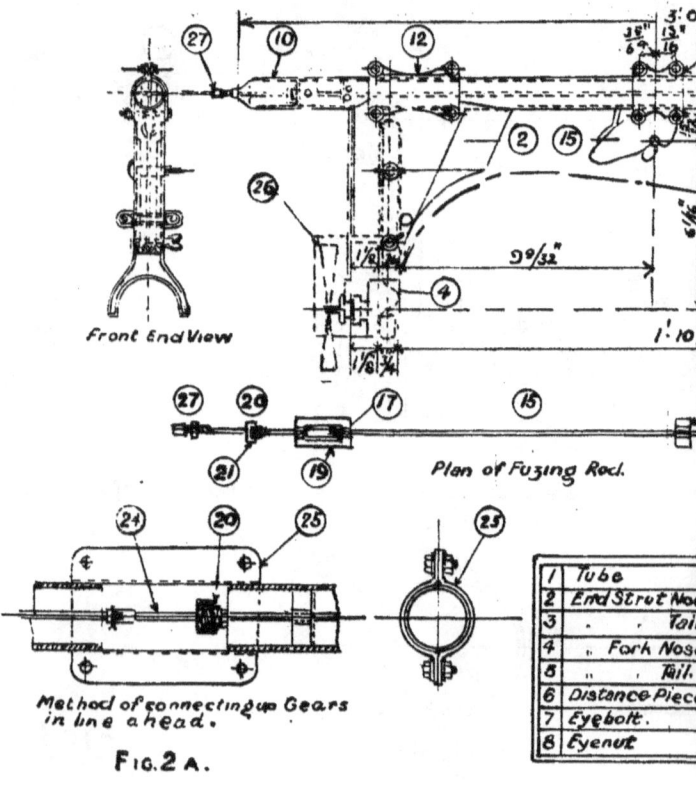

Front End View

Plan of Fuzing Rod.

Method of connecting up Gears in line ahead.

FIG. 2 A.

1	Tube
2	End Strut Nose
3	" " Tail
4	" Fork Nose
5	" " Tail
6	Distance Piece
7	Eyebolt
8	Eyenut

112. L.B. MARK III (F).

FIG 2.

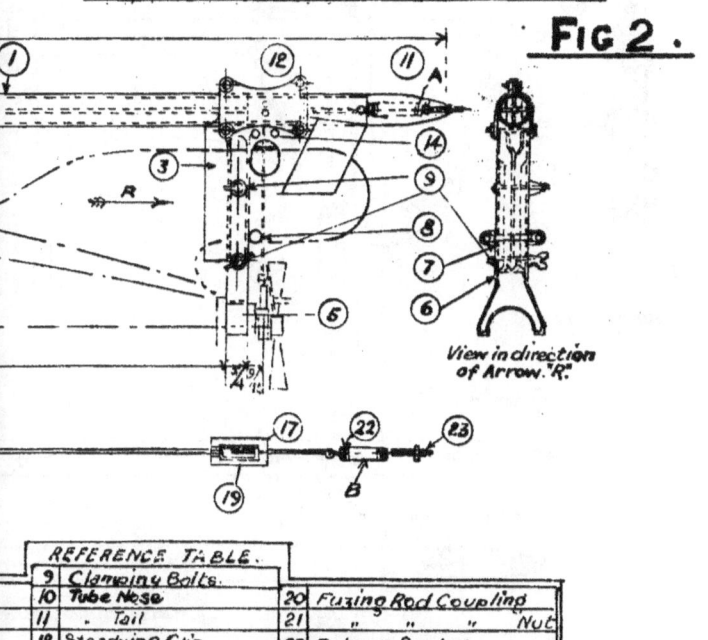

View in direction of Arrow "R".

REFERENCE TABLE.

No.	Part	No.	Part
9	Clamping Bolts.	20	Fuzing Rod Coupling
10	Tube Nose	21	" " " Nut
11	" Tail	22	Release Spring.
12	Steadying Clip	23	Tension Adjusting Screw
13	Supporting "	24	Coupling Link.
14	Fuze Wire Guide	25	" Clip.
15	Slip	26	Nose Fuze Guard.
16	Fuzing Rod	27	Nipple for Bowden Wire.
17	" Slide		
18	" Rod Guide.		
19	" Pin.		

Leaflet No. 26b (continued).

CARRIER SKELETON

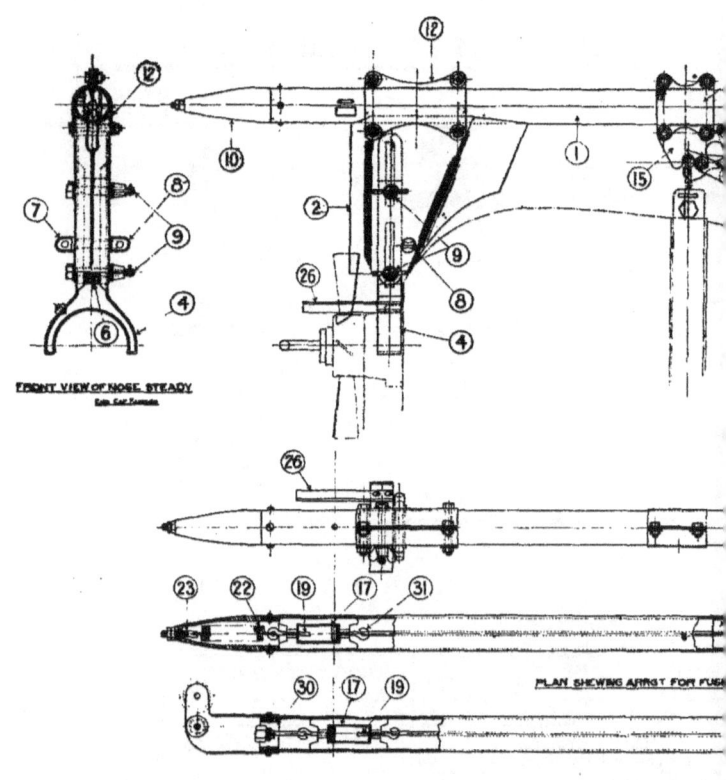

1. Tube.
2. End Strut (Nose).
3. ,, ,, (Tail).
4. ,, Fork (Nose).
5. ,, ,, (Tail).
6. Distance Piece.
7. Eye Bolt.
8. Eye Nut.
9. Clamping Bolts.
10. End Cap.
11. End Pulley Bracket.
12. Steadying Clip.
13. Supporting Clip.
15. Release Slip.

TUBULAR 112 LB. MARK V. (F.)

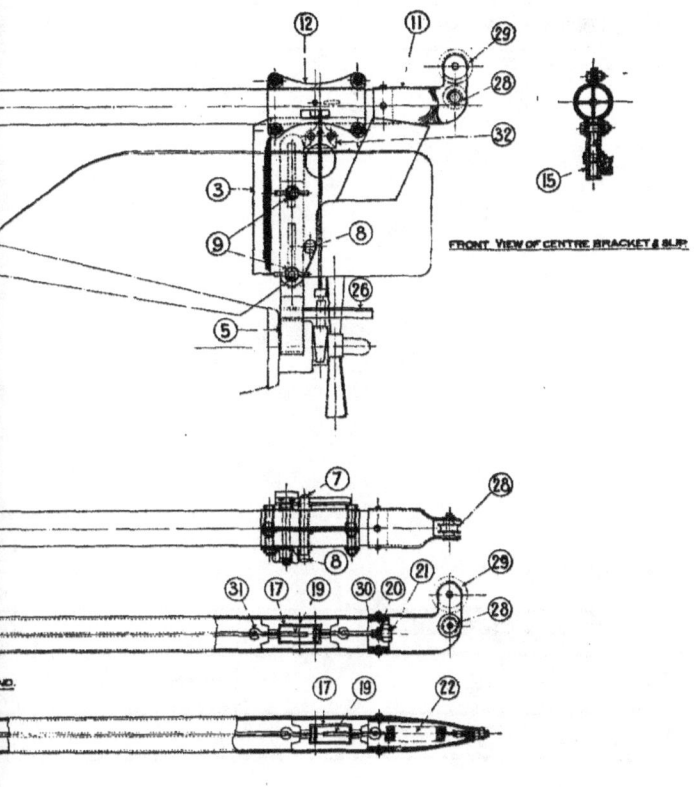

Fig. 3.

16. Fusing Rod.
17. ,,   Slide.
18. ,,   Rod Guide.
19. ,,   Pin.
20. Union for Wire Nipple.
21. Nut for Wire Nipple.
22. Fusing Spring.
23. Tension Adjusting Screw.
26. Arming Vane Stop.
28. Fuse Wire Pulley.
29. Release Wire Pulley.
30. Bush for Pulley Bracket.
31. Eye for Fusing Slide.
32. Fusing Wire Guide Block.

CARRIER SKELETON TUBULAR

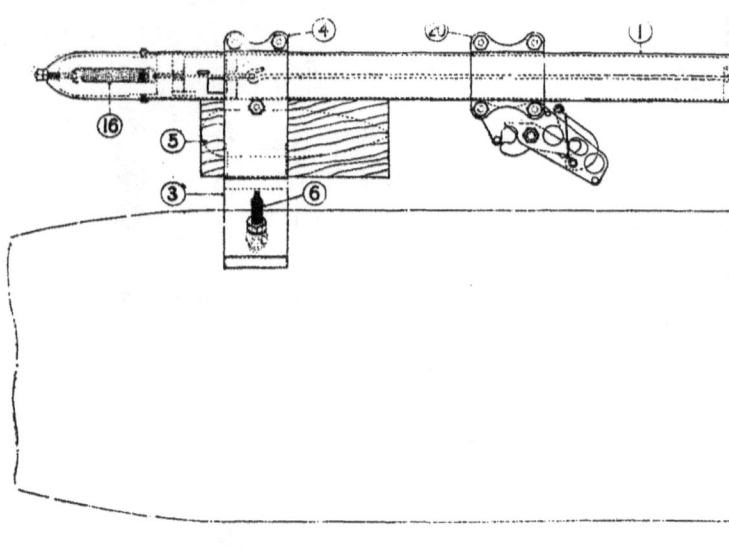

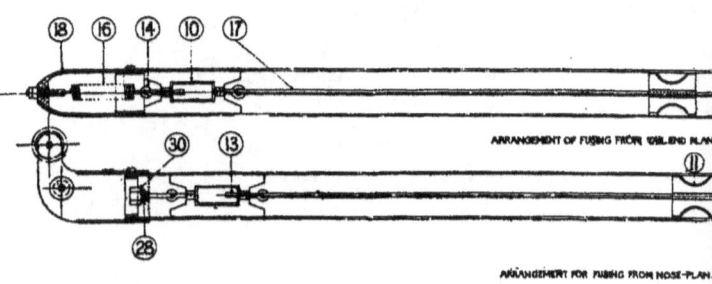

Fig. 4

1. Tube.
2. End Strut (Tail).
3. Nose Crutch.
4. Supporting Clip for Nose Crutch.
5. Wood Streamline Block.
6. Steady Screw.
8. End Fork Tail.
9. Wood Block.
10. Fusing Slide.
11. ,, Rod Guide.
12. ,, Pin (Rear).
13. ,, ,, (Front).
14. Eye for Fusing Slide.
15. Tension Adjusting Screw.
16. Fusing Spring.

230 LB. MARK IV. (F.)

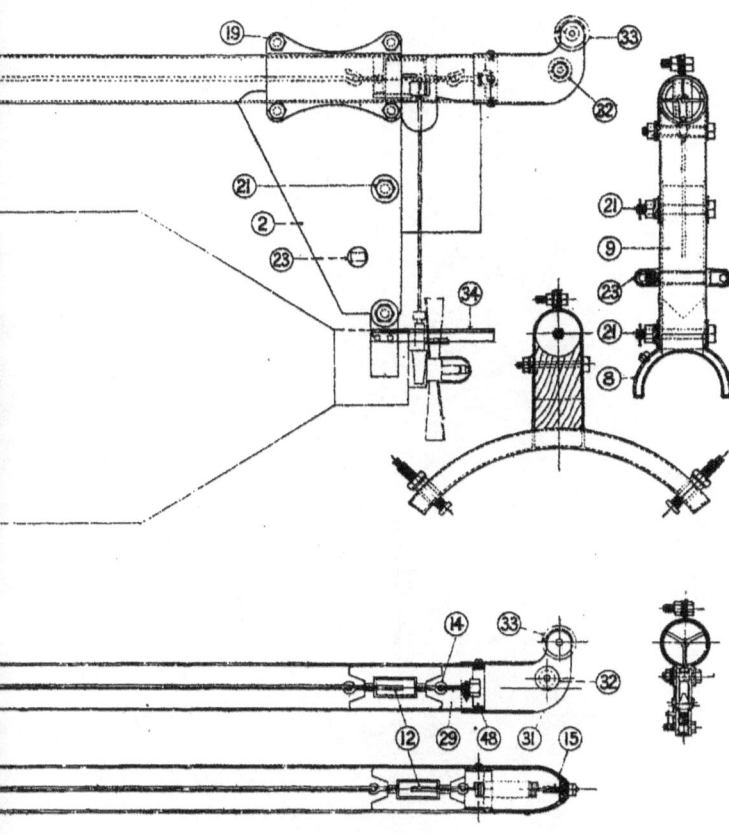

17. Fusing Rod.
18. End Cap.
19. Steadying Clip.
20. Supporting Clip.
21. Clamping Bolt.
23. Eyebolt and Nut.
28. Union for Wire Nipple.
29. Hook for Fusing Slide.
30. Nut for Union No. 28.
31. End Pulley Bracket.
32. Fuse Wire Pulley.
33. Pulley for Release Wire.
34. Arming Vane Stop.
48. Bush for End Pulley Bracket.

No. 26b *(continued)*.

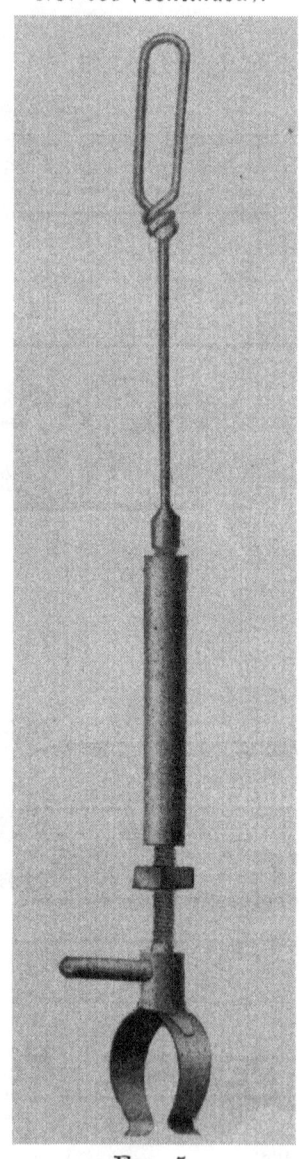

Fig. 5.

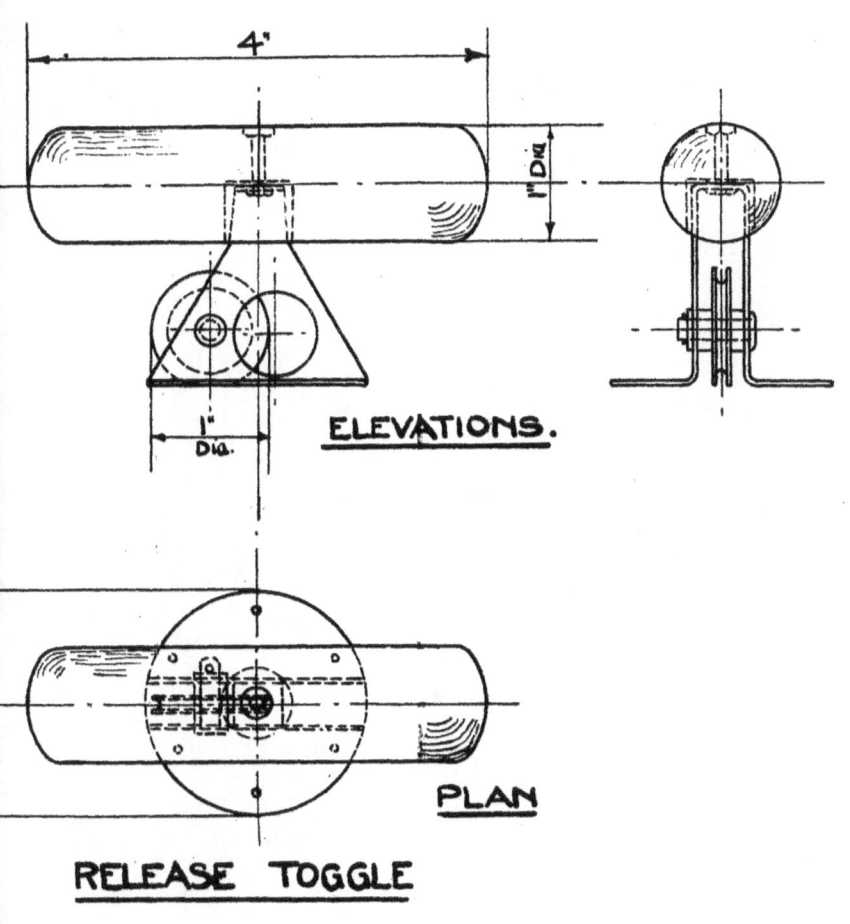

Fig. 6.

BOMB DROPPER, SALVO, MARK I.
Plan of Levers.

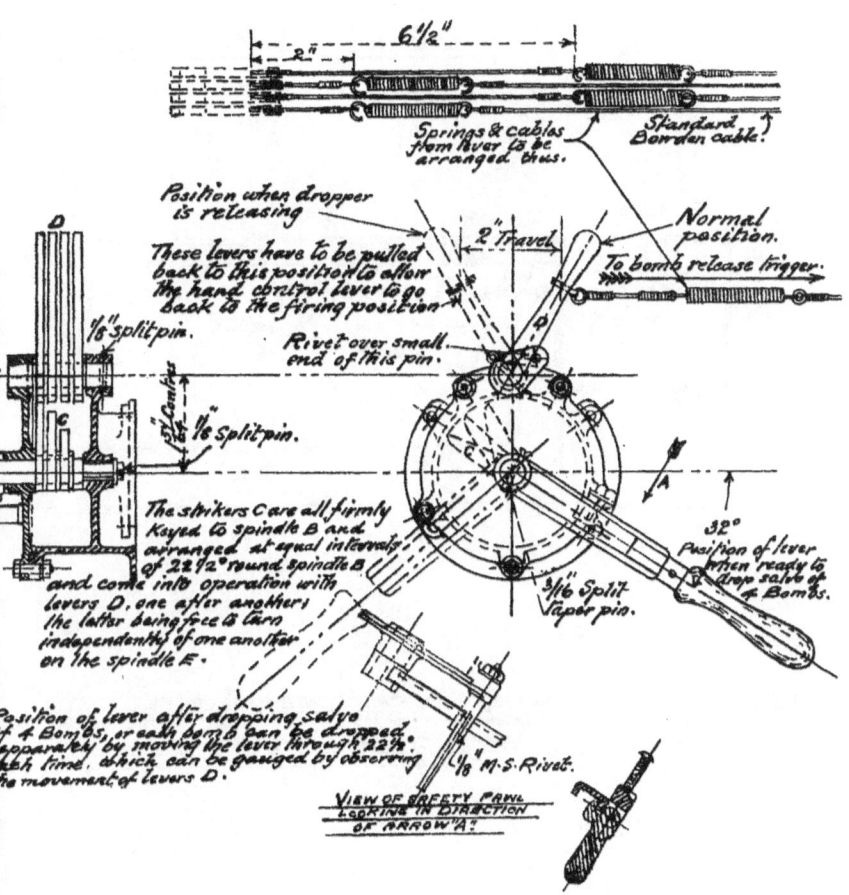

Fig. 7.

BOMB DROPPER.

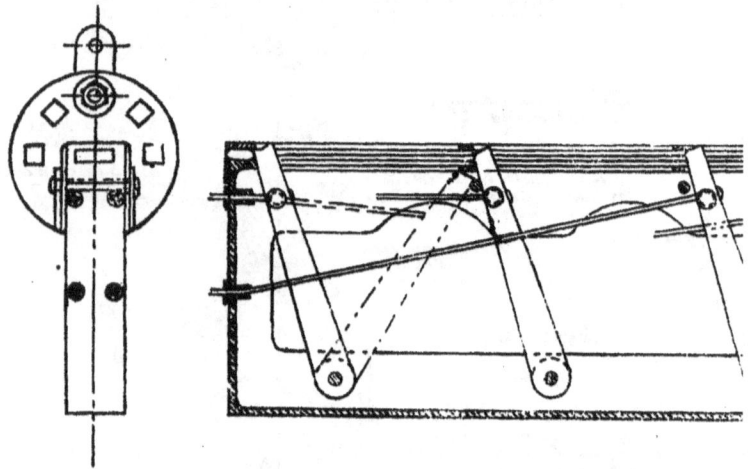

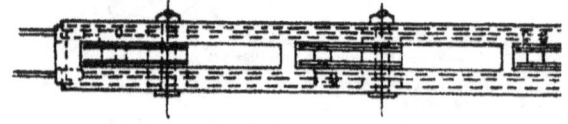

SALVO Mᴷ III.

Fig 8

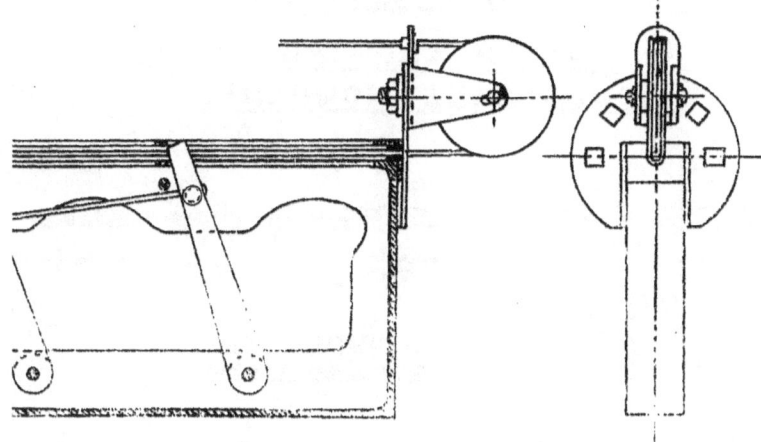

Leaflet No. 26b *(continued)*.

SALVO BOMB
SKETCH SHOWING ADJUSTABLE COUPLING

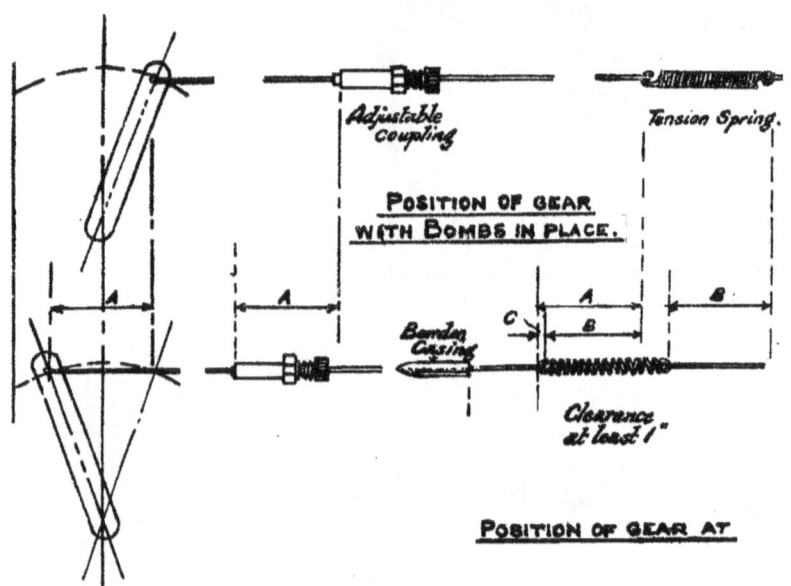

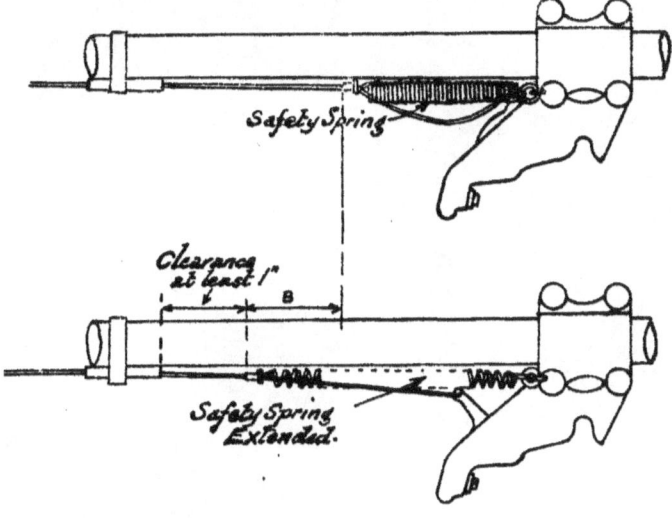

Fig 9

DROPPING GEAR.
AND OPERATION.
OF TENSION SPRING.

Safety Spring

Clearance at least 1"
B

Safety Spring Extended.

THE MOMENT OF RELEASE

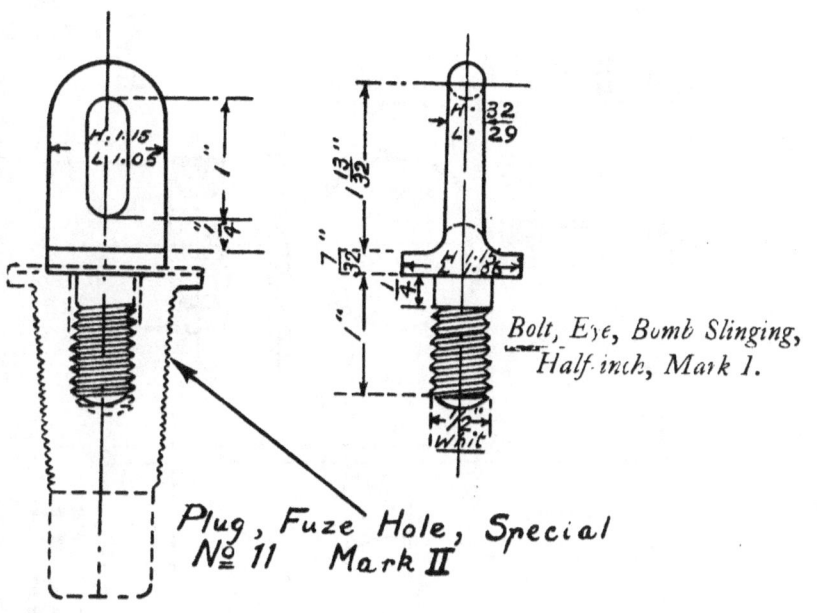

Fig. 10.

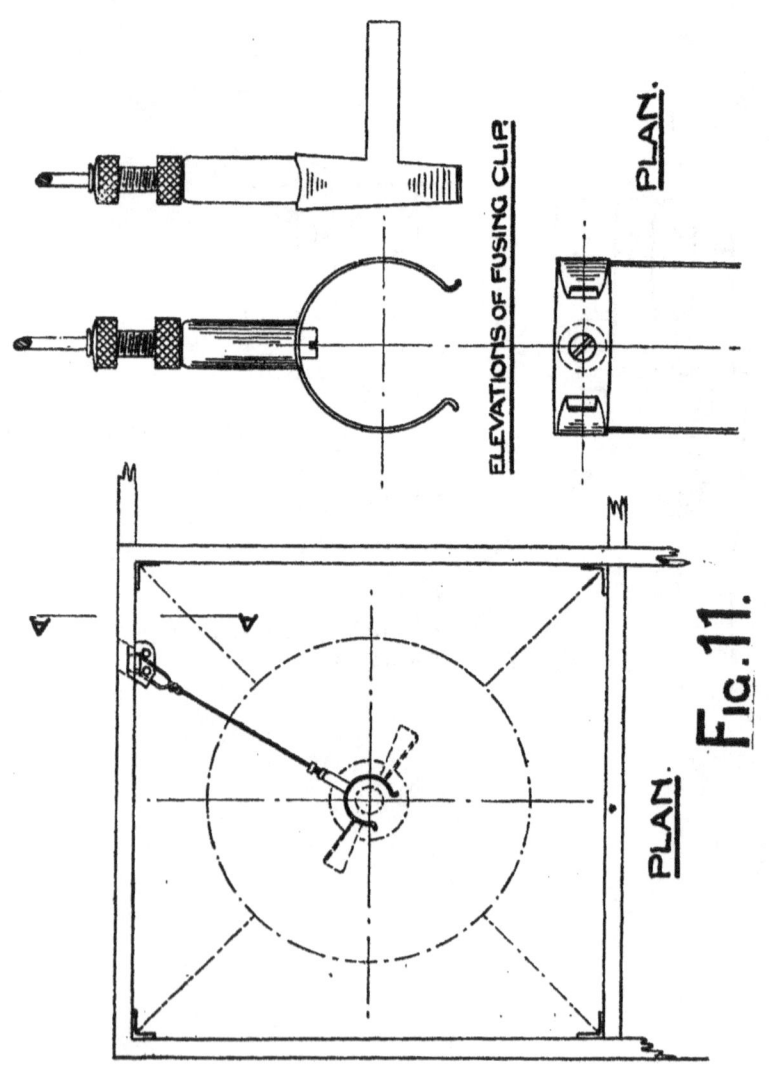

ELEVATIONS OF FUSING CLIP

PLAN.

PLAN.

Fig. 11.

Leaflet No. 26b (continued).

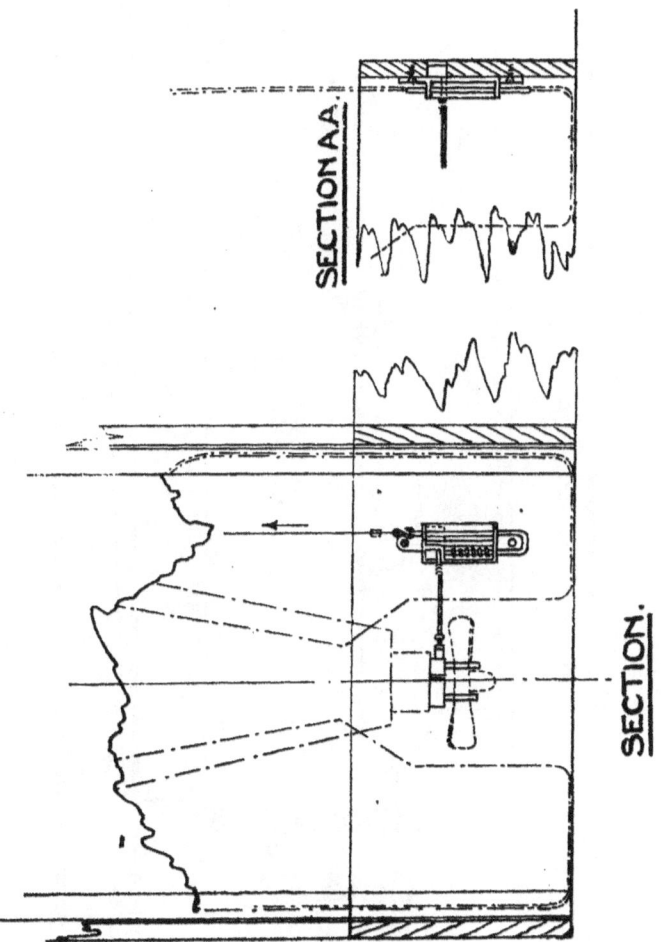

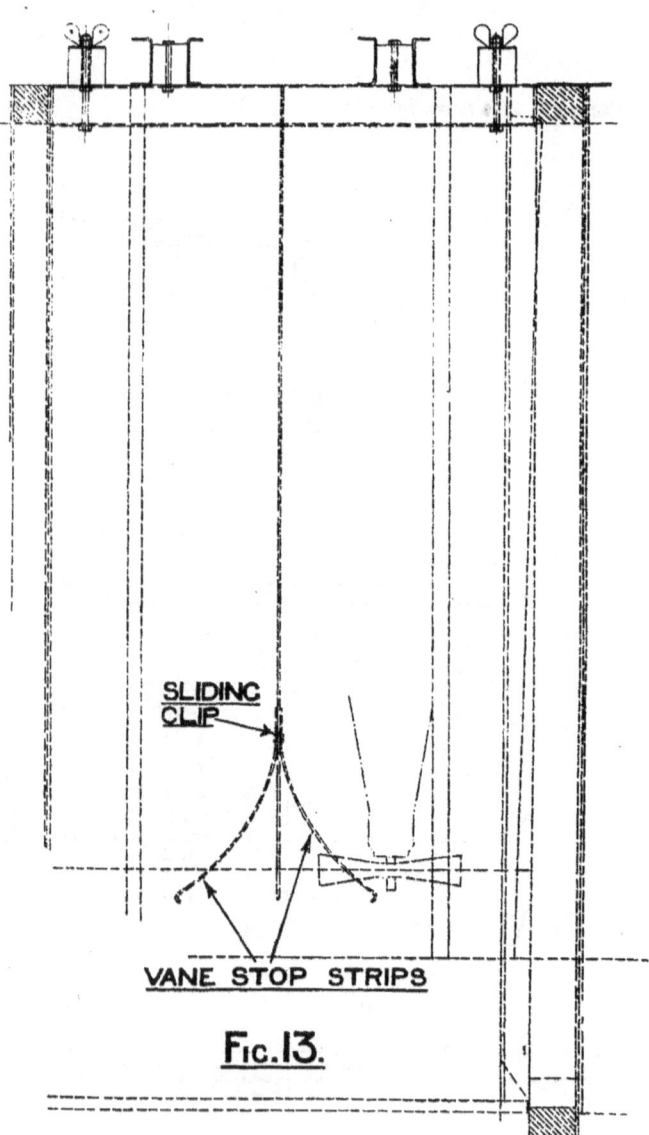

FIG. 13.

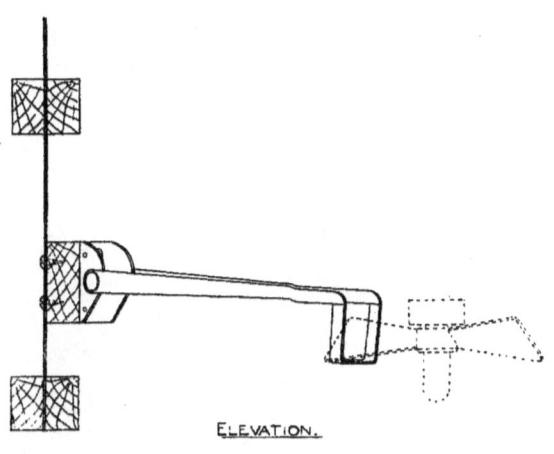

ELEVATION.

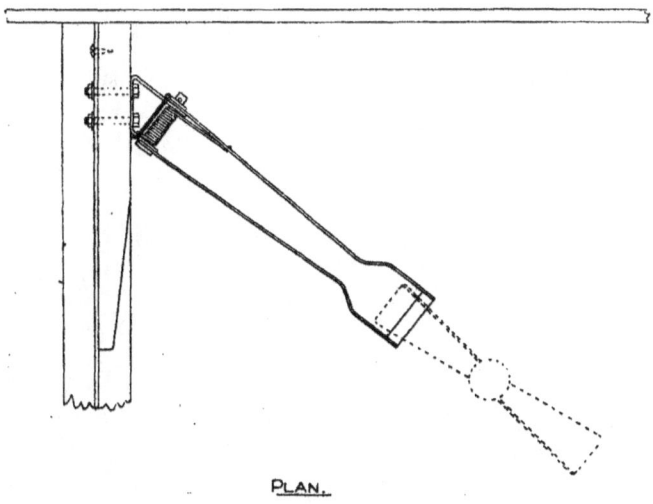

PLAN.

FIG. 12.

Leaflet No. 27.

Gledhill Bomb Gear.

GENERAL ARRANGEMENT.

Two sizes of this gear are being made at present. These will be issued as complete sets made up of the following units:—

- A. One fixed unit of two suspensions for 20 lb. bombs. (This unit is a fixed part in the D.H.9.)
- B. One movable unit of 12 suspensions for 20 lb. bombs.
- C. One movable unit of six suspensions for 50 lb. bombs.
- D. One operating mechanism and connection.

Units B and C are interchangeable, and may be fitted in turn according to the type of bomb it is intended to carry. Units A, B, and C, are placed in position immediately behind the engine and in front of the petrol tanks. Unit D is fitted in any convenient position for working by the pilot.

CONSTRUCTION.

In Units B and C, the bomb rails carrying the slips, which are three in number, are mounted on the top of the bomb crates. The bomb crates are made of three ply wood and afford the lateral support needed by the bombs when stowed vertically. The crate in Unit B, illustrated in Fig. I, consists of 12 cells, made to fit the Cooper bomb, the crate in Unit C is similar in construction, with the exception that it is formed of six cells constructed to fit the 50 lb. bombs.

THE BOMB SLIP AND RELEASE GEAR. (*See Fig. 2.*)

The slip is the mechanism on which the bomb is retained, and by means of which the bomb is released. It is self locking, and consists of a lever carrying the suspension hook B, and a trigger lever C, both of which are pivoted. The

Cooper bomb is suspended from the suspension hook B by a special wire loop which replaces the nut on the tail of the bomb. The 50 lb. bomb is suspended by an eye bolt which forms an integral part of the nose fuse.

It will be seen that the suspension hook B receives the suspension lug of the bomb to be stowed, and is then automatically locked by a trigger lever C, which projects through a slot in the sliding bar D. When this bar is pulled along in the direciton of the arrow, as is the case when operating the release, the end of this slot depresses the lever C, and so allows the suspension hook B to turn on its pivot and release the bomb.

The pilot's release lever, which is connected to the bellcrank lever G, Fig. 1, has seven positions, as follows:

1. " Locked " position.
2. " Free " position.
3. Release 2 Cooper bombs from fixed unit.
4. Release 3 Cooper bombs or 1—50 lb. bomb.
5. Release 3 Cooper bombs or 2—50 lb. bombs.
6. Release 3 Cooper bombs or 2—50 lb. bombs.
7. Release 3 Cooper bombs or 1—50 lb. bomb.

INSTRUCTIONS FOR LOADING.

Make sure that the gear is properly adjusted. The position of the pilot's lever should correspond to that of the sliding bar on scale S. Fig. 1; means of adjustment are provided on the operating cable.

Place the release lever in " free " position, and pull down the slides at the bottom of each bomb cell which hold the safety springs aside, push the suspension lug of the bomb to be loaded upwards through the cone A until a click is heard.

As already described, the bomb will now be automatically held in position. Care should be taken to make certain that the bomb is firmly engaged before allowing its weight to fall unsupported on the slip.

When all the bombs are stowed, place the release handle in the locked position; this renders it impossible for bombs to be jerked off when taxi-ing, unless the release handle be removed from the locked position. The safety springs must now be adjusted by pushing up the slides which hold them aside while stowing the bombs is in progress.

GLEDHILL BOMB GEAR (20 LB.) FIG 1

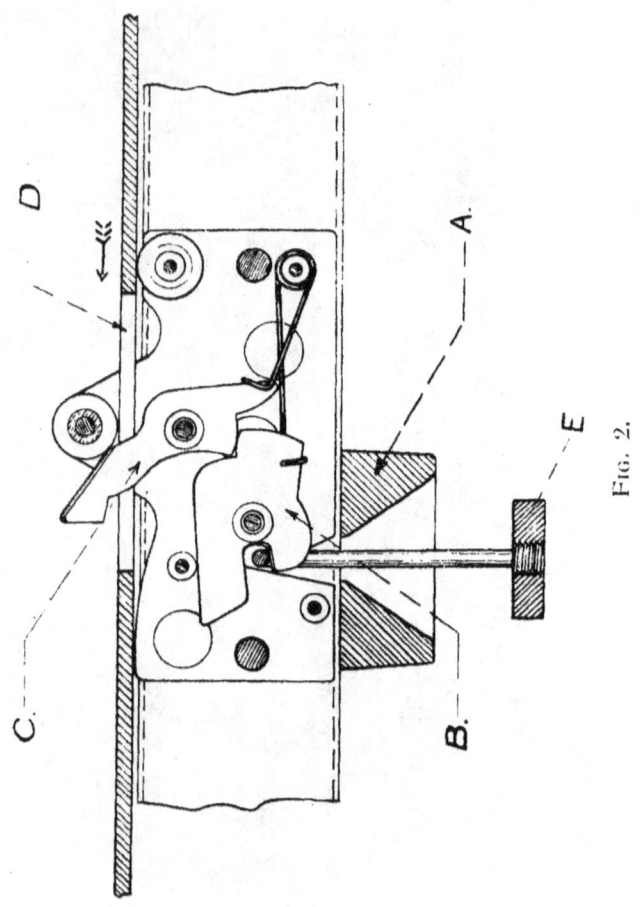

Fig. 2.

UNLOADING

If Cooper Bombs are to be unloaded their protecting cover should first be screwed into position over the fuse on the nose of each bomb.

The bombs are then supported from below, care being taken to take the weight of all the bombs included in the salvo to be released. The release gear is then operated for the first salvo, and the bombs are lowered out of the crate and laid gently on the ground.

This operation is repeated for each salvo. When all the bombs have been released in this way they should be placed at a convenient distance from the machine, and be unfused by screwing off their protecting covers and nose fuses and removing the detonators. This must be carefully done, and the detonators be immediately replaced in their tins.

Before releasing the 50 lb. bombs the safety pins must be replaced in the tail fuses; this done they are released singly, or in pairs, according to the order of the salvos, as previously directed for unloading the Cooper bombs. As soon as the bombs are lowered out of their cells their nose fuse safety pins must be replaced. The bombs are then removed to a suitable distance from the machine and carefully unfused. (See Leaflet 14.)

AIR MINISTRY,
    MARCH, 1918.

Leaflet No. 28.

Bomb Gear in Handley Page Machine.

GENERAL ARRANGEMENT.

The Bomb Crates are built into the fuselage and are not detachable, the framework on which the bomb slips are supported being built into the framework of the centre section. The framework of the Bomb Crate consists at its top of two longitudinal members of $3'' \times 4''$ spruce $5'\ 2''$ long, one on either side of the machine. On these two longitudinal members are carried four transverse members, also of spruce, termed *Bomb Beams*. The bomb beams are $2'' \times 5\frac{1}{4}''$ and $4'\ 9''$ in length. They are numbered from the front of the machine 1, 2, 3 and 4, for purposes of reference (Fig. 4).

From each of the bomb beams are suspended four metal supports or brackets; these brackets are called *Adapters*. The adapters extend downwards nine inches and at their ends are carried the bomb slips, on which the bombs are hung. (See Fig. 3.)

From each of these adapters is also supported a bomb cell skeleton framework constructed of four $\frac{3}{8}''$ steel tubes. The upper ends of these tubes correspond in position to the centres of the sides of the squares of the cells in the honeycomb immediately below them, which cells contain the bomb fins. The upper ends of the tubes are shaped to the approximate outline of the nose of the bomb. These tubes are termed the *Bomb Guides*, and are fitted with narrow strips of ash bolted to them, the latter being named guide plates. The function of the bomb guides and guide plates is to steady the bomb when it is released, preventing its falling sideways as it slips through the bomb crate. The lower ends of the bomb guides forming each bomb cell skeleton framework, are in each case secured to the centres of their corresponding squares in a series of shallow cells arranged on the floor level between the longerons immediately below the bomb beams. These enclosed cells are called the *Honeycomb*, their purpose being to give lateral support to the bombs as they fall through the crate when released, and also to check any tendency on the part of the bomb to rotate.

The walls of the honeycomb cells are of aluminium, reinforced with wood, and fill in the space between the bottom longerons.

RELEASE GEAR.

ORDER OF RELEASE.

Each bomb slip is actuated by an individual control cable consisting of Bowden Standard No. 51 wire of 270 lbs. strength.

The bombs are released in salvos of four, or separately as desired. Dropping bombs singly is not easy, and cannot be relied on, but they may be released positively in pairs, if the release handle is pulled over only one point on the ratchet on top of the control box in place of pulling it over two points, as in the release of a salvo. In either case the order of release is the same, *i.e.*, the aft port side bomb is the first to fall, and is followed in order by the next three bombs to starboard of it; this completes the first salvo. In the second salvo the port side bomb of the second transverse row of bomb cells working forward, is the first to be released, followed by the remaining three bombs of the second salvo. The third and fourth salvos are released in the same order, always from port to starboard, and always opening with the port side bomb.

CONTROL CABLES. (*See Figs. 1 and 3.*)

The control cables are 16 in number, and run from port to starboard in four distinct groups of four cables each. The port side control cable of each salvo is led through a wooden fairlead in position immediately above the bomb slip next to starboard, and held in the adapter supporting the bomb slip. The second and third control cables of each salvo are similarly led through separate guides in the wooden fairlead blocks fitted in the adapters above the bomb slips to their starboard. In this way the fairlead block above the starboard bomb slip of each salvo has three separate control cables led through it. These three control cables, together with the control cable of the fourth or starboard bomb slip, are passed through a set of four pulleys mounted one above the other on a single spindle, retained in a bracket bolted to the fairlead block, the latter being in turn bolted to a cross member. This applies to beams 1 and 2 only. In the case of beams 3 and 4, which have no fairlead blocks, they are bolted direct to a cross member. This set of four pulleys is termed the " *Pulley Nest Block.*"

From this point the control cables run forward through Nos. 1 and 2 fairlead blocks, on to, and through the main fairlead block, to the salvo release gear.

Each of the control cables of each salvo of four, after passing through its pulley nest block at the starboard side of the machine, has soldered to it one end of a light spring (see Fig. 5), whose other end is attached to its pulley nest block. The function of this spring, which is termed the "*Safety Spring*," is to keep a certain amount of slack in the cable next to the release trigger, so that the trigger spring is certain to keep the trigger in the " on " position, and thus prevent an accidental release.

In addition to these safety springs, a second spring is attached to each control cable at the control box end. This spring is known as the *Tension Spring*.

Beyond the tension spring, and attached by some six inches of cable to the control box levers is a small turnbuckle, one to each control cable.

With these turnbuckles the control cables are adjusted. The tension springs are introduced in case the control cables should be adjusted too tightly with the turnbuckles; the tension springs would in this event extend and prevent the releasing mechanism being jammed or strained.

The length of travel of the levers actuating the control cables from the control box is $1\frac{3}{4}$ inches, and the length of travel of the release trigger on the bomb slip only $1\frac{1}{4}$ inches. The difference is the amount of " bight " which the safety spring keeps in the release cable.

DETAILS OF SKELETON BOMB GEAR.

SALVO RELEASE GEAR, MARK IV. (See Fig. 5.)

The control box consists of a cast aluminium cylinder made in two parts (H), at the top of which is carried a ratchet (J) with eight points and a release handle (K) which serves to rotate a central shaft (L) by means of a pawl (M) which engages with the ratchet points.

·The release handle (K) is limited in its backward and forward travel by the two stops (N). The complete travel of the release handle is equal to one quarter of the circumference of the circle formed by the eight ratchet points. The travel of the release handle is equal to two ratchet points.

Each ratchet point represents the release of two bombs, thus the rotation of two points represents the release of a salvo of four bombs. After the release of each salvo the release handle is drawn back to its full extent, when it will again be in position to release another salvo. This operation of the release handle is to be repeated for each salvo dropped.

If it is required to release only two bombs, that is, half a salvo, the release handle should be drawn back half way into such a position that when pushed forward to its full extent only one point of the ratchet (P) is rotated, and so only two bombs are released. To release bombs singly is a matter of guess work, and cannot be relied upon.

The central shaft (L) has sixteen fingers (O) arranged equi-distant along a spiral curve; these are held in position on the shaft by a key. The function of the central shaft fingers is to operate the release levers (Q).

The release levers are also 16 in number, and are carried on a common shaft (R) placed in a position in the cut away portion in the wall of the control box. Each release lever has a lug (S) extending within the control box (H) operated by being engaged in turn by the central shaft fingers (O), as the central shaft itself is rotated by the release handle (K). Each finger in passing the lug of its corresponding release lever pushes the lug back causing the lever arm to be drawn forward. The control cables (T) being attached to the arms of the release levers are caused to move forward, so pulling back the triggers of the bomb slips in turn, and releasing the bombs.

From the foregoing it is seen that when the release handle is operated for the release of a salvo, the upper salvo release levers are pushed back in sequence by the four corresponding central shaft fingers. The release levers of the remaining three salvos are operated in turn as the central shaft completes its rotation together with the central shaft fingers fixed to it.

CONTROL CABLES.

TO ADJUST CONTROL CABLES. (See Figs. 1 and 2.)

When adjusting the control cables, care must be taken that the release triggers (C) are in turn placed as near the end of their travel as is possible without allowing them to return to the closed position. This must be done by working the release handle gently over half a ratchet point for each

Leaflet No. 28 (continued).

control adjusted. When in this position the triggers should be hard over, and if they are not, the turnbuckles between the control box and No. 1 fairlead must be adjusted. The control cables must be tested systematically, beginning with the control cable running to the aft port side bomb slip, and working through the release of each salvo from this point.

When correctly adjusted, there should be $\frac{1}{2}''$ of slack on each cable taken up by the safety spring at each cable's pulley nest block. This slack is required for the following reason. The length of travel of the bomb slips trigger arm is only $1\frac{1}{4}''$, whilst the length of travel of the release lever arm at the control box is $1\frac{3}{4}''$; thus, if too little slack is allowed, undue strain is put on the release mechanism. The adjustment should be rather on the tight than the loose side. In the case of its being a shade too tight the extra strain will be taken on the tension spring, but if the adjustment allows too much slack, the bomb slips will fail to release.

ALTERATIONS FOR STOWING 250 lb. BOMBS.
(See Fig. 4.)

The adapters on Nos. 1 and 2 bomb beams are removed, together with their pulley nest blocks and control cables complete.

It will then be seen that a set of eight bomb slips are in position immediately beneath the bomb beams. The control cables for these bomb slips will be found in position. These unconnected cables should then be attached to their respective tension springs between the main fairlead and the control box, and adjusted as directed on page 4. The 250 lb. bombs may then be stowed.

HANDLEY PAGE BOMB SLIP.

The bomb slip is the mechanism on which the bomb is retained, and by means of which the bomb is released.

The slip has five parts, as follows (see Fig. 2).

(a) The framework of the slip.
(b) The suspension hook.
(c) The retaining trigger.
(d) Retaining trigger spring.
(e) Electro-explosive release.

METHOD OF ACTION.

The electrical release is never used and need not be considered. It will not be present in the latest designs.

The suspension hook (A) is pivoted in the framework of the slip at (F), and has two positions, one open and one closed. (See Figs. 1 and 2.) When closed the arm of the suspension hook (B) is retained in the shaped slot in the trigger (C). When the trigger (C) is opened by being pulled back towards the cylinder (E), against the spring (D), the arm of the suspension hook (B) is freed, and carried into the open position by the weight of the bomb, which is thus released. Fig. 3 is a view of the slip when it is just on the point of releasing.

In loading, the release is automatically closed from the open position, by the bomb lug engaging with the top of the suspension hook, so pushing the arm of the suspension hook (B), back against the trigger (C), until opposite its slot, when the trigger (C) is pushed forward by the spring (D) so closing the release as shown in Fig. 2.

INSTRUCTIONS FOR LOADING.

The bombs are loaded from beneath the centre section, being pushed up into their cells by hand. The slip is automatically closed, as explained above.

It is, however, imperative to make certain that the arm of the suspension hook (B) is firmly retained and locked by the trigger (C) (Fig. 2) before the weight of the bomb is allowed to fall unsupported on the slip.

The nose fuse safety pin is only to be removed as the bomb is being handled for loading. When engaged on the slip no safety pin is required, as the arming vanes are automatically prevented from rotating by the fact of the nose fuse suspension lug being engaged on the suspension hook of the slip.

(The arming vanes and suspension lug are one part—see leaflet 17)). The tail fuse arming vanes are prevented from rotating by a locking arm resting over one of the vanes.

AIR MINISTRY,
May, 1918.

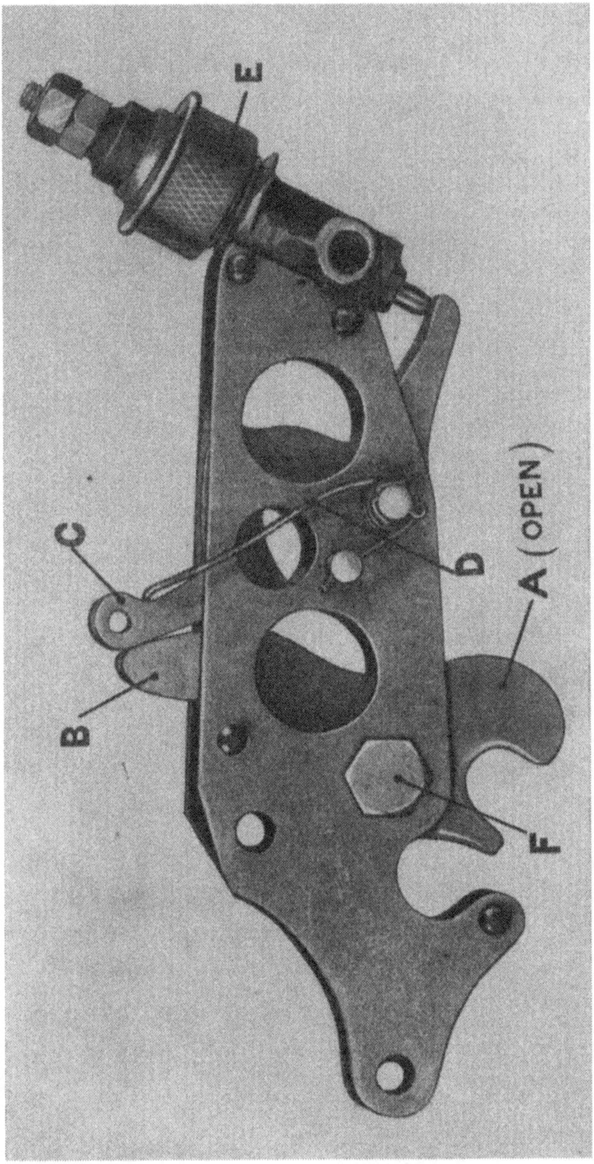

Fig. 1 (Open.)

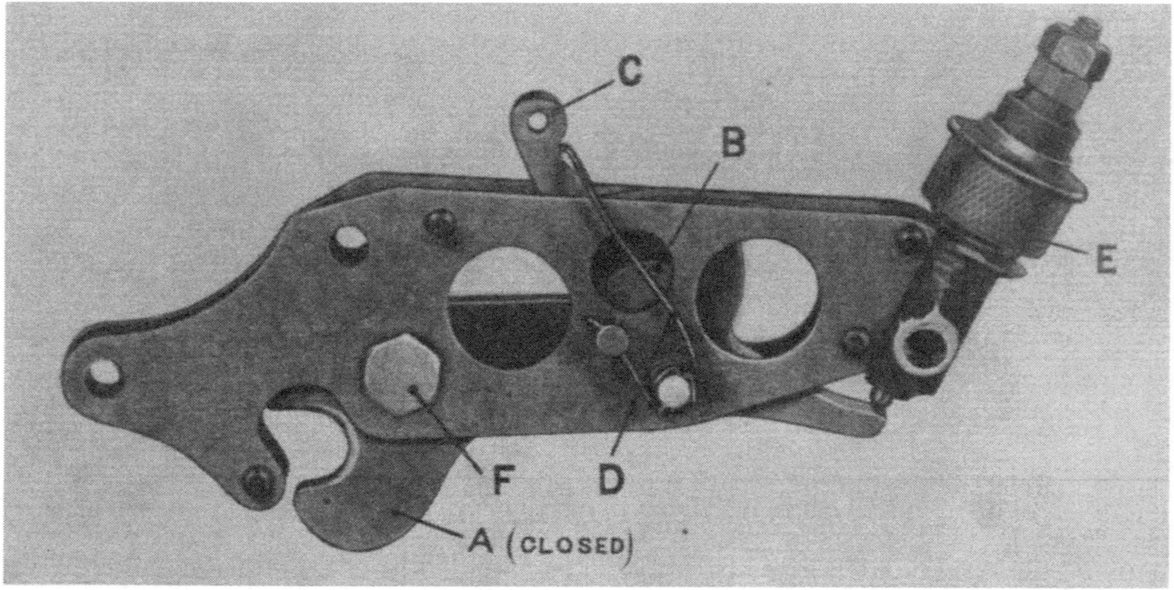

Fig. 2 (Closed.)

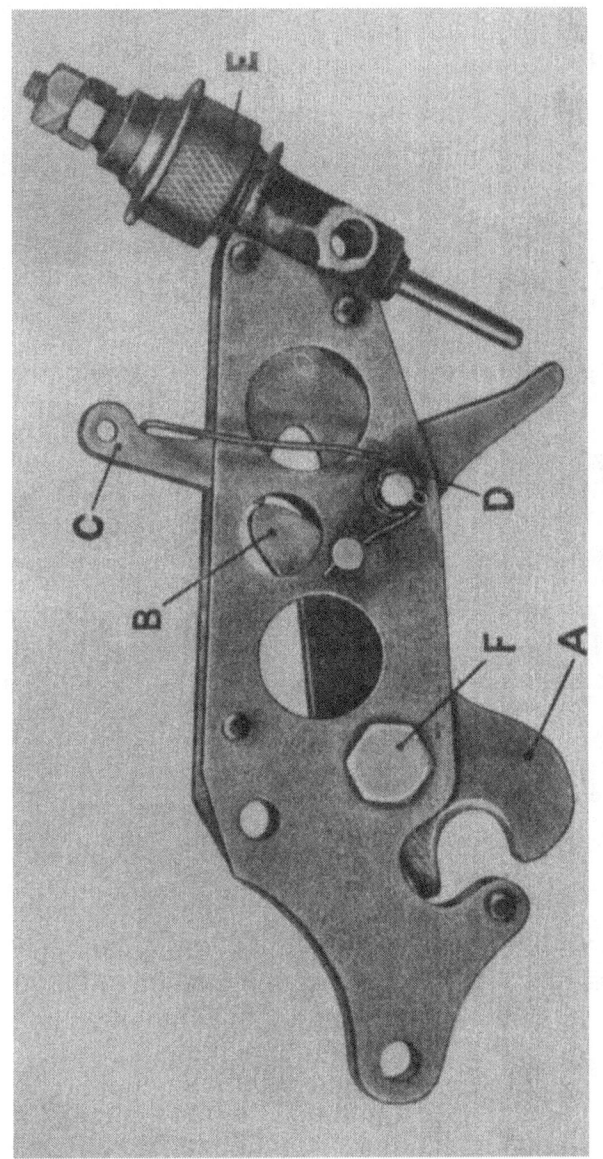

Fig. 3 (On point of Release.)

Leaflet No. 28 (continued).

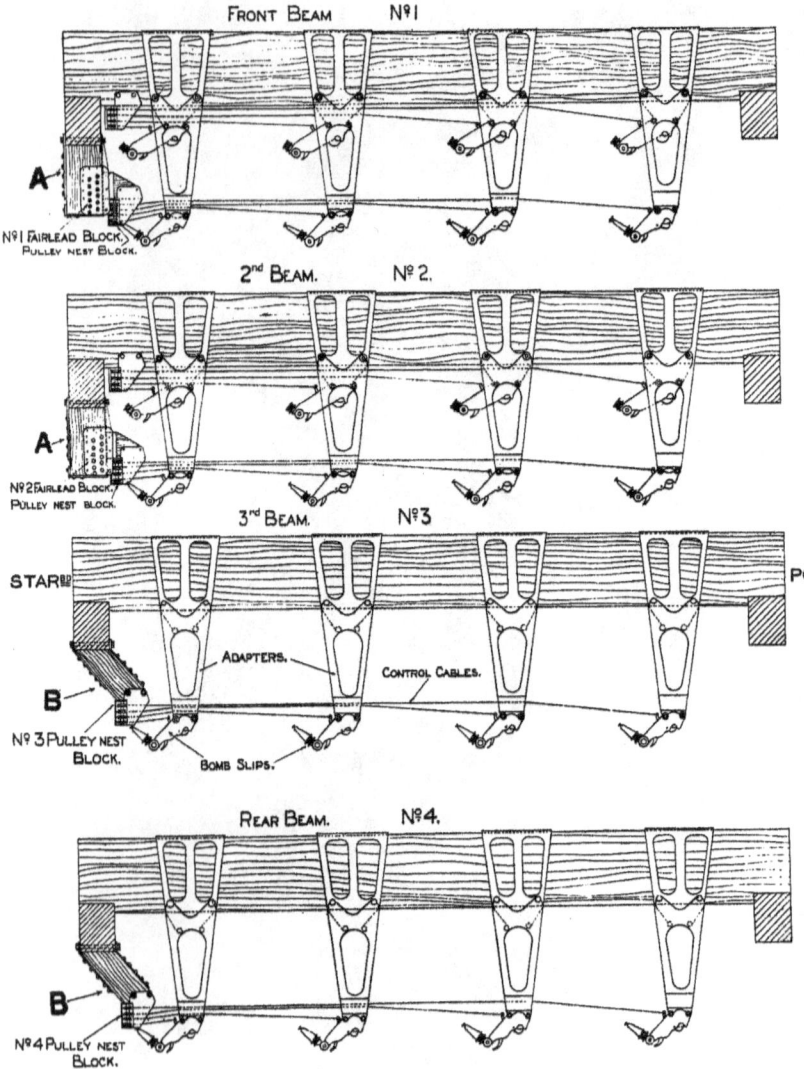

Fig. 4.

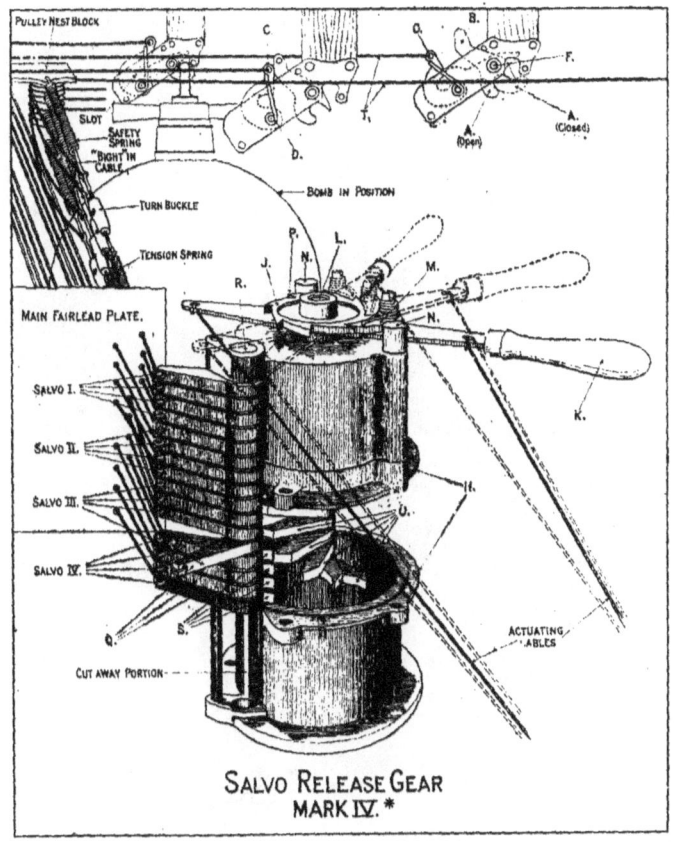

Fig. 5.

LEAFLET 29.

NEGATIVE LENS BOMBSIGHT.

GENERAL ARRANGEMENT.

A, E, Steering wires (fore and aft).

B, C, D, Back sighting wires.

The sighting wires, D, C, B, are fixed for the following air speeds by the Pitot tube at different heights.

	Height.	Air Speed.
D.	6000 feet	90 m.p.h.
C.	10000 feet	80 m.p.h.
B.	15000 feet	70 m.p.h.

(The air speed referred to is the *apparent* air speed as recorded by the Pitot tube. Owing to the decrease of density of the air at great heights, this air speed is considerably below the *true* air speed.)

J, Brass angles on which are engraved three wind scales corresponding to heights 6,000 feet, 10,000 feet and 15,000 feet respectively.

G, Range sighting wire which can be set on any one of the scales depending on the height from which bombs are dropped.

U, Undershield to which brass angles are fitted.

T, Tin cowl which fits through the bottom of the fuselage and into which the framework carrying the negative lens fits.

B—G Line of sight for bombing from 15000 ft.
C—G Line of ,, ,, ,, ,, 10000 ft.
D—G Line of ,, ,, ,, ,, 6000 ft.

NOTES ON USE OF SIGHT.

The accuracy of the negative lens bombsight is small, owing to its dependence on the loading, engine power, rigging and correct Pitot reading of the machine in which it is fitted.

The sight is calibrated for use at three heights—6,000, 10,000 and 15,000 feet. There is only one position of the aeroplane at each of these heights in which the sight is correctly placed.

The correct position of the machine is obtained at each of these heights by flying at a definite air speed. For each of these air speed readings the aeroplane has a corresponding normal flying position, for which positions the sight is calibrated.

The heights and corresponding air speeds to be maintained are shown on page 1.

To obtain good results with this sight the same elementary factors must be taken into consideration as when using any other type of sight. These factors are (a) the height of the aeroplane and (b) the direction and velocity of the wind.

The height of the aeroplane will be known by the altimeter reading, but to find the direction and velocity of the wind is not so simple a matter.

The following is a *resumé* of five ways in which the direction and velocity of the wind may be ascertained.

(a) By the weather forecast. This is often an accurate method and is widely used. It should not be relied on closely when flying above clouds. At 10,000 feet the wind may be blowing in a reverse direction to the wind on the ground.

(b) By observation of the direction and velocity of the wind on the ground. This method is usually founded on pure guess work as regards the speed of the wind; this may, however, be ascertained acurately if an anemometer reading is available. The direction will be found by compass.

(c) By the direction and velocity of the wind in the air at a given height, as observed from the ground. This is done as follows:—A machine flies over the

Fig. 1.

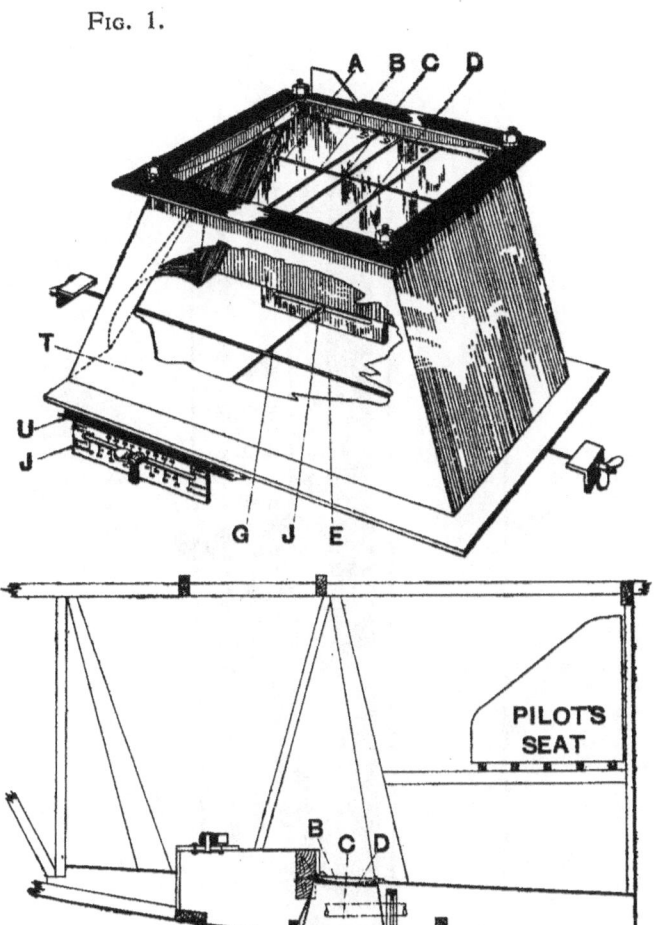

Sight fixed in D.H.4, R.A.F., B.H.P., Fuselage.

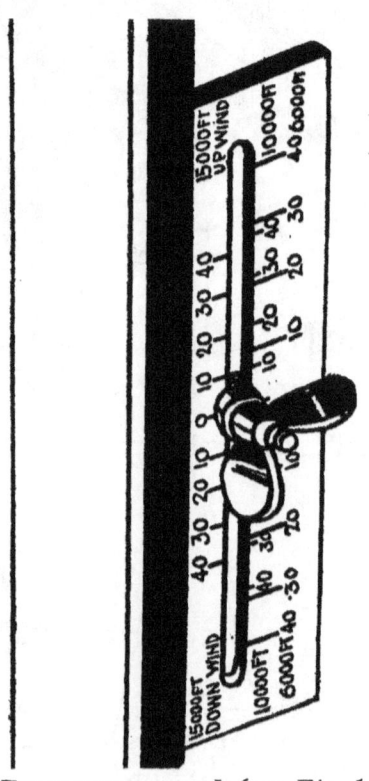

Enlargement of J *(see Fig. 1)*.

camera obscura at a given height, and fires a Very's cartridge or smoke cartridge. The direction and speed of the wind can then be calculated from the time taken in tracing the path of the smoke, so formed, across the lens of the camera obscura.

(d) By the direction and velocity of the wind as actually observed and measured from a machine in the air. To enable this to be done a series of small phosphorous shells are put up by an A.A. gun at given intervals of, say, 30 secs. All these shells are timed to burst at a given height. This results in the formation of a sequence of smoke bursts in line, in a direction immediately up and down wind. These smoke bursts will be separated from each other by intervals equal to the distance which each smoke burst has travelled down wind before being followed by another burst. In the case under consideration the distance travelled by the wind in 30 seconds is represented by the intervals between the smoke bursts.

The direction and velocity of the wind can now be recorded by an aeroplane flying down wind, down the line of smoke bursts.

The velocity of the wind is calculated from the time in seconds which the aeroplane takes to fly from one smoke burst to the next; the true air-speed of the aeroplane being known the calculation is a simple one.

(e) By trial and error in flying over given marks on the ground. This method is not practicable for use in light winds at heights, but may prove of assistance under exceptional circumstances, as when flying without a compass under clouds.

The following methods are applied:—

Keep the fore and aft steering wires A and E coincident beneath the eye, and picking up any prominent object on the ground, note if the machine drifts to the port or starboard.

Now it may not be known if the wind is a following wind or a head wind, but this can be found out by careful observation of the effects produced by ruddering.

Take the case of the aeroplane appearing to drift to starboard; to correct this the pilot rudders to port, and then notices that the drift in place of diminishing increases; he will, from this result, know that the wind *was* behind him, and is now beginning to blow on his beam. Having made this discovery he should slowly reverse his rudder to starboard until he finds the machine in such a position that all drift is eliminated, and there is no difficulty in keeping any prominent object on the ground, travelling along the coincident steering wires A.E. The direction of the wind should then be noted on the compass.

If in the above instance the effect of ruddering away from the drift had reduced the drift, it would have proved the wind to be ahead; the pilot would then have continued slowly ruddering to port until he had eliminated the drift.

From this it is seen that if ruddering away from drift increases the drift, the wind is behind, but if it decreases it, the wind must be ahead.

The following examples illustrate the use of the sight:—

(1) Suppose the air speed of the machine is 90 m.p.h. and that bombs are to be dropped from 6,000 feet. If there is no wind, set the foresight G (Fig. 1) to zero on the range-finding scale (Fig. 1). The pilot climbs to 6,000 feet with his sight thus set, places his eye so that the back sight wire D coincides with the foresight G, and releases his bombs when the target crosses this line of sight.

Similarly, if the pilot were to fly his machine at 10,000 feet with an air speed of 80 m.p.h., he would use the line of sight CG for bombing. If he flew at 15,000 feet, at air speed 70 m.p.h., he would use the line of sight BG.

(2) Let us suppose the pilot flies down wind at air speed 90 m.p.h., at 6,000 feet in a wind of 20 m.p.h. His ground speed is now 110 m.p.h. The range of the bomb will be greater. The sight is adjusted before the pilot leaves the ground, so as to take into account this wind, by setting the foresight G forwards to the mark 20 on the scale marked 6,000 feet (see Fig.   ). The line of sight for bombing is DG when G is set to this 20 mark (forward). If the pilot were flying up-wind at 6,000 feet his ground speed would be $90-20=70$ m.p.h. The foresight would be set to mark 20 behind the zero, on the 6,000 scale, and DG is again the line of sight for bombing.

Similarly, if the pilot flew his machine at 10,000 feet, with air speed 80 m.p.h. in a wind blowing 20 m.p.h., the foresight would be set to 20 on the 10,000 feet scale, either forward or back, depending on whether he flew down or up wind. CG would then be the line of sight for bombing. Or, again, he might fly at 15,000 feet in this wind. If his air speed were 70 m.p.h., he would use the line of sight BG, when G has been set to 20 on the 15,000 feet scale, either forwards or backwards, depending on whether he flew down or up wind.

(3) Suppose now a pilot flew at 90 m.p.h. at 10,000 feet, there being no wind. We may regard this as 80 m.p.h., air speed at 10,000 feet, and take the machine as moving in a down wind, whose velocity is 10 m.p.h. Therefore, set the foresight G forward to 10 beyond the zero on the 10,000 feet scale and use the line of sight CG for bombing.

(4) To take the most general case, suppose a pilot is told to drop bombs from 15,000 feet up wind. Suppose the estimated wind is 10 m.p.h. At 15,000 feet the air speed of the machine is 75 m.p.h. (say). The sight can be set before the pilot leaves the ground. We may regard an air speed of 75 m.p.h. as equivalent to one of 70 m.p.h. with a superimposed wind of 5 m.p.h. in the direction

of motion of the machine. The setting of the foresight G for this *imaginary* wind is on the forward mark 5 of the 15,000 feet scale. But the machine is moving up wind in a *real* wind of 10 m.p.h., and to correct the setting of the foresight for this we must set G to mark 5 behind the zero (*i.e.*, 10 behind the forward setting 5) on the 15,000 feet scale. This final position of G gives the line of sight BG for bombing from 15,000 feet up wind, when the wind speed is 10 m.p.h., and for air speed 75 m.p.h., shown on the pitot tube.

This is the most general case in practice, so that if a pilot knows the air speed of his machine for a given altitude, and has an approximate idea of the wind strength at that height, his sight can be set before he leaves the ground.

AIR MINISTRY,
March, 1918.

Leaflet No. 30.

BOMB H.E., R.L. 520 lbs., Mk. 1/N/.

(Light Case).

GENERAL DESCRIPTION.

Approximate weight of bomb (fused)	525 lbs.
Approximate weight of case	180 lbs.
Approximate weight of explosive	340 lbs.
Approximate weight of fusing components ...	5 lbs.
Explosive substance ...	40/60 Amatol.
Case material ...	Body, sheet steel. Dome, steel plate pressing.
Thickness of case ...	Body, No. 12 S.W.G. (.104″ thick). Dome, No. 3 S.W.G. (.252″ thick).
Overall dimensions of bomb	Length 61″, maximum diam. 19.5″.
Diameter of circle containing fins	19.5″.
How stowed	Horizontally.
Type of fuse	Nose and tail.
Construction	See diagram.

All further instructions as for Bomb. H.E., R.L. 550 lbs. See leaflet No. 31.

Note.—This bomb is obsolescent, to be replaced by a modified design with new fusing components.

Air Ministry,
May, 1918.

BOMB H.E., 520 LBS., MARK I/N., LIGHT CASE.

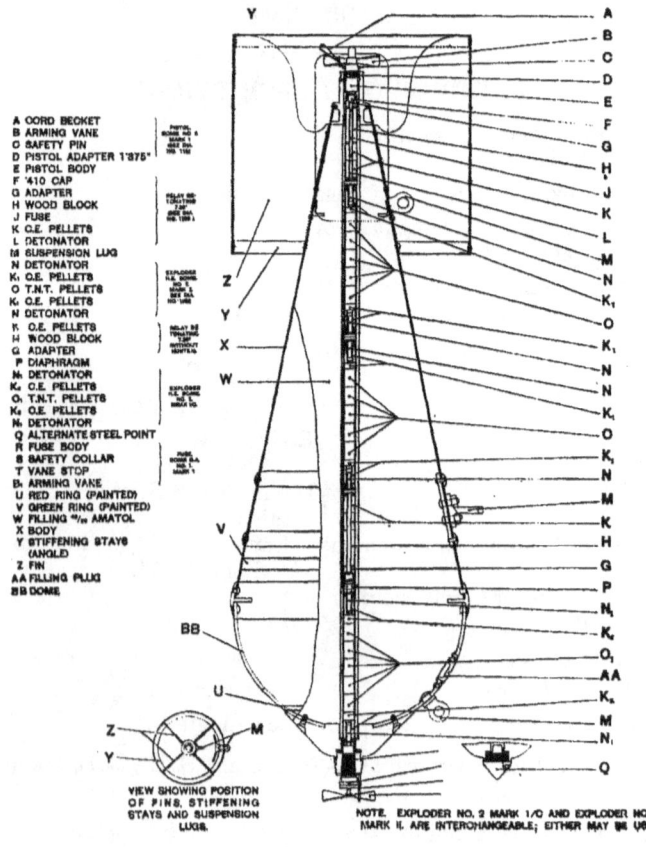

A CORD BECKET
B ARMING VANE
C SAFETY PIN
D PISTOL ADAPTER 1·875"
E PISTOL BODY
F ·410 CAP
G ADAPTER
H WOOD BLOCK
J FUSE
K C.E. PELLETS
L DETONATOR
M SUSPENSION LUG
N DETONATOR
K₁ C.E. PELLETS
O T.N.T. PELLETS
K₂ C.E. PELLETS
N₁ DETONATOR
K C.E. PELLETS
H WOOD BLOCK
G ADAPTER
P DIAPHRAGM
N₁ DETONATOR
K₁ C.E. PELLETS
O₁ T.N.T. PELLETS
K₂ C.E. PELLETS
N₁ DETONATOR
Q ALTERNATE STEEL POINT
R FUSE BODY
S SAFETY COLLAR
T VANE STOP
B₁ ARMING VANE
U RED RING (PAINTED)
V GREEN RING (PAINTED)
W FILLING ⁴⁰/₆₀ AMATOL
X BODY
Y STIFFENING STAYS (ANGLE)
Z FIN
AA FILLING PLUG
BB DOME

VIEW SHOWING POSITION OF FINS, STIFFENING STAYS AND SUSPENSION LUGS.

NOTE. EXPLODER NO. 2 MARK I/O AND EXPLODER NO. 2 MARK II. ARE INTERCHANGEABLE; EITHER MAY BE USED.

Leaflet No. 31.

BOMB H.E., R.L. 550 MARK 1/N/.
(Heavy Case).

GENERAL DESCRIPTION.

Approximate weight of bomb (fused)	550 lbs.
Approximate weight of case	365 lbs.
Approximate weight of explosive	180 lbs.
Approximate weight of fusing components ...	5 lbs.
Explosive substance ...	40/60 Amatol.
Case material	Cast steel.
Thickness of case	Body $\tfrac{3}{4}''$, nose $1\tfrac{1}{2}''$.
Overall dimensions of bomb	Length 60". maximum diam. 15".
Diameter of circle containing fins	15".
How stowed	Horizontally.
Type of fuse	Nose and tail fuses.
Construction	See diagram.

BOMB, H.E. 550 lbs., HEAVY CASE, MK. I/N.

MARK 1/N.
(HEAVY CASE).

A CORD BECKET
B ARMING VANE
C SAFETY PIN
D PISTOL ADAPTER 1·375″
E PISTOL BODY
F ·410 CAP
G ADAPTER
H WOOD BLOCK
J FUSE
K C.E. PELLETS
L DETONATOR
M SUSPENSION LUG
N DETONATOR
K_1 C.E. PELLETS
O T.N.T. PELLETS
K_1 C.E. PELLETS
N DETONATOR
K C.E. PELLETS
H WOOD BLOCK
G ADAPTER
P DIAPHRAGM
N_1 DETONATOR
K_1 C.E. PELLETS
O_1 T.N.T. PELLETS
K_2 C.E. PELLETS
N_1 DETONATOR
Q ALTERNATE STEEL POINT
R FUSE BODY
S SAFETY COLLAR
T VANE STOP
B_1 ARMING VANE
U RED RING (PAINTED)
V GREEN RING (PAINTED)
W FILLING 40/60 AMATOL
X CAST IRON BODY
Y STIFFENING STAYS
   (ANGLE)
Z FIN

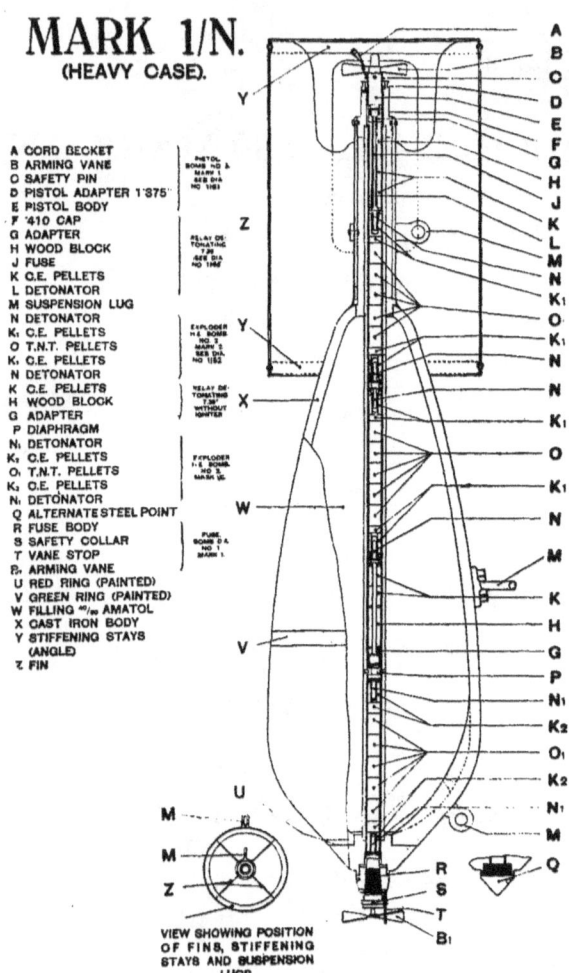

VIEW SHOWING POSITION OF FINS, STIFFENING STAYS AND SUSPENSION LUGS.

NOTE. EXPLODER NO. 2 MARK 1/C AND EXPLODER NO. 2 MARK II. ARE INTERCHANGEABLE; EITHER MAY BE USED

Leaflet No. 31 (continued).

To Prepare for Action (With Nose and Tail Fuse).

This form of fusing is transitional, and will be modified for use in both existing and redesigned Marks of this bomb in the course of a few months.

The following will be required:—

Pistol Bomb, No. 4 or 5, Mark I.	1	
†Pistol Adapter 1.375″	1	
Relay Detonating 7.39″, Mark I. or Mark II., complete with Igniter combining a 15 sec., 2.5 sec., or .05 sec. delay as required	1	Tail fuse.
Relay Detonating 7.39″, Mark I. or Mark II., *without igniter*	1	
*Exploder Bomb, H.E. Long, Mark I. or Mark II.	2	
Detonators Bomb H.E. 56 gr., Mark I. or Mark II.	4	
Fuse Bomb D.A. No. 1, Mark I.	1	
*Exploder Bomb H.E. Long No. 2, Mark I. or Mark II.	1	Nose fuse.
Detonators Bomb H.E. 56 grain, Mark. I. or Mark II.	2	

FUSING BOMB.
With Nose and Tail Fuse.

TAIL FUSE.

(1) From the tail end of bomb insert one or more felt washers as required into the central tube. The washers will lie against the diaphragm and are placed in this position for the purpose of keeping the fusing components closely packed in the central tube, when the tail pistol is screwed into position.

(The number of washers required may be calculated by inserting a rod in the central tube and measuring its length. The length occupied by the fusing components being known (41.78″), the number of washers required may then be estimated).

---

*Exploder No. 2, Mark I., is issued with two Mark I detonators in position, one at either end, stuck in with shellac. Exploder No. 2, Mark II., is issued without detonators; Mark II detonators, being of a screw in type, are drawn separately.

†For use with Pistol Bomb No. 5, Mark I., only.

(2) Insert a 7.39" Relay detonating, adapter end first, into central tube (no igniter is required in this relay).

(3) Take two 12" exploders from their tins (if Mk. II exploders are used screw in a Mk. II detonator at both ends of each exploder) and in turn gently push the exploders into the central tube.

(4) Untie cord becket from Pistol vane and test vane for ease of spinning. Push igniter with 15 sec., 2.5 sec. or .05 sec. delay, as selected, into relay detonating and screw pistol on to relay.

(5) If Pistol Bomb No. 5 Mark I is being used screw Pistol Adapter 1.375" on to pistol. (If Pistol Bomb No. 3 or 4 Mk. I is being used no Pistol Adapter is required.)

(6) Screw fuse into tail of bomb and tighten grub screw.

NOSE FUSE.

(7) Remove nose plug from nose of bomb.

(8) Remove a 12" exploder from its tin (if Mk. II exploder, screw in a Mk. II. detonator at each end) and gently push exploder into central tube from nose end.

(9) Remove safety pin, safety collar and striker spindle from nose fuse, and test striker spindle for ease of spinning. Screw nose fuse into bomb and replace striker spindle, safety collar and safety pin, seeing that the red line on the striker spindle is flush with the face of the pressure plate.

(10) Wire safety collar to bomb carrier.

(11) Just before leaving the ground remove safety pins from nose and tail fuses.

WITH TAIL FUSE ONLY.

As above, but replace nose fuse by screwing into the nose of the bomb the steel point provided for this purpose.

Note.—As in the case of any other bomb fused with nose and tail fuse, 550 and 520 lb. bombs should not be dropped with nose fuse only. Should a nose fuse fail to function, it is improbable that the tail fuse will also fail; thus in cases where direct action is required, it is better in the event of a failure of a D.A. fuse, to secure a delayed burst from the functioning of the tail fuse, rather than obtain no burst at all.

Leaflet No. 31 (continued).

ACTION OF FUSE AND SAFETY DEVICE.

On the skeleton carrier, the vanes of the nose and tail fuses are held from rotating by two fusing wires fitted with safety collars at their lower ends, and suspended from the carriers.

NOSE FUSE (SEE LEAFLET 20).

(1) On dropping, the safety collar is pulled off nose fuse by wire attached to the carrier, and the vane is spun round by air pressure.

(2) On striking the ground, the blow comes on the vanes and the pressure plate, shearing pins are sheared and the striker hits the cap. This detonates the Tetryl in nose fuse and this in its turn detonates 56-grain detonator and exploder which sets off the bomb.

TAIL FUSE.

When the bomb is dropped the vane is free to rotate and spins off, the fusing wire being retained on the carrier, together with its safety collar.

On impact the bomb is checked, but the striker being free to move forward, compresses the striker spring and fires the cap of the igniter. This burns for 15 seconds, 2.5 seconds, or .05 second, according to type, and then fires its detonator which in its turn fires the detonator in exploder, and so sets off the bomb.

LOADING BOMB ON CARRIER.

These bombs are carried on the 520/550 lb. Skeleton tubular carrier Mark II (F). The slip and adjustment of release should be carefully tested for correct functioning before loading the bomb on the carrier. The bomb should not be fused until secured on the carrier in which position it should be firmly housed. This object is attained by the adjustment of the nose and tail pieces at either end of the carrier. These bombs are man handled in loading, the usual method being to place a bomb on a suitable stretcher, and with some six or more men to lift it into the necessary position to engage the bomb's suspension lug in the slip.

UNLOADING.

1. Replace safety pins in fuses.
2. With the number of men required, lower the bomb off carrier.

3. Unscrew and remove fuses or nose plug. (In removing nose fuse, first take off safety collar, and unscrew striker spindle.) Replace fuses in their tins.

4. Gently shake exploders out of central tube, and if Mk. II. detonators are used remove detonators. Replace exploders and detonators in their tins.

5. Replace nose plug in bomb.

Targets engaged :—Towns, Factories, Railway Centres.

AIR MINISTRY.
May, 1918.

LEAFLET No. 32.

BOMB INCENDIARY CASELESS.
MARK 1.

GENERAL DESCRIPTION.

Total weight fuzed	Approx. 30 lbs.
Weight of frame and fins	,, 4 lbs.
Weight of incendiary substance	,, $24\frac{1}{2}$ lbs.
Incendiary substance ...	Thermalloy.
Overall dimensions ...	Length of bomb 27.8″ × 5″ side of square on maximum section. Side of square of vane frame 5″.
How carried	Horizontally or vertically, nose up.
Type of fuze	Tail fuze with special igniter.
Construction	See fig. and description below

CONSTRUCTION.

This bomb is caseless, the incendiary substance being formed in a mould to the required shape and dimensions.

A framework is employed consisting of a cast iron end cap (1) through which passes the rod (3) screwed at both ends. The forward end of this rod is retained by the disc nut (2) and provides the slinging lug connection when the bomb is carried vertically; the rear end is screwed into the connecting piece (4).

Two tie rods (6) pass through the connecting piece and are retained by nuts, the other ends being screwed into the pistol adapter (10).

The connecting piece (4) has a screwed extension which takes the disc nut (5) and provides the slinging lug connection when the bomb is carried horizontally.

The vanes are rivetted to a box shaped vane frame (8) and are serrated on the inner edges which engage with the incendiary substance.

The framework and vanes are set up in an iron mould and the thermalloy rammed in while hot. On cooling, the thermalloy sets quite hard. A former is employed to give the central recess for the igniter and pellet.

The shape of the bomb is designed to be "streamline" from nose to tail, with a rounded off square section for most of its length. This can best be seen in the sectional figures of the diagram.

TO PREPARE FOR ACTION.

The following will be required:—
   (1) *Pistol, Bomb*, No. 5, Mark I.
   (2) *Special Igniter.*

The igniter consists of an Eley 28 bore cap with vent hole on top, into which is fitted a copper sleeve crimped over a short length of instantaneous fuze.
   (3) *Adapter, Standard* $4\frac{1}{2}''$ *Relay*, with celluloid tube.

The adapter will be recognised as the top part of Relay Detonating H.E. Bomb, 4.5", Mark I., and is issued complete with celluloid tube. The latter takes the copper sleeve and instantaneous fuze when the igniter is pushed into place, and has a tapered end containing about five grains of match composition.
   (4) *Ignition Pellet*, 4".

This consists of a 4" length of instantaneous fuze, impregnated with Match Composition (issued in the bomb).

It should be noted that although called a "pellet," it is actually of a form which may make this term misleading unless its composition is borne in mind.
   (5) *Lug, Slinging Cooper Bomb, Mark I.*

FUZING BOMB.

   1. Untie cord becket from tail pistol and test vane for ease of spinning.
   2. Push igniter into adapter and screw adapter on to pistol.
   3. Screw pistol assembled as in (2) into bomb.
   4. Just before leaving the ground, remove safety pin from pistol.

LOADING BOMB.

The bomb can be loaded on to the standard Carrier, 4—20 lb. Mark I., and for this purpose the slinging lug is screwed on the connecting piece projection. When stowed vertically, the lug is screwed on to the threaded portion of the framework rod at the nose.

For horizontal stowage, the carrier should first be tested by loading unfuzed bombs and dropping them by means of the release gear.* The bombs should then be fuzed in the manner described and reloaded on the carrier. The nose crutch and tail clip should then be firmly tightened down for each bomb. The tail clip bracket on this carrier will act as a vane stop for the tail fuze. Finally, all the bombs should be examined to see that they are securely and firmly housed.

ACTION OF THE FUZE AND SAFETY DEVICE.

On the carrier the vane of the pistol is held from rotating by the tail clip bracket. When the bomb is dropped, the vane is free to rotate, and spins off.

On impact the bomb is checked, but the striker in the pistol continues its forward motion, compressing its spring, and firing the cap of the igniter.

This ignites the short length of instantaneous fuze, and through it the celluloid tube with its match composition, which fires in turn the ignition pellet. These finally ignite the thermalloy composition surrounding them.

UNLOADING.

1. Replace safety pin in fuze.
*2. Drop bomb off carrier.
3. Unscrew fuze from bomb and unscrew adapter from pistol. Remove igniter from adapter and replace pistol. Replace igniter and adapter in box.

*NOTE.—It is advisable to drop bomb into a mechanic's hand when testing the carrier or unloading.

AIR MINISTRY,
    July, 1918.

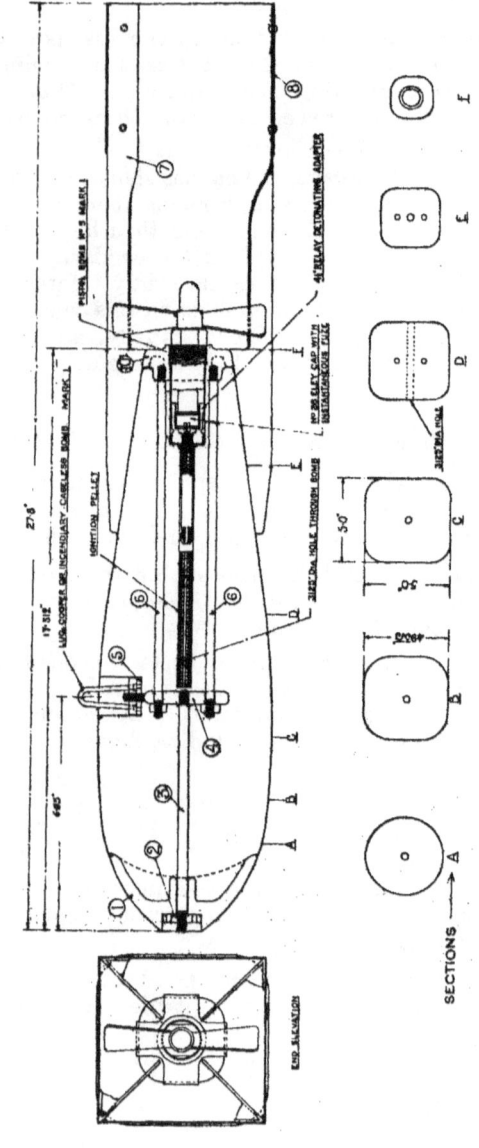

Bomb, Incendiary Caseless, Mark I.

Leaflet No. 33.

BOMB, H.E. 9.45 IN. TRENCH HOWITZER (CONVERTED).

GENERAL DESCRIPTION.

Approximate weight of filled bomb	160 lbs.
Approximate weight of case ...	90 lbs.
Approximate weight of explosive	70 lbs.
Explosive substance	80/20 Amatol.
Case material	Cast steel.
Thickness of case	.3" all over.
Overall dimensions of bomb ...	Length 35.5". Maximum diameter 9.43".
Side of square containing fins	12.6".
How stowed	Vertically.
Type of fuze	Nose fuze only.
Construction	*See* diagram.

TO PREPARE FOR ACTION.

The following will be required:—

Pistol Bomb D.A., No. 8, Mk. I. (with hanging eyebolt): 4.5" Relay Detonating, Mk. I/L, and Detonator, Aerial Bomb, No. 4, Mk. I. (instantaneous): issued with pistol screwed into relay, but detonator separate.

FUZING BOMB.

1. Remove nose plug from bomb.
2. Assemble the nose fuze, by unscrewing pistol from relay and inserting detonator then screwing on pistol again.
3. Remove safety pin from nose fuze, and test arming vane for ease of spinning.
4. Replace safety pin.
5. Screw fuze into nose of bomb.

ACTION OF FUZE AND SAFETY DEVICE.

NOSE FUZE. (See Leaflet 17.)

1. The arming vanes of the nose fuze being a fixed part carried on the pressure plate cover, can only rotate with this cover. The suspension lug is also a fixed part on the top of the pressure plate cover. The pressure plate cover and arming vanes can then only rotate when the suspension lug is free to turn. From this it is clear that when the bomb is stowed vertically, no safety pin or stop on the carrier is required to secure the arming vanes against rotating; the suspension lug being once secured on the release slips, the arming vanes can no longer rotate. When stowed horizontally, the arming vanes are to be held from rotating by a stop on the carrier.

2. On release, the arming vanes are rotated by air pressure, which results in the spinning off of the pressure plate.

Erratum Slip. Leaflet No. 33.

Page 2.—Nose Fuse, Section 3, Line 1: For " shearing pins are sheared " read " shearing pin is sheared."

) Relay acts as the sole exploder in this bomb.

LOADING BOMBS.

On Bomb Gear as Carried in the Handley Page.

This bomb is primarily designed for vertical stowage only, and to be carried on the same slips as the 250 lb. bomb on above and similar bomb gears.

The total number of bombs to be carried, having been carefully fuzed, should be laid gently on the ground with safety pins in position at a convenient distance from the aeroplane on which they are to be stowed.

The release slips on the carrying gear should now be tested (*see* Leaflet 28) before stowing the bombs. If the slips are found to be working satisfactorily, the suspension hooks of all slips should now be placed open in readiness for stowing bombs.

The bombs may then be stowed in the order of the salvos, from port to starboard. The safety pin in the nose fuze of each bomb should not be removed until it is actually being handled for stowing, when, with the nose fuze safety pin removed, the bomb is pushed up into its cell from beneath the centre section by two or more men, as required. The suspension lug on the nose fuze now engages with the suspension hook of the release slip, which it automatically closes and locks, so retaining the bomb. Before allowing the weight of the bomb to fall on the release slip, the greatest care must be taken by the Officer or N.C.O. superintending the stowing to ascertain that the arm of the suspension hook is securely locked by the trigger.

UNLOADING.

1. The weight of the bomb is taken by two or more men from below.

2. The release trigger in which the bomb being supported is engaged should now be pulled back by hand. This must be done by a man in position just behind the bomb crate within the fuselage. The release handle must not be operated in unloading bombs, since in doing so bombs other than the one being supported may be released. The bomb is now gently lowered to the ground.

3. Replace safety pin in nose fuze.
4. Unscrew and remove fuze.
5. Replace nose plug in bomb.

AIR MINISTRY,
July, 1918.

Leaflet No. 33 (continued).

BOMB H.E. 9·45

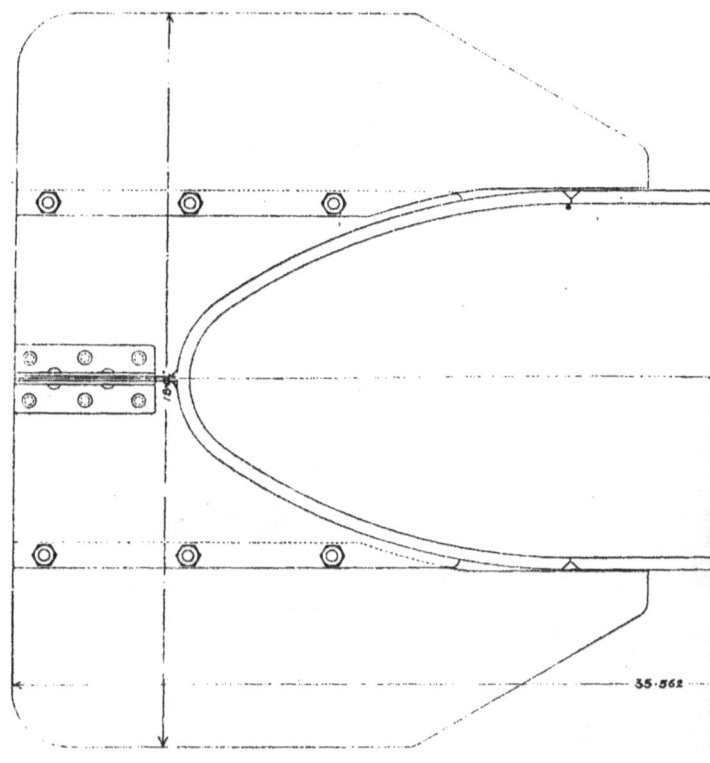

TRENCH HOWITZER (CONVERTED).

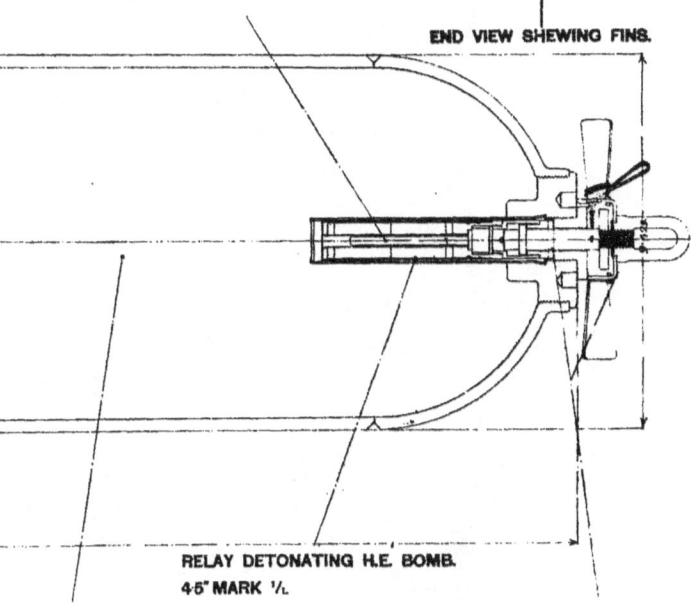

DETONATOR AERIAL BOMB Nº 4 MARK I. (INSTANTANEOUS),

END VIEW SHEWING FINS.

RELAY DETONATING H.E. BOMB. 4·5" MARK I/L

FILLED AMATOL 80/20

PISTOL BOMB D.A. Nº 8. MARK I.

Leaflet No. 34.

BOMB INCENDIARY R.L., MARK III.

(Carcass Mark II. Modified.)

GENERAL DESCRIPTION.

Actual weight of bomb (including pistol)	23¼ lbs.
Weight of case	6 lb.
Weight of incendiary substances	{Carcass: 3¼ lbs. } Total, {Thermalloy: 13¼ lbs. } 16½ lbs.
Incendiary substance (for ignition of the Thermalloy)	Carcass.
Main Incendiary substance	Thermalloy.
Case material	Tin plate.
Overall dimensions ...	Bomb—19.25" × 5" maximum diameter. Fins—Side of square containing fins, 5.2".
How carried	Horizontally.
Type of fuze	**Tail fuze.**
Construction	See diagram.

TO PREPARE FOR ACTION.

The following will be required:—
 (1) *Pistol Bomb No. 4 Mark 1.*
 (2) *Special Igniter.* The igniter consists of an *Eley 28 bore cap* with vent hole on top, into which is fitted a *copper sleeve* crimped over a short length of *Instantaneous Fuze.*
 (3) *Adapter, Standard 4½ Relay, with celluloid tube.* The *Adapter* will be recognised as the top part of Relay Detonating 4.5" Mark I/L and is issued complete with celluloid tube. The latter takes the copper sleeve and instantaneous fuze when the igniter is pushed into place, and has a tapered nozzle end containing about 5 grains of Match Composition. (*See* Fig.)

FUZING BOMB.

1. Untie cord becket from pistol and test vane for ease of spinning.

2. Push igniter into adapter and screw adapter on to pistol.
  3. Screw pistol into bomb.
  4. Just before leaving ground remove safety pin from pistol.

ACTION OF FUZE AND SAFETY DEVICE.

When the bomb is loaded on carrier, the vane of fuze is held from rotating by a stop on the carrier.

When the bomb is dropped, the vane is free to rotate, and spins off.

On impact the bomb is checked, but the striker, being free to move forward, compresses the striker spring and fires the cap of the igniter.

This ignites the short length of instantaneous fuze and through it the celluloid tube with its match composition, which fires in turn the Carcass composition surrounding it. This fiinally ignites the main Thermalloy filling.

LOADING BOMB ON CARRIER.

The bomb must be securely housed on the carrier, and on no account be free to move in either the horizontal or vertical planes.

This object is attained by the adjustment of the nose and tail pieces. This adjustment must be repeated in the case of every bomb loaded.

Before the bomb is fuzed it must be loaded on the carrier and dropped at least once, to ascertain that the carrier is functioning correctly. When this has been done, and provided the carrier is found to be working satisfactorily, the bomb is to be reloaded on the carrier, fuzed as described.

UNLOADING.

  1. Replace safety pin in fuze.
  2. Drop bomb off carrier.
  3. Unscrew fuze from bomb and unscrew adapter from pistol, remove igniter from adapter, replace adapter and pistol, and replace igniter in its box.

AIR MINISTRY,
    July, 1918.

BOMB INCENDIARY R.L., MARK III.
(Modified Carcass).

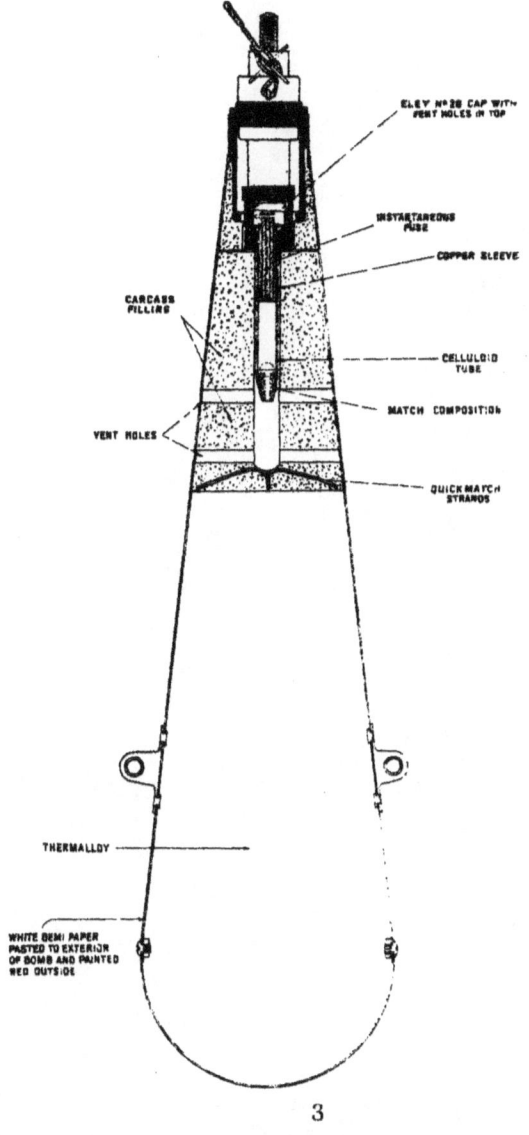

Leaflet No. 35.

BOMB: H.E.R.L. 180 lbs. MARK I.

Heavy Case (Armour Piercing).

GENERAL DESCRIPTION.

Weight of case ...	... 160 lbs.
Weight of explosive	... Trotyl 21.1 lbs.
	Amatol 40/60 20.6 lbs.
Explosive substance	... Trotyl or 40/60 Amatol.
Case material ...	... Cast steel (with mild steel cap).
Thickness of case :	
Nose	... 3.3 inches.
Body	... 0.9 inches.
Overall dimensions	... Overall length 29"; maximum diameter, 9.4".
	Side of square containing fins, 12.6".
How carried ...	... Horizontally.
Type of fuse ...	... Tail fuse.
Construction ...	... See diagram.

TO PREPARE FOR ACTION.

The following will be required:—

1, Pistol bomb, No. 4, Mark I, or

1, Pistol bomb, No. 3 or No. 5 Mk. with adapter 1.375".

1, Detonator Aerial Bomb, No. 4, Mk. I (instantaneous), or No. 5 Mk. I (2.5 secs. delay).

1, Relay detonating, H.E. bomb 7.39", Mark III.

1, Exploder, H.E. Bomb, 10.1" No. 7 Mark I. with

1, Detonator, H.E. Bomb, 56 grs. Mark II.

The Relay, Detonating 7.39" Mark III. is used for the tail fuse assemblage which is of the " B " type (Leaflet No. 19a). The equivalent Stokes Assemblage or "A" type may also be employed.

FUSING BOMB.

1. Screw Detonator H.E. Bomb into the exploder.
2. Push the exploder gently into the central tube, detonator outwards.
3. Test arming vane of tail pistol for ease of spinning, and assemble the tail fuse.
4. Screw the tail fuse into the bomb.

NOTE.—In screwing the tail fuse into the bomb, care should be taken to ensure that all components are in contact. This can be done by carefully feeling the tail pistol abutting on the exploder when screwing home, and glazeboard washers should be inserted at the base of the exploder to adjust if necessary.

5. Tighten the grub screw.
6. Before leaving the ground, remove safety pin from tail pistol.

ACTION OF FUSE.

The action is as described fully in previous leaflets.

LOADING ON CARRIER.

This bomb is loaded on any carrier designed to take the 112 lb. bombs, and the procedure in loading is similar. The bomb should be fused after loading on to the suspension hook, and then the nose and tail steadies can be pushed home and clamped. The mild steel nose cap is shaped to comform to the shape of the nose steady.

TARGETS ENGAGED.

This bomb will be used for special operations.

AIR MINISTRY,

July, 1918.

Bomb: H.E.R.L. 180 lbs. Mark I.

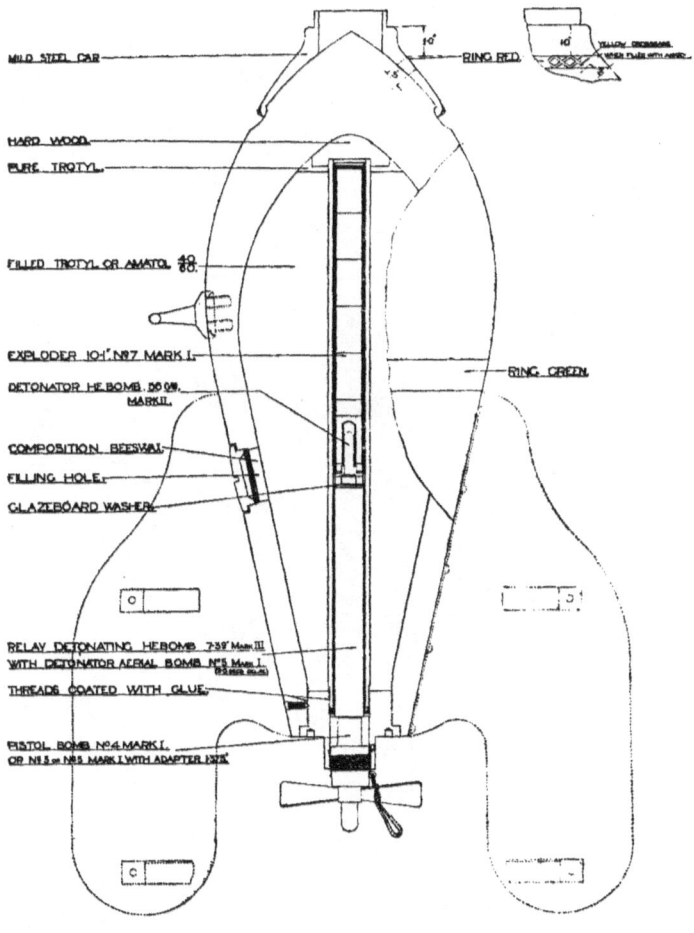

LEAFLET No. 36.

BOMB, H.E., R.L., 50 lb. Mark II.

HEAVY CASE.

NOTE.—The 50 lb. bombs Marks I, II, and III are cast steel bombs, used previously in Naval Stations exclusively. The Mark II is the one most commonly in use, the Mark III has never been actually manufactured, and the Mark I only differs from the Mark II in small manufacturing details which it is not necessary to describe here. They are all diaphragm bombs as distinct from the 50 lb. Mark IV which is cast iron and has no diaphragm.

GENERAL DESCRIPTION.

Weight of fuzed bomb	50 lbs.
Weight of case	38 lbs.
Weight of explosive	11.9 lbs. Trotyl.
	11.6 lbs. 40/60 Amatol.
Explosive substance	40/60 Amatol or Trotyl.
Case material	Cast steel.
Thickness of case:	
Nose	} 0.5" all over.
Body	
Overall dimensions:	
Bomb	28¼" long by 7" maximum diameter.
Fins	Side of square containing fins, 10¼".
How carried	Vertically, nose up.
Type of fuze	Tail fuze or nose and tail fuze.
Construction	*See* diagrams.

TO PREPARE FOR ACTION.

The following will be required:—

Tail fuze only.

B {
1, Pistol Bomb, No. 3 or No. 5 Mark I.
1, Detonator Aerial Bomb, No. 4 Mark I. (instantaneous), or No. 5 Mark I. (2.5 secs. delay).
1, Relay detonating H.E. Bomb, 7.39" Mark III.
}

1, Exploder H.E. Bomb, No. 1, Mark I or Mark II. with
1, Detonator, H.E. Bomb, 56 grs., Mark I. or Mark II.

Plug bomb nose 1.105", Mark II. (This plug is drilled and tapped for slinging eye-bolt and is issued with the bomb).

1, Bolt, eye, bomb slinging ½", Mark I.

The Assemblage marked " B " corresponds with that detailed in Leaflet No. 19a for the 230 lb. bomb. The " A," or Stokes' Assemblage may also be employed.

Nose and Tail Fuze.

Assemblage " B " for Tail as detailed above together with

1, Pistol bomb, D.A., No. 8, Mark I.
1, Relay Detonating H.E. Bomb, 7.39", Mark III, with
1, Detonator Aerial Bomb, No. 4, Mark I. (Instantaneous),
1, Wood block, 4.5".

FUZING BOMB.
With Tail Fuze Only. (*Fig. 1.*)

1. Remove nose plug from bomb.
2. Test arming vane of tail pistol for ease of spinning, and screw in tail fuze.
3. Tighten the grub screw for tail fuze.
4. Screw or push the detonator H.E. Bomb into the exploder (No. 1), if not issued with detonator in place.
5. Push exploder, detonator end first, gently into the bomb from the nose end.
6. Screw nose plug with slinging eyebolt into place.
7. Just before leaving the ground, remove the safety pin from the tail fuze.

FUZING BOMB.
With Nose and Tail Fuzes. (*Fig. 2.*)

1. Remove nose plug from the bomb.

2. Test arming vane of the tail pistol for ease of spinning, and screw in the tail fuze.
3. Tighten grub screw for tail fuze.
4. Push in wood block through nose as far as the diaphragm.
5. Assemble the nose fuze; *i.e.*, insert " detonator aerial bomb " into " relay detonating 7.39" " and screw in the pistol No. 8, Mark I.
6. Screw nose fuze into bomb.
7. Before leaving the ground take out safety pins from tail and nose fuzes.

ACTION OF FUZES.

(*a*) *With Tail Fuze Only.*—The striker of the pistol sets forward on impact in the usual way on to the cap of the " detonator aerial bomb " which detonates the relay detonating. This is transmitted to the "detonator H.E. Bomb" of the exploder on the other side of the diaphragm and finally to the main explosive filling. It should be noted that owing to the construction of this bomb, it is necessary to get a primary detonation by means of the exploder well below the diaphragm, as otherwise there is danger of the tail portion only being blown off, without setting off the main filling.

(*b*) *With Nose and Tail Fuzes.*—In this case the functioning to be relied on is that of the nose fuze, which is as described below.

The arming vanes rotate as soon as the bomb is released and dropping off expose the pressure plate. This is driven in on impact, the shearing pins are sheared and the " detonator aerial bomb " is struck by the point of the striker. This detonates the relay detonating which communicates the detonation to the main filling.

LOADING BOMBS.

This bomb will usually be carried suspended vertically by the nose in cells with the Gledhill Bomb Gear. Instructions for loading are given fully in Leaflet No. 15. The tail fuze arming vane is prevented from rotating while the bomb is in the machine by a strip of leaf spring; and care should be taken to see that the clip for manipulating this strip is pushed up in every cell after the bombs are loaded.

AIR MINISTRY,
July, 1918.

BOMB, H.E., R.L. 50 LBS. MARK II.

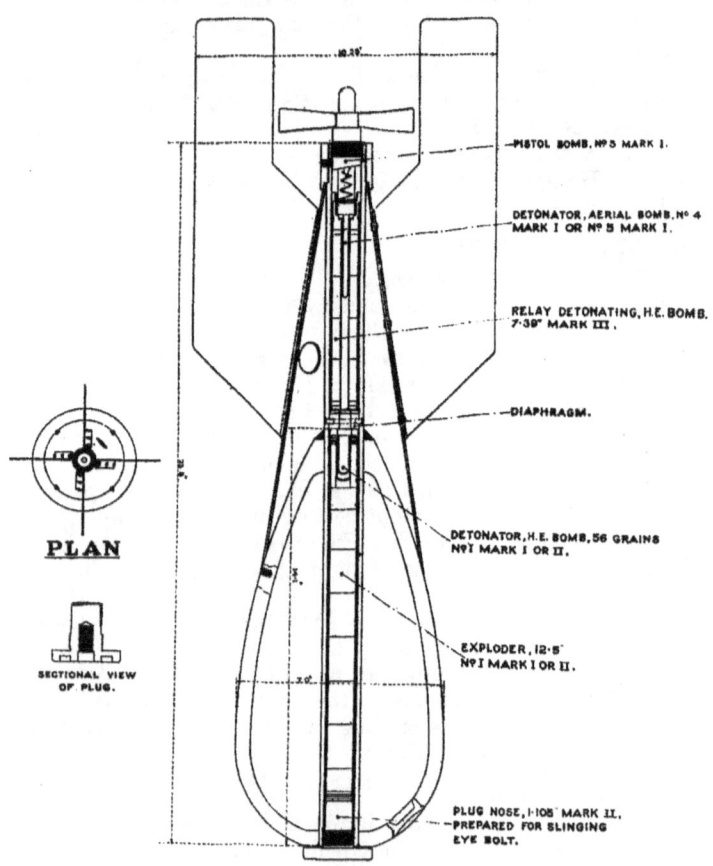

Fig. 1.

BOMB, H.E., R.L. 50 LBS. MARK II.

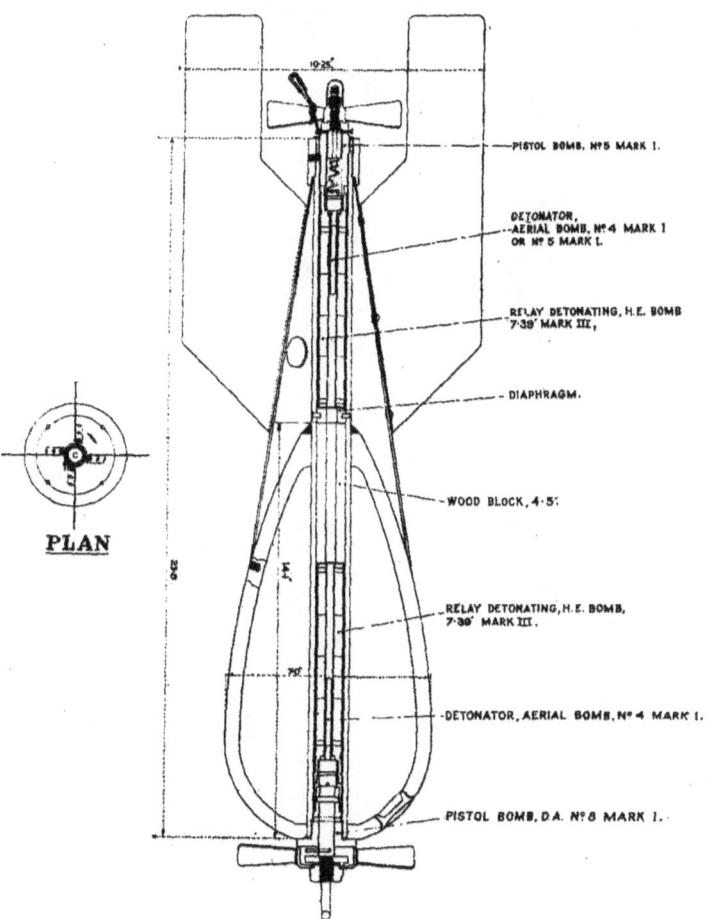

FIG. 2.

Leaflet 37.

ROCKET: 1 lb., MAGNESIUM METEOR.

Note.—This Rocket is issued for the purpose of indicating the position of aerodromes to returning aircraft.

GENERAL DESCRIPTION.

The Rocket is 14" in length by $1\frac{5}{8}$" diameter and consists of a *Brown Paper Case* (*See* Fig.), about 10" long, having walls $\frac{1}{4}$" thick, at the front end of which is a brown paper *Cylinder* about $2\frac{3}{4}$" long, having walls $\frac{1}{16}$" thick. The front end of this cylinder has a hollow brown paper *Cone*, $1\frac{1}{2}$" in height, attached by glue and the joint covered by paper pasted over. The cylinder fits over a cut-away portion at the front end of the brown paper case to which it is secured by glue and the joint covered with a band of paper pasted over. The brown paper case has a *Choke* about $1\frac{1}{2}$" from the lower end. Above the choke is a *Clay Plug* forming a vent. The choke is secured with pack-thread on the outside so as to form a vent $\frac{1}{2}$" in diameter. The case is screwed (8 threads per inch), on the inside below the choke to receive a *Beech Wood Plug*.

FILLING.

The brown paper case is filled with *Rocket Composition* which is driven in, a cavity about $6\frac{1}{2}$" long and tapering from $\frac{1}{2}$" at the vent to $\frac{3}{16}$" at the front being left in the centre. Clay is driven on top of the composition; a hole is bored through the clay into the composition, and two pieces of quick-match are passed through the hole into the composition. The vent at the lower end of the brown paper case is painted with shellac varnish and sprinkled with L.G. powder while damp.

The brown paper cylinder at the front end of the case contains the star. The *Star Composition* is charged into a cylindrical *Aluminium Case* with a closed base to within $\frac{1}{4}$" of the top. The remainder of this case is charged with a priming composition of slightly varied ingredients. The exposed surface of the composition is covered with *Gauze* which is primed with H.G. powder paste. A piece of quick-match is secured transversely across the gauze. The space between the closed base of the aluminium case and the end of the brown paper cylinder is filled by a *Cardboard Packing Piece* $\frac{1}{4}''$ thick.

EXTERIOR FITTINGS.

A *Socket* about 4" long made of tinned iron sheet is fixed to the exterior of the rocket with glue and secured with pack-thread at each end. The front end of the socket has a small piece 0.35" in width projecting to fit into a notch in the stick when inserted, to prevent the stick falling out in flight. The stick is about 5' in length and suitably shaped at the end to fit into the socket.

A piece of stout paper about $1\frac{1}{2}'' \times \frac{5}{16}''$ coated with Brock's patent *Friction Composition* is pasted on the side of the brown paper case above the choke on the opposite side to the socket.

A piece of *No. 12 Small Gutta Percha Fuze* about 2" long is passed through the case just below the choke, the outer end being splayed and turned down into the *Friction Surface* and held in position with pack-thread. The other end of the fuze is turned into the vent of the rocket and held in position by a disc of paper pressed in below it. Fuze and friction surface are covered with a piece of paper pasted to the case and arranged with a *Tear-off Tape* to expose the friction surface before firing.

Ignition is effected by means of an *Igniter Plug*. This consists of a small hardwood plug $2\frac{1}{8}''$ long and $\frac{5}{16}''$ tapering to $\frac{3}{16}''$ in diameter. The small end is covered with a layer of amorphous phosphorus. The igniter plug is attached to the body of the rocket by being inserted in a paper cylinder about $1\frac{3}{4}''$ long and of sufficient diameter to hold it. The smaller end of the cylinder is secured by a *Clay Plug* and it is secured to the body of the rocket above the metal socket. In older types the igniter plug is kept separately from the rocket in the box containing rocket.

The whole exterior of the rocket is painted grey or stone colour and a label showing method of fixing stick, and method of firing, is pasted on.

The date of manufacture and contractor's initials are stencilled on the body. The contractor's initials are also stamped on the beech wood plug.

TO FIRE THE ROCKET.

Force the stick well into the socket and press the projecting piece into the notch in the stick.

Insert the free end of the stick in a tube buried in the ground, or other suitable support.

Before firing unscrew the beech wood plug from the vent.

Withdraw igniter plug from its cylinder. Tear down the tape on the rocket and draw the igniter plug smartly across the exposed friction surface.

ACTION.

The action of the igniter plug on the friction surface is similar to that of a safety match. The resultant flame fires the No. 12 gutta percha fuze which in turn fires the L.G. powder in the vent. The flame from this ignites the rocket composition and the resultant gaseous product escaping through the central cavity and the vent propels the rocket. Combustion ultimately extends to the quick-match, passing through the clay plug in the front end of the brown paper case which fires the priming at the base of the star composition, the star appearing at a height of about 1,000 feet.

AIR MINISTRY,
August, 1918.

Rocket: 1 lb., Magnesium Meteor.

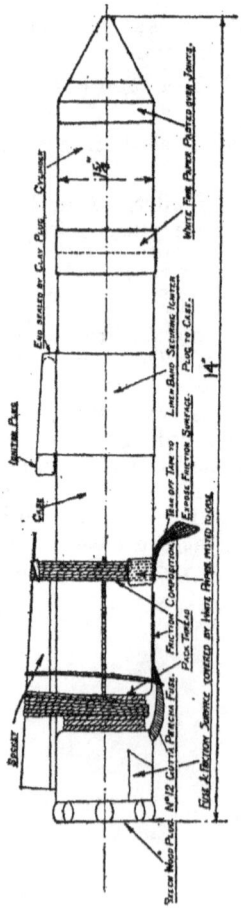

— OUTSIDE ELEVATION —

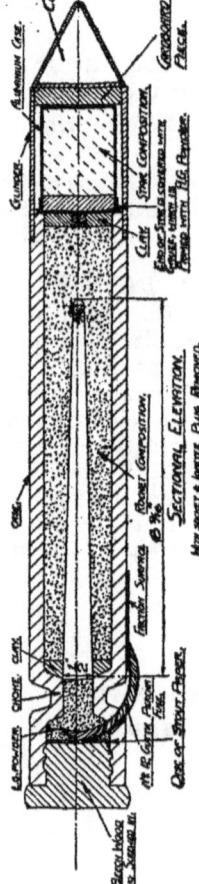

SECTIONAL ELEVATION.

Leaflet 38.

Bomb, 3.45 inch, Parachute Flare, (Mark V.) Electric Ignition.

Overall dimensions	17.2 inches long × 3.45 inches diameter.
Weight of complete flare	5 lbs. 4½ ozs.
Weight of empty case with wood head	1 lb. 10 ozs.
Weight of one filled candle	10½ ozs.
Weight of candle unit	3lbs. 2 ozs.
Illuminating element	Four aluminium candles.
Method of ignition	Electric (launching tube).
Time of burning	2½—3½ minutes.
Candle power	About 40,000.
Case material	Tinned plate.
Parachute material	Japanese silk (fire-proofed).
Size of parachute	5′ 6″ diameter approx.
Weight of parachute	3½ ozs.

This flare is a landing flare, and is used to light up position for the purpose of enabling pilots to land at night. It is launched through an *Electric Launching Tube* fixed to the outside of the fuselage.

CONSTRUCTION. (*See Fig. 1.*)

The flare consists of a bundle of four *Candles* each about 11″ long. The candles are rolled paper tubes containing pressed *Aluminium Composition*. They are each primed at one end with pressed *Magnesium Composition*, through which are passed two strands of six-thread *Quickmatch* at right angles, the open end of the candle being closed by a paper disc, with a *Linen Cap* shellaced over the top. The other ends of the candles are screwed into tinned plate *Candle Cups*, which are rivetted and soldered to a tinned plate *Base Disc*. To this disc is attached an *Iron Wire Loop* to take the flexible steel wire rope of the *Parachute*. The candles are held together by means of four longitudinal *Wood Strips* of sector section, secured in position with glue, the whole being bound together transversely by two bands of iron wire.

The candle cups are surrounded by felt treated with soda, while beneath the base disc is a thick felt disc similarly treated. These prevent the singeing of the parachute on discharge.

The whole flare is contained in the tin *Cylinder*, 15.5" long. This is closed permanently at one end by the *Wood Head*, and at the other by a tinned plate *End Cup*, the latter being driven off when the flare is fired. This cup has three rivets which engage in bayonet slots in the tin cylinder, and is placed in position after the flare itself and the parachute have been inserted.

The wood head is closed with a tinned plate *Head Cup*, secured to the body of the cylinder with solder and rivets. A brass *Pellet Holder*, containing a pressed delay pellet (delay 1 sec.), is screwed into a brass *Ferrule*, which is soldered to the head cup. The top surface of the delay pellet is roughened and covered with *Powder Priming*. Above the delay pellet is the *Electric Tube*, which contains a platinum-silver *Wire Bridge*, soldered to the ends of wire *Leads*. The wire bridge is surrounded by *Priming Composition* in a paper tube. Four *Gas-escape Holes* 0.1" in diameter are bored through the top of the wood head.

Beneath the head cup is the steel *Top Disc*, 0.1" thick, resting on top of the wood strips, and separated from the cup by two felt strips, secured to the disc with shellac. On top of this steel disc is the *Powder Puff*. This consists of two muslin discs, stitched together concentrically and transversely, the space between them being filled with pistol powder. Two strands of six-thread quickmatch are passed through the puff and primed at the edges. These strands are led down through slots on either side of the top disc, through white paper envelopes, and connected with the quickmatch in the priming magnesium composition of the candles.

The cylinder has a *Guide Rib* down its whole length to fit the groove in the launching tube. It is covered with brown paper, which acts as an insulator, and is fitted with two longitudinal cupro-nickel *Contact Strips* to engage the spring contacts on the launching tube. These strips are 6.5" long × 1.5" wide, extending up from the base of the flare, and being continued from there to the wood head by brass *Connecting Strips*, 0.25" wide, the latter covered with

Leaflet 38 (continued).

paper, which acts as an insulator. The connecting strips join on to the leads previously mentioned, which pass on to the electric tube through sawcuts in the head.

THE ELECTRIC LAUNCHING TUBE. *(See Fig. 2.)*

The electric *Launching Tube* (A) is a japanned tin tube of sufficient internal diameter to enable the flare (M) to drop freely through it. It has a groove (D) formed longitudinally in its interior. This is engaged by the guide rib on the flare, thus ensuring the alignment of the contact strips (L) on the flare with the *Contact Springs* (J) on the tube. The tube is provided with three external *Securing Flanges* (B), having holes (K) which enable it to be attached to the aeroplane by means of screws or wires. These flanges also serve to stiffen the tube. A working *Electric Battery* (E) is secured by a leather strap round the tube, a spare battery (O) being attached above in the same manner. The batteries issued may be of various types, each put into a wooden box for the sake of protection and fitted with screw terminals. The wooden box is carried in a waterproof case. The *Leads* (F) from the working battery are carried down to the contact springs, which are insulated from the tube by means of the detachable *Insulating Blocks* (G), which are fixed in place by split pins (N). The insulating blocks have prolongations (H) to protect the contact springs. Two *Safety Springs* (C) are arranged opposite each other near the top of the tube and are so shaped that they ensure the insertion of the flare point downward. Where an accumulator is used on the aeroplane, the contact springs may be coupled in the circuit through a switch.

The launching tube is attached in different ways according to the type of aeroplane. Sometimes it may project through the bottom, sometimes be attached to the outside of the fuselage. The tube should be so fixed that it will be at an angle *at least* 20° to the vertical, the lower end to the rear and the spring contacts fore and aft. The top of the tube should be in a position where it can easily be reached and the lower end with the spring contacts should be below the fuselage, so that the flare has a clear drop downwards. If considered necessary, it can be roughly streamlined by securing aeroplane fabric over it when in position on the machine.

Bomb 3·45 Inch. Parachute Flare. Mark V. Electric Ignition

DIMENSIONS IN INCHES

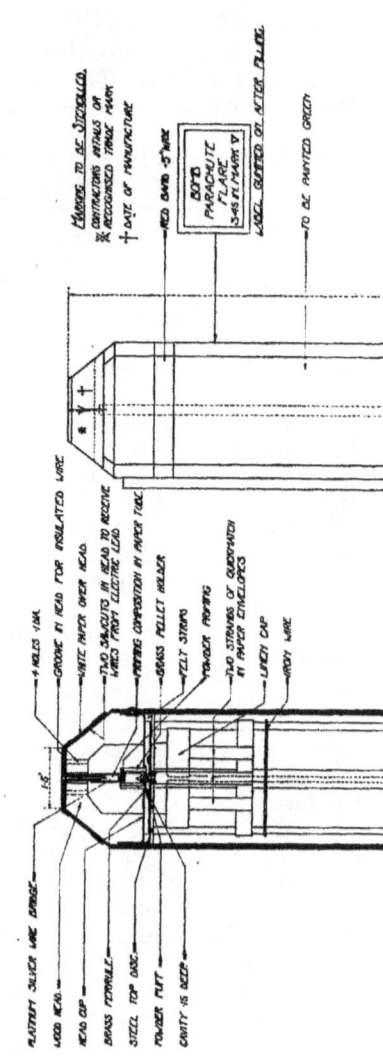

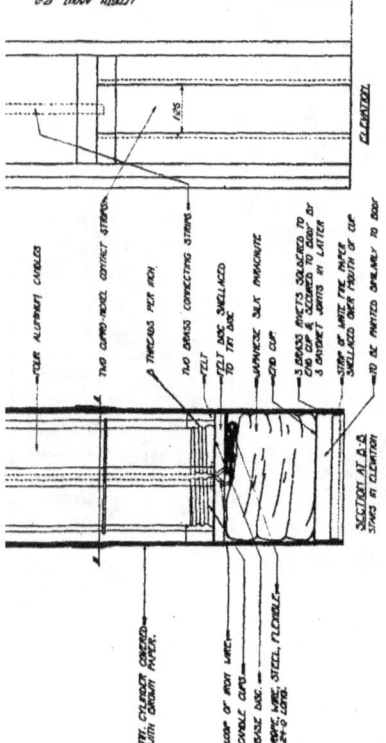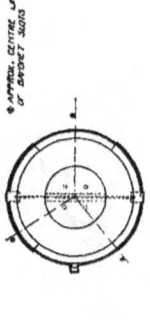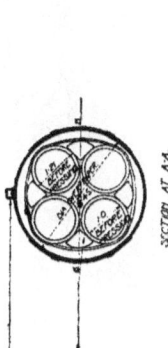

Fig. 1.

Bomb 3.45 inch. Parachute Flare. Mark V. Electric Ignition.

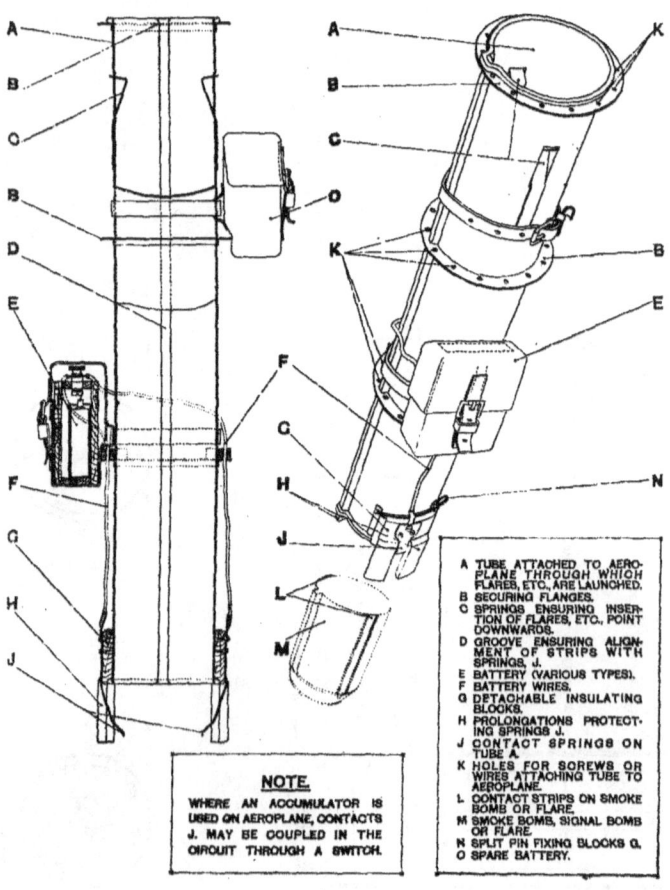

A TUBE ATTACHED TO AEROPLANE THROUGH WHICH FLARES, ETC, ARE LAUNCHED.
B SECURING FLANGES.
C SPRINGS ENSURING INSERTION OF FLARES, ETC, POINT DOWNWARDS.
D GROOVE ENSURING ALIGNMENT OF STRIPS WITH SPRINGS, J.
E BATTERY (VARIOUS TYPES).
F BATTERY WIRES.
G DETACHABLE INSULATING BLOCKS.
H PROLONGATIONS PROTECTING SPRINGS J.
J CONTACT SPRINGS ON TUBE A.
K HOLES FOR SCREWS OR WIRES ATTACHING TUBE TO AEROPLANE.
L CONTACT STRIPS ON SMOKE BOMB OR FLARE.
M SMOKE BOMB, SIGNAL BOMB OR FLARE.
N SPLIT PIN FIXING BLOCKS G.
O SPARE BATTERY.

NOTE
WHERE AN ACCUMULATOR IS USED ON AEROPLANE, CONTACTS J. MAY BE COUPLED IN THE CIRCUIT THROUGH A SWITCH.

Fig. 2.

ACTION.

The flare is inserted nose downwards in the launching tube, the guide rib on the flare engaging the groove in the launching tube. This ensures the alignment of the longitudinal contact strips with the contact springs on the tube, as explained above. The flare is then let go, or given a slight downward push. As the flare leaves the tube, the electric circuit from the launching tube battery is completed through the contact springs on the tube and the cupro-nickel contact strips on the flare, thence by the connecting strips to the leads and electric tube. The latter is thus fired, giving a small flash, and after the short delay (to allow the flare to drop about 20 feet), the powder puff is fired. This ignites the quickmatch of the candles, and at the same time by the pressure exerted on the top disc projects the whole flare with its parachute clear of the cylinder, the end cup being forced out in this process. The flare should then remain burning in the air for two and a half minutes or upwards.

> NOTE.—Each flare, complete in its cylinder, is issued in a tin case, fitted with a tape-banded lid, so as to protect it as far as possible from damp.

PRECAUTIONS AND CARE OF APPARATUS.

(1) Test the battery. The battery is small and compact. It must not be used for giving a continuous current. It should give a voltage of at least 3 volts between the spring contacts, or it may be tested by seeing whether it will make an ordinary small flash lamp glow brightly, but care must be taken that contact is only made *instantaneously*.

(2) Care must be taken that the launching tube has not become dented. To test this a flare may be dropped through and caught below, but in this case *the battery must be disconnected* or the flare will fire.

(3) Care must be taken that the flares will pass quite *freely* through the launching tube. They may be tried through the tube, but must be caught below, and, of course, the battery *must first be disconnected*. If both launching tube and flare are in good order, there is little or no chance of a flare sticking between the con-

tacts, but to make doubly sure a stick could be carried to ram the flare out in the unlikely case of its not dropping free.

(4) Care should be taken that all contacts, both on the flare and on the launching tube are quite clean and bright and free from grease.

(5) See that good contact is made at the battery terminals. Here also the points of contact should be clean and bright and free from grease.

(6) See that the groove in the launching tube is clear and the guide rib on the flare is clean and not dented.

(7) The flares should be handled with the greatest care and not knocked about in any way, as the platinum-silver wire bridge of the electric tube is very easily broken.

AIR MINISTRY,
  September, 1918.

www.ingramcontent.com/pod-product-compliance
Lightning Source LLC
Chambersburg PA
CBHW031251230426
43670CB00005B/126